"Gregory de la Haba's memoir is in the tradition of *Portrait of the Artist as a Young Man.* In a narrative that is engaging, insightful and precise—much like the drawings and sketches by de la Haba that adorn the book—he tells a story of artistic enlightenment, first through youthful attempts to enhance *the work* through life experience, and then, finding his muse within the people and places that matter most. Read this book to discover what it takes to be an artist, a friend, a husband – a man. Curriculum Vitae is a keeper."
—T.J. English, New York Times best-selling author of The Westies and Havana Nocturne

"*Curriculum Vitae* is a wild book, as eccentric and electric as the talented artist that wrote it. Fantastic."
—James McBride, NY Times bestselling author of *The Color of Water* and *The Good Lord Bird*, winner of the National Book Award for Fiction.

"I don't recall the last book I read continually, maybe because they've all been dry nonfiction, as opposed to what Gregory de la Haba has done with *Curriculum Vitae*. Aside from W*hat Happens Next* in the life of a memoirist (wanting to know), I have to be surprised, at least once a page or so, by the language, meaning, I have to be thinking 'I didn't see THAT coming...' then this follows: 'but somehow it's just right-perfect' in nuance. This way each vignette becomes a story with an ending and ENDINGS ARE EVERYTHING. No ending, no story. Period. Apart from being an incredible artist, Mr. de la Haba is a natural writer and storyteller. Anyway, a great service has been done, but only for those who love life... no wait, not necessarily that.... but a service to those who have an intense INTEREST in it... it.... it's doings, the cause and effect of it."
—Allan Weisbecker, author of *Cosmic Banditos* and *In Search of Captain Zero*

"Several writers have turned their focus toward capturing the ghosts and glory, the tradition and tenderness, the sweat and the soused of McSorley's Old Ale House — from myself to my father, Geoffrey "Bart" Bartholomew, to the great Joseph Mitchell. None of them have had the ace up Gregory de la Haba's sleeve, which is to include prints of his gorgeous, soulful art alongside his big-hearted prose (which remains wrapped in just the right amount of New York toughness). *Curriculum Vitae* is a powerful song of family, creativity, and bar life, and a vital addition to the literature of McSorley's."
—Rafe Bartholomew, author of *Two & Two* and *Pacific Rims*. rafebartholomew.com

CURRICULUM VITAE

GREGORY DE LA HABA

MEMOIR

C&R Press

Conscious & Responsible

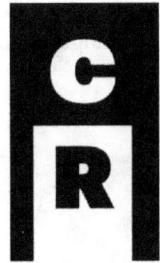

CONTENTS

For Matthew & Sebastian

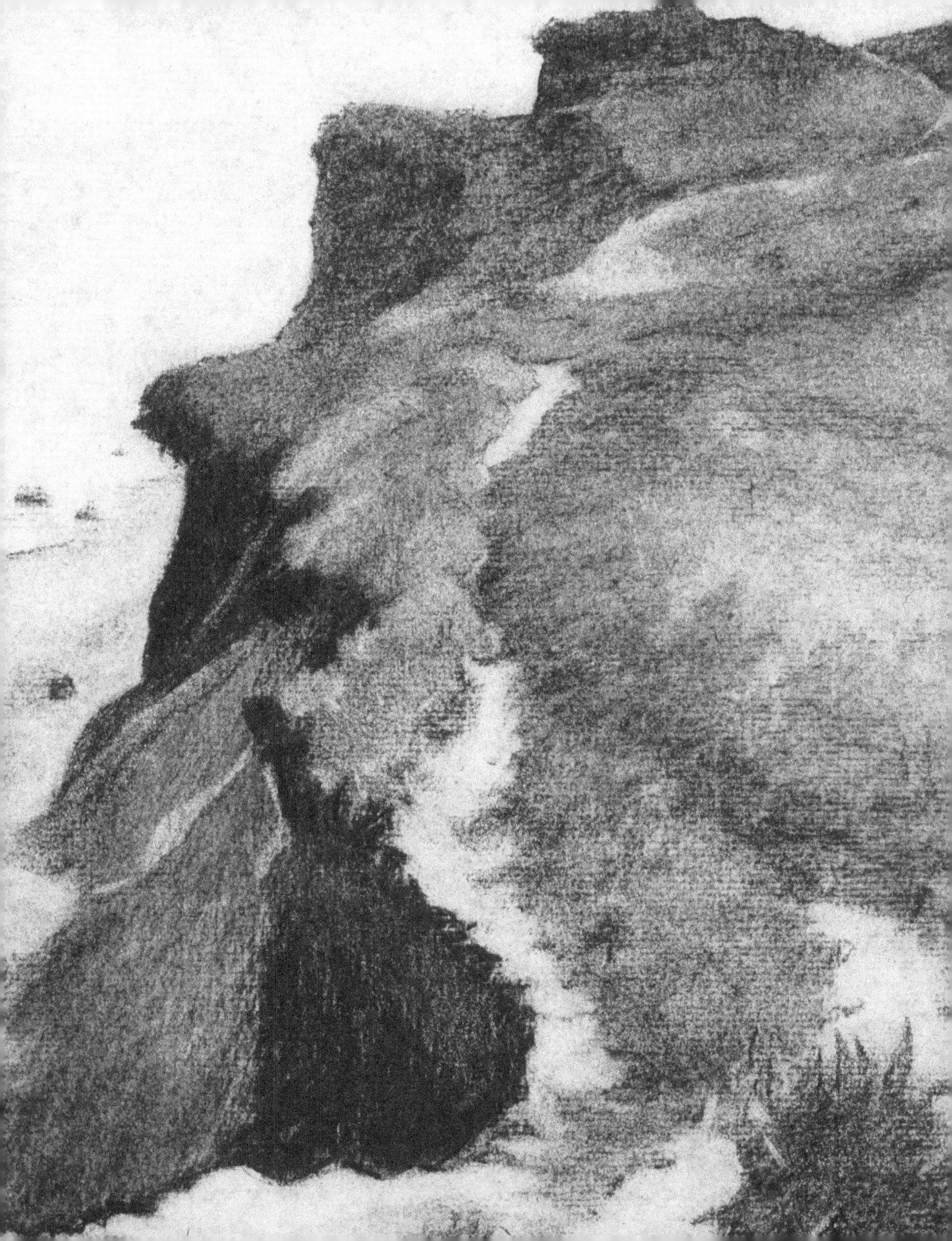

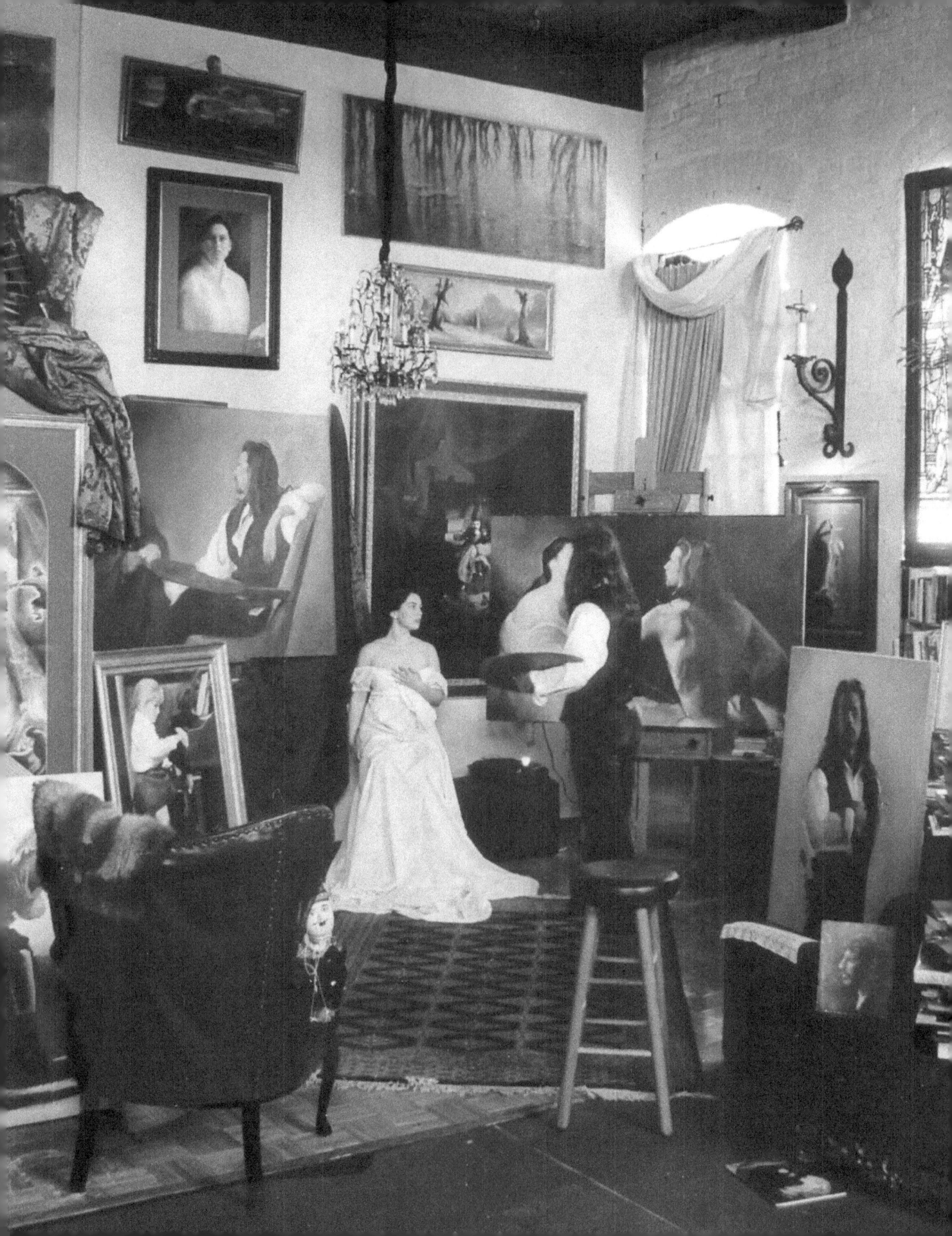

GENERAL INFORMATION

Gregory: "CVs are all horse shit."

Teresa: "Why does this bother you so much?"

Gregory: "Because it does. It isn't supposed to be this way."

Teresa: "You mean you're not supposed to have to do what everyone has to do to be a commercially successful artist? Learn to listen, Gregory, to those who've already made it.

It was early Summer 2001, and I needed a CV, a "curriculum vitae," a resume, a document for a gallery in East Hampton that wanted to show drawings I executed in Montauk beginning that Spring. I didn't have one. I had never read Caravaggio's CV, or Goya's, so I had nothing to go on. Those artists, like others I admired, went around showing their work, or their work was talked about, and back then that was enough. But "The Gallery Man" said that if he was going to show my work, I must have one. So I asked a friend to write something and make what little art-world-experience behind me sound better than what really was, because what really was, was better suited to a Vegas pawn broker than a New York gallery artist.

"What art affiliations do you have?"

"None."

Never had any. Never wanted any because artists, real artists, are supposed to be, I believed, fiercely independent, loyal to no one but themselves and their art. But that was a romantic answer. That much I recognized. I was told to join art clubs: The Portrait Society of America, The Pastel Society, and the Salmagundi Club. These affiliations would look good on a CV.

Over several weeks, the thought of having to write a CV continued to summon vomit to the back of my mouth. Meanwhile, the notion of joining the Pastel Society (even though I loved pastels and attempted to use them in the same vein as Degas) tied knots in my stomach. The Pastel Society, a lower crust of old ladies and retirees who color all day in a last-ditch effort to live life to the fullest, and not, in any way, a cadre of artists working to discover new vernaculars. And the Salmagundi Club? Ha! The place smelled of rotting old ass, bad art, and mildew; it hadn't offered the world a show of any significance since the 1920s.

The Gallery Man: "It will look great on your CV. People love this stuff. They love seeing that you're active in the art community."

"How about just loving the art?"

The Gallery Man: "It doesn't work that way, Gregory. If you're going to sell work for a high price, you need more than just the picture to sell. You need an active auction record. Has your work been in any auctions?"

"No."

The Gallery Man: "Is your work in any big institutions? Part of any permanent collections? Any major collectors know who you are?"

"No, no, and no."

The Gallery Man: "You're not offering me anything. I need a hook. I need to sell them you as much as I need to sell them these pictures. What kind of frames are you putting on them? Have you thought about that?"

"No. I haven't."

The Gallery Man: "Frames are important. You should go to my wife's shop next door. She'll do a fine job. We'll work something out. Get them looking like the valuable works of art I think they are. These are really good drawings."

Fine by me. After all, he said he'd give me a show. I would just have to follow through on his advice—join some clubs and societies and assemble a CV.

"A show in the Hamptons? Very nice, Gregory. I'm so proud of you," my wife said.

She really was proud; I was proud. And a bit relieved: something to look forward to, and where were we looking if not forward? I would do what was asked of me. I would do it because I was 30 years old and had never had a gallery exhibit. I would do it because I was starting to feel what I'd previously only read about—the anxiety of artists who remain unnoticed and unembraced—and because of that, suddenly and dramatically older. I was, in fact, beginning to question the choices and decisions I'd made. And on most days, many of those choices seemed poor at best.

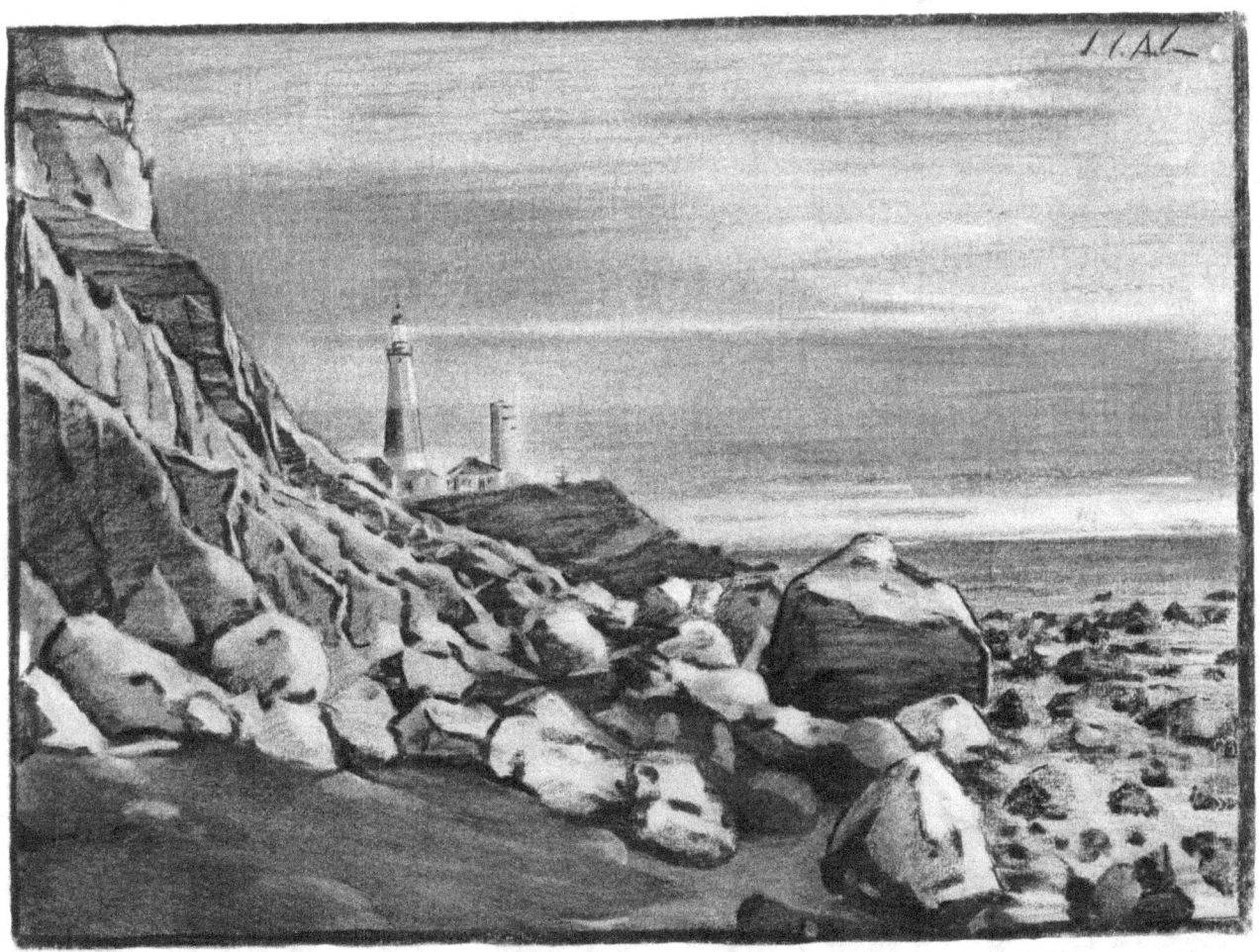

QUESTIONS
(LINGERING, ONGOING, AND AT THE TIME, NEW):

Why did I stop painting on a daily basis? Why did I buy a fucking racehorse? Why did I buy a second racehorse? Why did I buy a second fucking racehorse on a credit card? Who puts a racehorse on a credit card, as if it's a carton of OJ or pallet of sod?

Why did running back to Boston to party with old friends on Newberry Street take precedence over picture making? Why was I collecting art with every penny earned instead of buying canvases, paints, and brushes? Why was I habitually ditching the studio to do something other than paint? What's the page limit for a CV anyway? There's more: Why did the excitement at the prospect of a show in the Hamptons so easily override my preconceived, albeit naive, principles regarding CV's and art clubs? Had I no pith, no courage, to refuse the first dealer wishing to show my work? Which course to take, what path to chart? I hated myself for feeling so fucking needy and for not having an interesting art life, an "active one," at the jittery age of 30—ancient in the world of contemporary fine art. And what the hell exactly was an "active" art life anyway? I wasn't projecting myself the way, say, an experienced and weathered mariner does when standing confidently at his helm. I was much more the mere sailor, forlorn and shipwrecked, quailing at the simple life choices and tasks that lay ahead.

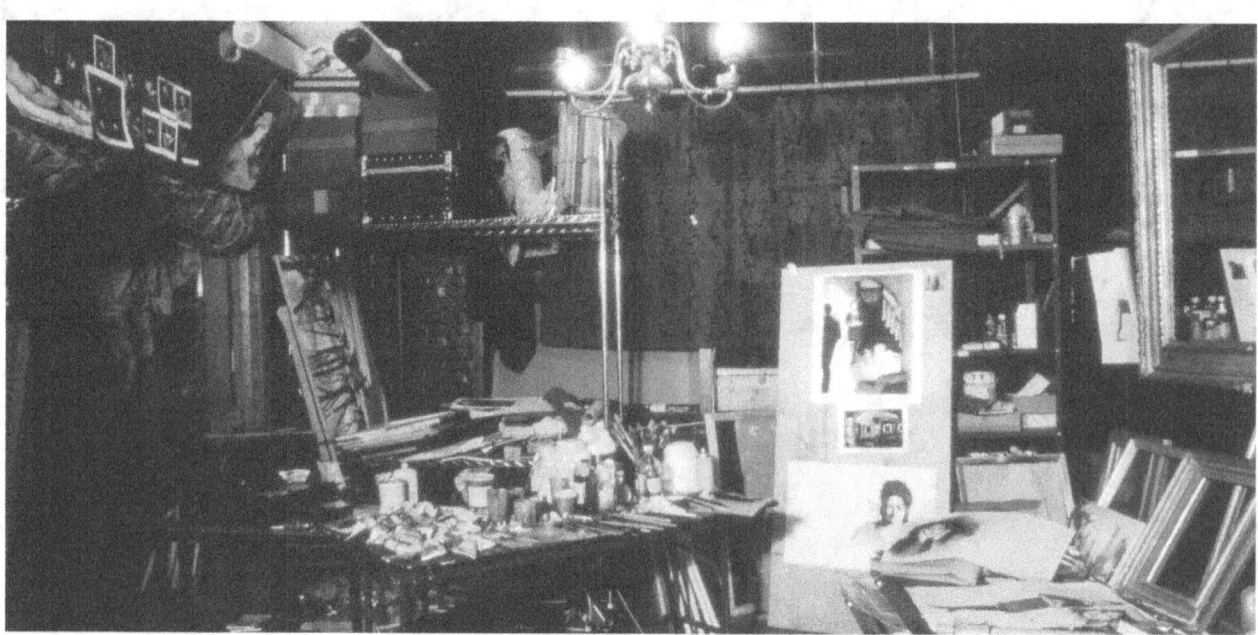

ANSWERS (PARTIAL, GLIB, AND ASTUTE):

Luck answers much of the above. The second horse? Because I was so goddamned lucky with the first. The first horse? Because I was lucky to have a new girl who said "yes, I love you, too," and because that love brought us to the race track in Saratoga Springs, where, with all our love and money staked on horses belonging to others, we both hit big that day. Luck, in fact, seemed to soften and shape every edge of every moment back in those days. Our first horse, according to the auction catalog, entered the world on March 17th, St. Patrick's Day, and was named Some Irish Legend, offspring of Gold Legend. Like the horse, my new girl, Teresa, my new love, was Irish and pure gold. How could we not make Legend ours? How could I not? Teresa loved that I was crazy, and that turned me on—made me feel even luckier. So I bought this first horse after dinner that night at Sperry's on Caroline street, after the tremendous day at the track, even though Teresa, her gambling father, and every horse-racing lover at the table insisted, "No, you're crazy." It's true, everyone insisted, everyone except, that is, for the luckiest, winningest Irish trainer in Saratoga at the time, Leo O'Brien, whose advice was pithy, "She's a fine horse." And so with O'Brien egging me on, and driven by the thought of all the races he'd won with Four Star Dave, his most famous, I shook on it, extending my hand like a paddle at auction and with just as much adrenaline, seeing honor, glory, and riches in a wobbling chestnut yearling long before ever considering, or believing, that the same could be true for my art.

"We need to get this Some Irish Legend, Teresa. How can a horse, born on St. Patrick's Day for Christ's sake, not bring us more luck? And when we get it, we'll get box seats at the track and sit next to other owners like Barry Schwartz [Calvin Klein's business partner and major thoroughbred owner], and we'll mingle with him and others like him—who'll become future patrons—and we'll make the money back in no time 'cause I'll be able to charge more for my pictures since rich people don't buy inexpensive things." (I've always liked speaking in future tense, where the totally unpredictable sounds absolute and flawless.)

"That's crazy, Gregory. There's no guarantee the horse will be fast or that they'll buy your work," the future and cautious Mrs. de la Haba contributed.

"Teresa, trust me, this horse is going to win, and they'll buy. All I need is a box seat and some carrots and everything will be amazing."

But horse people, I learned, only buy more horses and are a breed apart from art people. Moreover, I soon picked up that when sitting amongst such wealth in fine places, you need more than carrots; plus, it's best to have someone else to speak on your behalf. But what did I know then? I didn't even have a CV. I did, however, boast a winning racehorse, and that complicated things for an artist trying to find his way.

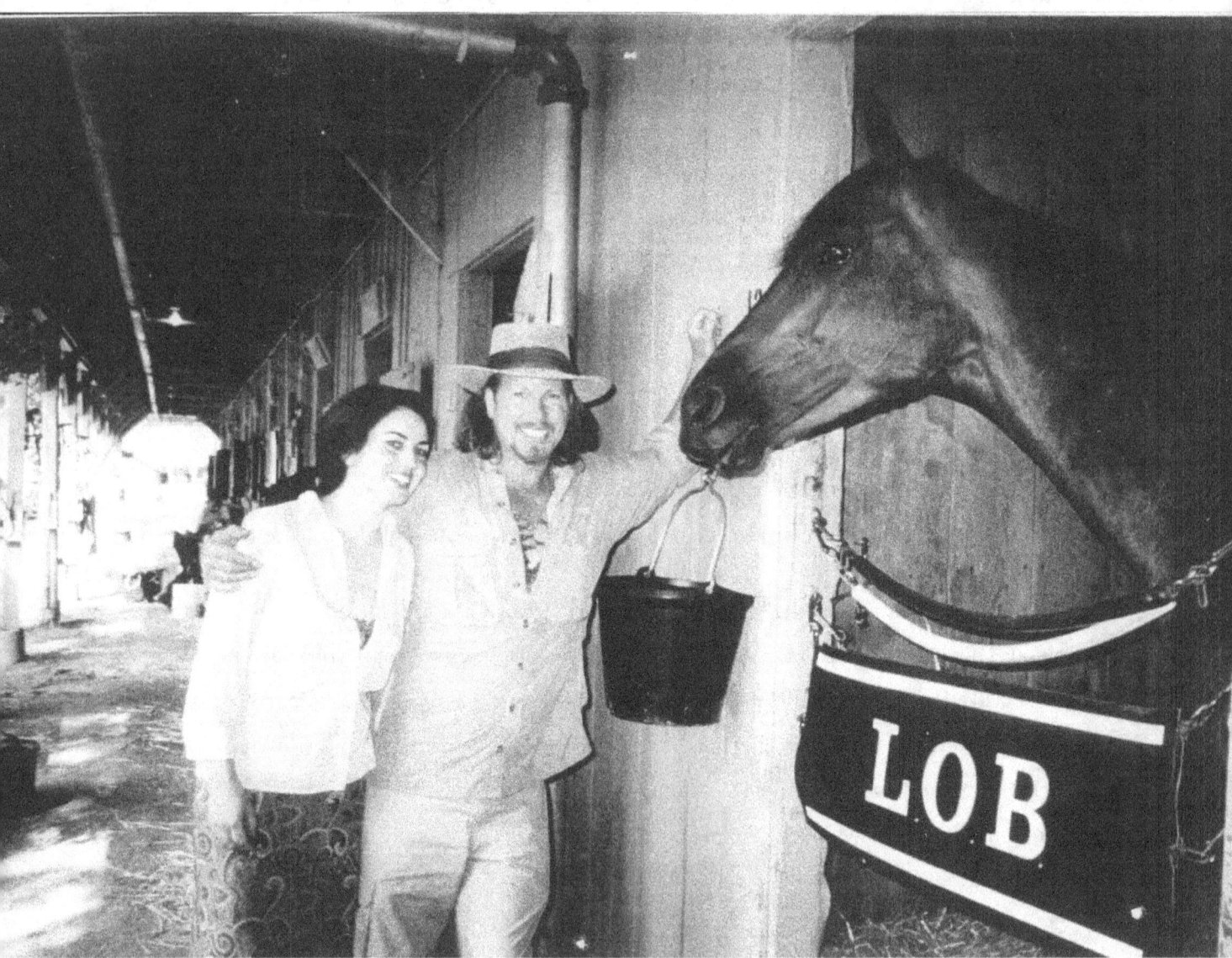

CONTACT (CRITICAL) INFORMATION

Keep reading. Keep reading. Keep reading.

You don't care yet, but you will.

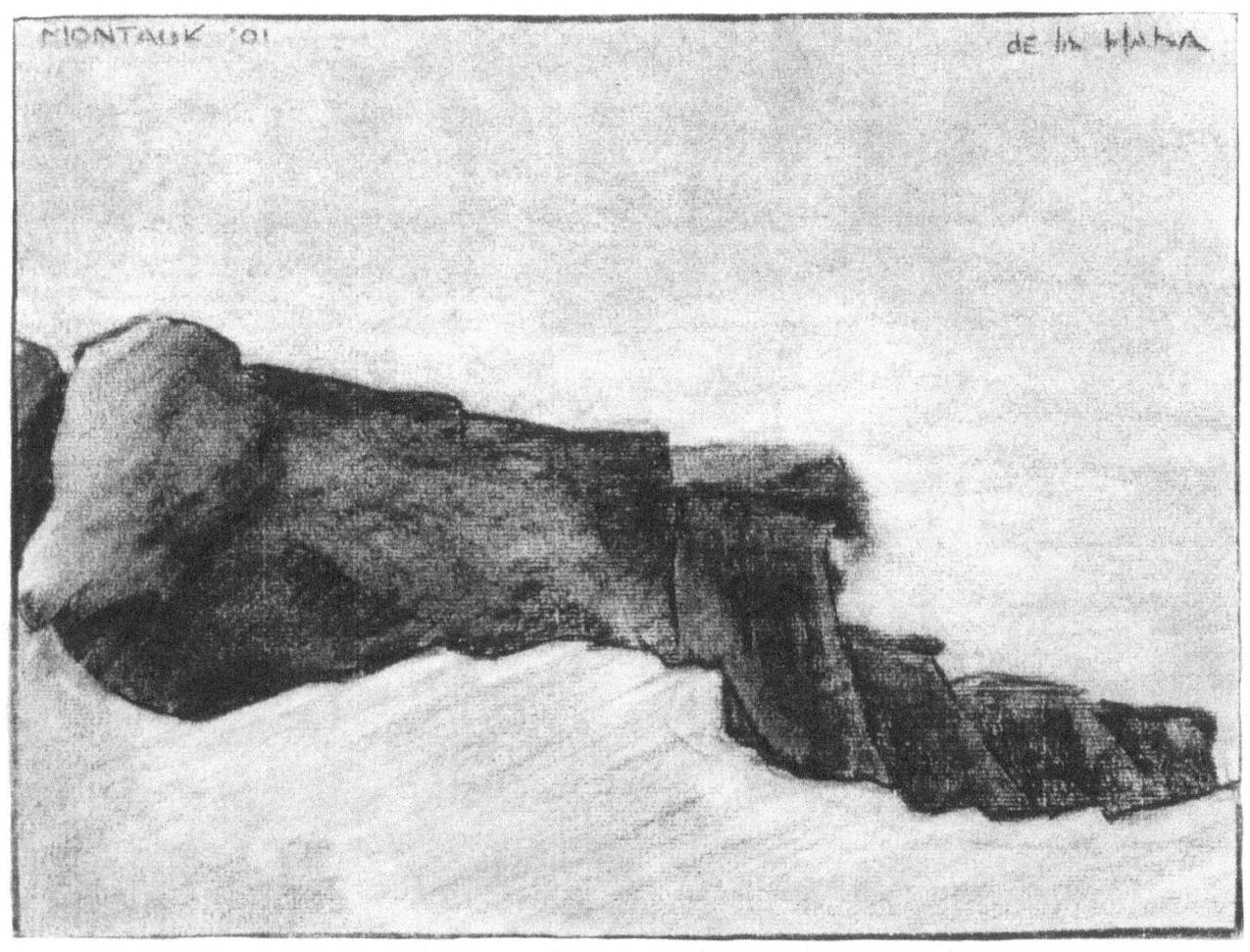

Nature is very rarely right, and must be improved upon by the artist, with his own vision.
  –James Whistler

EDUCATION

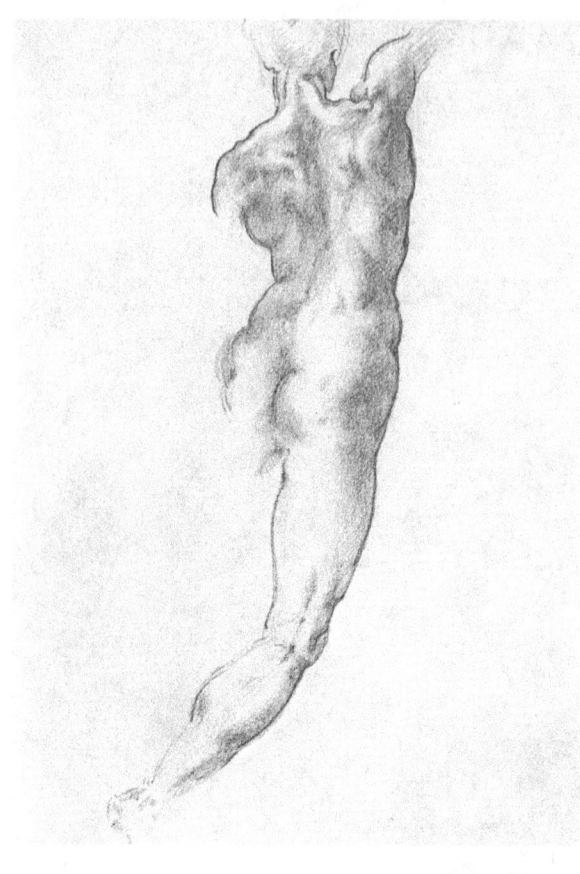

First art competition: Sophomore in high school. Won.

Prize: Partial scholarship to St. John's University.

St. John's is known for basketball, not art, and by junior year of high school, places like Cooper Union were more appealing. Also, Cooper cost nothing for the lucky few who got in. Getting in, however, was not in the cards. Convinced that it had everything to do with the poor draftsmanship displayed in the admittedly lackluster drawings submitted for portfolio review, I enrolled in Queens College upon completing high school in '87 and immediately signed up for figure drawing with Professor B. He was the best, I was told, and I had high hopes of getting more aligned as an artist: acquire skills, develop artistic habits, gain knowledge—on art, art history, anything. After a few classes with Professor B., he told me how well I drew. When I looked at the work of the other students, I believed him. No trace of an Old Master anywhere in class, especially not in the hand of Professor B., a crackpot, a disciple of the German Expressionists, where "crude" had been mislabeled "gestural" and "scribbles" were mistaken for "fine line." What Professor B. meant, then, when complimenting his students' figurative drawings, was that they had achieved an overall gesture that was correct—"On the money," he'd say—in regard to the grand movement of the model, who was standing in a five-minute pose, naked, silently watching in horror as her fit body got mutilated by the dozens of glazed eyes, indifferent from the morning's reefer buzz. That much about class I enjoyed.

"You must get the big sweeping gesture of the figure in your drawings as soon as possible!" Professor B. pounded the table with that one. These drawings, rapid sketches, really, consisted of nothing more than long lines that flowed right off the paper, from the top left-hand corner out the bottom right, or vice-versa, depending on the pose of the model, but always straight off the page. "I want to see sweeping lines!" Those lines gave him a fucking hard-on.

"Where do the feet go?" I asked.

"No worries about that, get the gesture first and foremost, keep working on the gesture, the details will be worked out later," he assured me.

But all I wanted was something that looked like an actual figure, with feet—or at least an independently verifiable arm with attached hand. The class was like a soup kitchen that belonged to a cook claiming to be a chef be-cause he's got all the same ingre-dients as Alain Ducasse. Soon, Professor B.'s compliments fell on deaf ears; I felt my time wasting away. I began to skip class, and after one year at Queens College, refused an education altogether, dropped out, and contemplated the next move. Art life at college wasn't cutting it, and with edu-cation seemingly arbitrary, with so little structure, it simply didn't seem worth it to stay.

Seeing is believing and I believed that learning to draw was feasible and that I could do it on my own time. On my own dime. That if I set out to copying

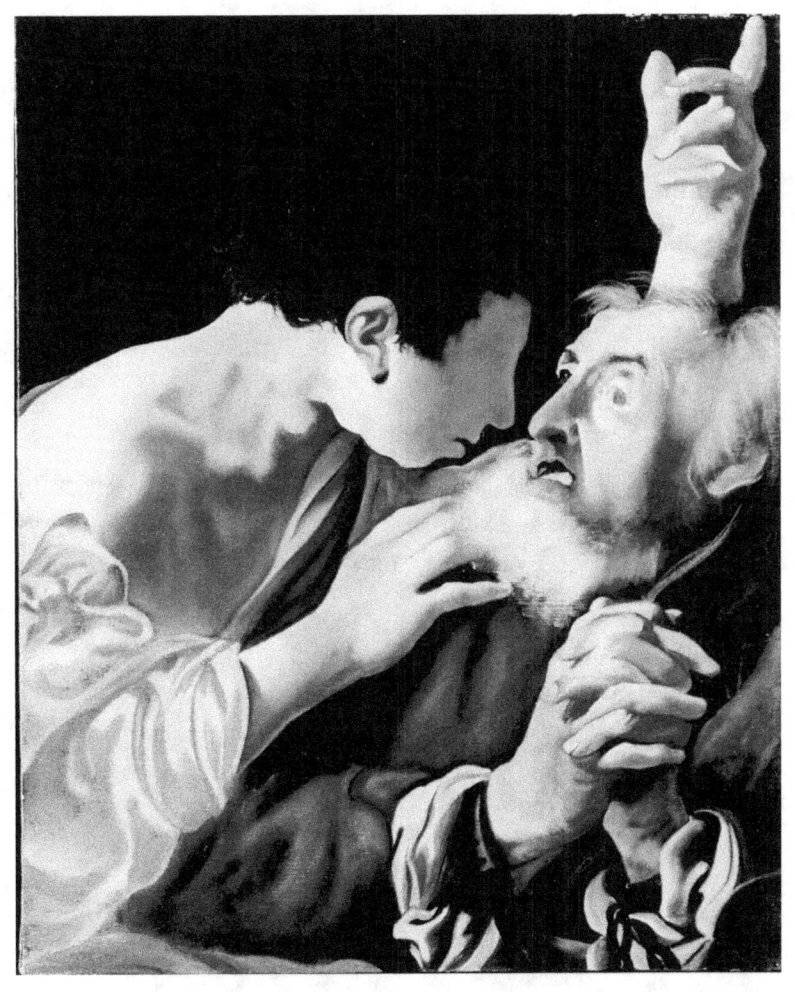

from the old masters, I could unravel their secrets and acquire their grace and ease in draftsmanship. During my early teens, Vasari's Lives of the Artists was my bible, the preeminent "tell-all" book on the greatest artists of the early Renaissance, and I learned from its pages who apprenticed with whom, before each set out on his own and inevitably surpassed his teacher in fame and greatness. As a devout student of Vasari's Lives, I'd later go on to copy almost every drawing by Michelangelo and Raphael—but none by Titian, who was too painterly—and only a few of Leonardo da Vinci—the ones of beauty and of warts, not those of science and invention—mimicking each artist's quality of line and precision.

Later in life, I'd find myself holding in my hands some of the very same masterworks I once copied from books, unframed, bequeathed and available for all to examine on certain days or by appointment at the Fogg Art Museum in Cambridge, MA; and I'd see, first hand, qualities in the work no facsimile in a book could replicate: laborious reworking and reshaping of line and form (Flaws? Yes! They were mortal after all!), by way of rubbing-out and erasing. And I had no idea that they used bread as erasers back then, so I held up the sheet to my nose but could only make out the musky smell of library. And instead of faint Italian bread aroma, I noticed how the paper trapped the red-chalk pigment in its crevices much the way a Thomas' English Muffin locks-in

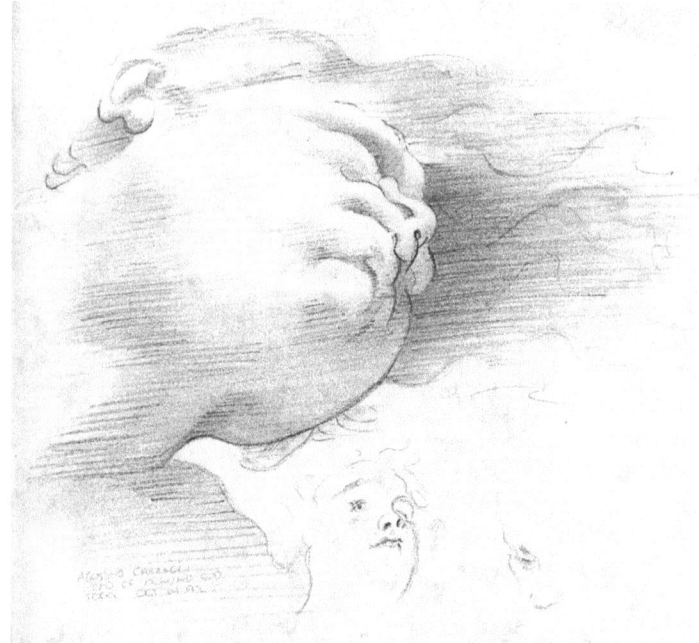

melted butter. I kept marveling at how these masters drew over and over again the same simple, outstretched arm or turning neck. Drew them no bigger than a silver dollar, while in my head I saw these works, viewed them, as larger than life; but to life they nonetheless came, magically, across the folio sheet. My hands nearly trembled, taking in the feeling of all 500 years separating their work from mine, half a millennium of talent and skill apart.

In some cases, their fingerprints were left visible: mark of the man at work while achieving mastery. And while no one in the Fogg Art Library looked, I committed a mischievous act: I rubbed my finger on a stick of charcoal stashed at the bottom of my sweater pocket and gently pressed the dusted digit next to that of the Old Master (can't say who), as though the priceless, rare, and fragile artifact were a big oak in a public park where young lovers inscribe their names after an intimate picnic on the lawn, hoping of forevermore.

Seeing is believing. I needed to see more. I remember going to an old art supply store, L. Cornelissen & Son, in London, in the early 90's, and buying the last batch of antique paper from a mill that shuttered its doors after World War II when countless trade and craftsmen were killed and with it their knowledge of fine paper making. The store, therefore, had a certain air of death; of something that survived too long past its shelf life or of someone that never bathed any longer— stale. And the countless jars of oils and turpentines, therefore, could easily have been mistaken for formaldehyde, with the large wooden drawers that held the paper eerily reminiscent of the drawers that kept dead bodies chilled at the morgue.

Yet there was something special and charmingly seductive about holding and feeling hand-made paper, the same paper, supposedly that these Renaissance artists had used in their sketches of apostles and dukes, of young Italian maidens.

My knowledge of antique paper, of its varying weights and origin of source, and that trip to London and the handling of masterworks at the Fogg, would all come later, well after moving to Boston in 1990 to study with a master painter in his atelier. Prior to that, I used inexpensive sheets of paper attached with spiral rings. And I'd use any crayon or stick of charcoal—$6 boxes of Windsor & Newton—for I had not yet discovered or encountered a need to spend for such material as Nitram Academie Fusains charcoal, which cost $70 a box, the dur sticks of which I'd one day sharpen on a fine-toothed square of sandpaper attached to a hand-held paddle, so I could make a point as fine as that of a hypodermic needle and turn form exquisitely, like an Old Master, on hand-made paper from France.

But before knowledge and awareness of quality in craft and material were realized, I'd sit in my room at home in Queens or in a wooden chair at a wooden desk in any library available and wonder, just wonder, how they did what they did. I'd ask myself was it just through constant repetition, as the drawngs hinted, that they achieved such skill? Or was it something more and of which I was totally lacking?

I searched in vain for a teacher or art school that offered a fundamental grounding in traditional picture making: the sort of knowledge unearthed in books, many books, but mostly in the "lives" of those 15th and 16th century artists that Vasari recollected. It existed elsewhere, too, or at least it had—in 19th-century French ateliers where John Singer Sargent learned from Carlous Duran and Manet obtained secrets from the great Couture; where the methods of working with paint and brush from life, from models, was fundamental and not nearly as dull as the language would suggest: "natura morta"—dead life in Italian—which came to be translated as still life in English. All apprenticeships must start somewhere, and there was a time when that was recognized; in most ateliers, before moving up to the live model, one had to start with a still-life or a cast from antiquity, because everyone understood how hard it is, first, to draw a straight line, and then, once mastered, a line that breathes, that moves and goes on and finally breaks just as the viewer's eye is starting to capture it. Yes, painting from life is difficult. Putting life into painting, more so.

There were many elements to master. Line, yes, but also light. Chiaroscuro, as the Italians called it—clear and obscure. The Italian who did it best was Caravaggio. His darks incredibly dark, lush and translucent, unlike amateurs who tend to produce opaque and vulgar patches of blackness, because the Italians (and the Dutch as well) knew, Caravaggio knew, through years of trial and error, that lead-white paint, when used as a ground, creates color interaction, depth, and a translucence that is the painting's membrane, through which artist and viewer and subject interact.

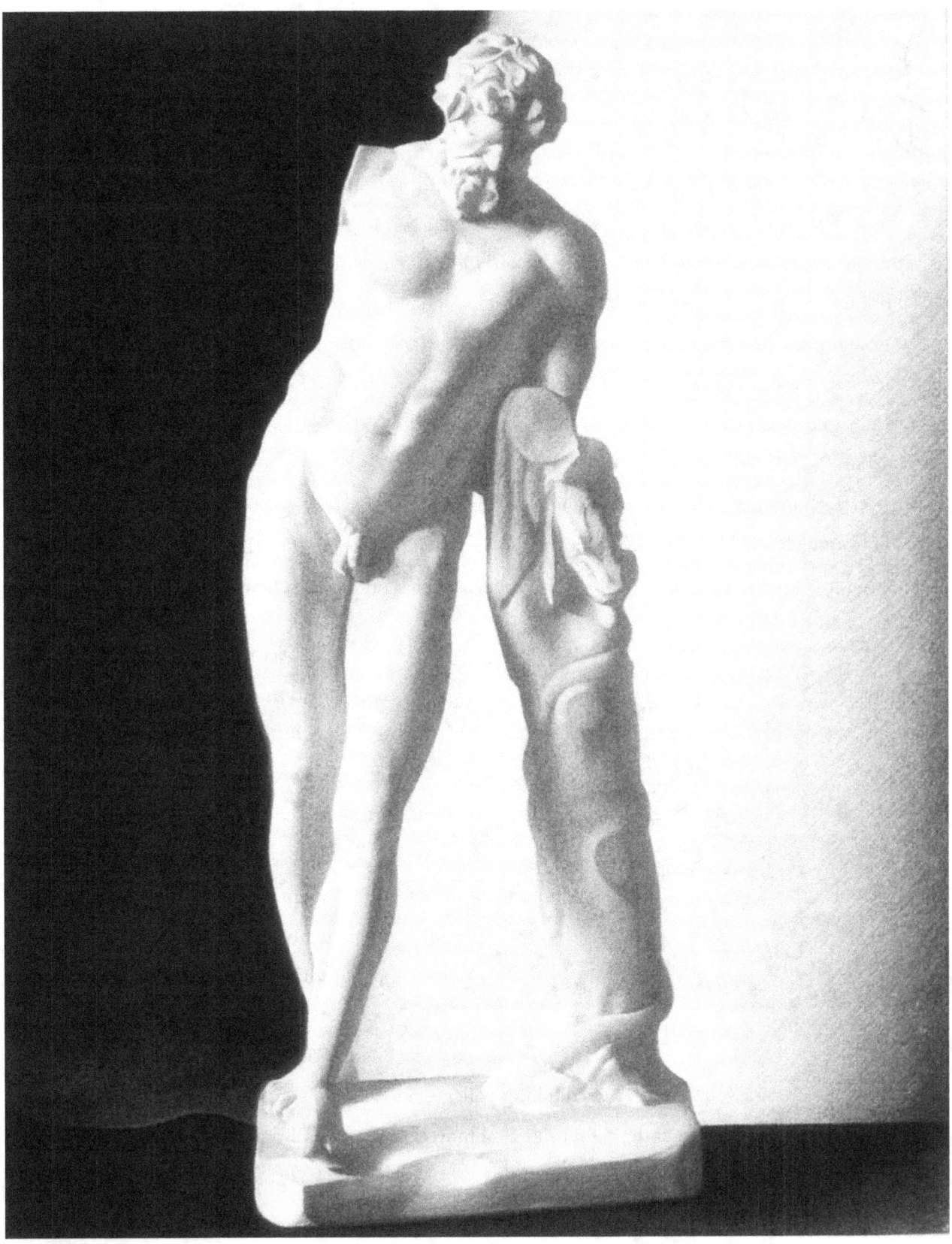

The study of light teaches the artist that everything is relative and in relation: negative space as important as positive space; cool colors versus warm colors; soft edges and hard ones.

As a teenager hungry for knowledge, none of this was yet made aware to me by anyone. Yes, one teacher sold me some of his art books, another his old paint set with half-filled tubes of oils and hardened brushes barely useful. But before I learned how the eye runs a marathon through a painting's process from beginning to end, there was no old and living master to teach me the gait, the pacing, the posture, not one that I could find at least. Anno Domino and Greece, Before Christ, the great Greco/Roman periods of art that all the great masters mimicked and looked to for inspiration, when form began to turn and breath life in marble and ideal beauty had standards worthy a pedestal, and all those other things, tricks of the trade, secrets, passed down from master to pupil, generation after generation for thousands of years, it all seemed lost, gone for good, upon graduation from high school in 1987. My drawings were flat and lifeless, just as the photos printed in the books purchased were and from which I studiously copied on toothless, run-of-the-mill paper.

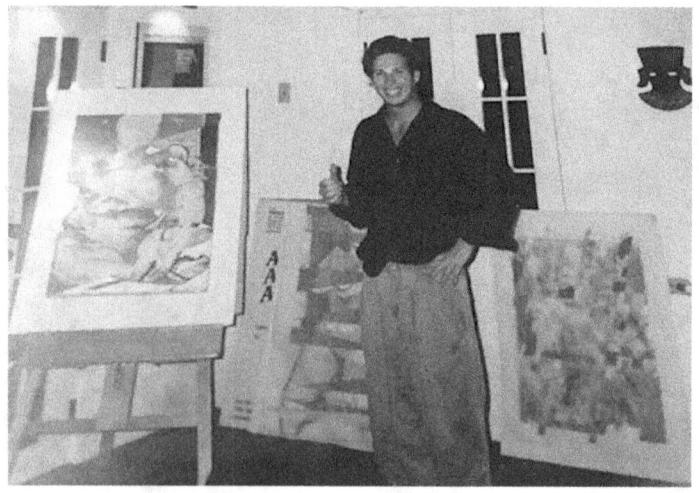

It was time to begin working from life, to hire my own models, to begin living life like other artists I had read about, and to start traveling in search of that someone, or something, that can bring destination within sight of purpose. Gauguin sailing to Tahiti drifted through my mind. Maybe, just maybe, paradise was still attainable even if a proper art teacher wasn't. I'd visited Puerto Rico twice a year, at Easter and Christmas, from a young age. After ditching college, my cousin Javier suggested I live there. It sounded like the right idea at the right time. So I moved, and La Isla Bonita became home for one raucous year: Christmas of '88 to the end of '89.

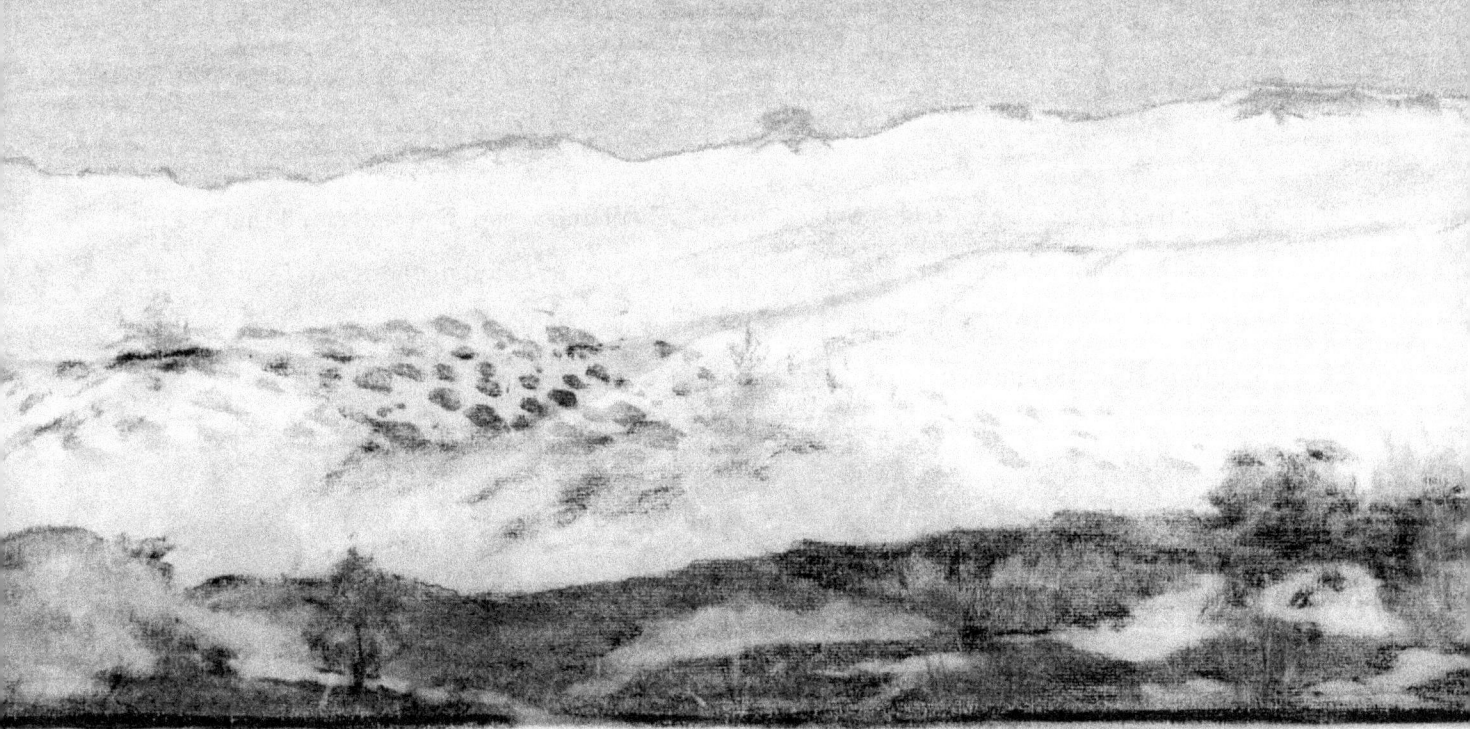

HIGHER EDUCATION

Paint what you see. Paint what is real to you.
   —Robert Henri

I was learning to rage, which is surprisingly important. Where is your passion without your anger?
   —Journal notation, Puerto Rico, 1989

The early 20th century brought the advent of Modernism. The avant-garde saw urinals as art, and ideas rose to greater importance than craft.

What was being offered in art schools, and the New York art scene in general during the 1980's, was no different, in my view, from complete and utter garbage. Held up for the budding artist to emulate was everything from Eric Fischle's pictorial representations of life with friends and family, painted—entirely, and unrefined—from projected photographs, to Julian Schnabel's broken-plate paintings, in which he smashed up a bunch of plates, attached the shards to a surface with industrial-grade bonding agent, and then painted atop it all in such a god-awful manner that one was left suspecting that the artist was, indeed, a child who had skipped his daily Ritalin dose. The only thing more vulgar than the pictures these 1980s art stars painted was the hundreds of thousands of dollars they fetched. Why go to art school and spend thousands if all that's needed is video projector and hammer? It seemed that traditional teaching methods and figure painting and the beauty of the Classical ideal had gone the way of bell-bottom pants. Five hundred years of painting tradition flushed down the drain. Rendered irrelevant. I needed to find my own Shangri-la, an art school or painter's studio where craft and skill still mattered.

After a few weeks as artist-in-the-tropics, all I did, though, was go completely and utterly batty over all the beautiful women. I reveled in the constant holidays and partied until the sun came up. And it always came up while on the beach with a fine novia, whom I had danced with all night at Loiza Street, which had the best live music then, or Neons in Old San Juan, which played the loudest. The roadside kiosks, which you could hit all night, sold lechon: roasted pig on the spit with skin perfectly crunchy, and made best by Jose Luis, who you could find on the side of the road, off the highway that ran east from San Juan to El Yunque, the national rainforest of Puerto Rico. That's where Javier and I would often go with lady friends to spend afternoons climbing up waterfalls, drinking ron y coke, and fishing for fresh-water shrimp in the clean pools of rain that collected in cavernous pockets of bedrock. We'd set traps: squirrel cages filled with large chunks of fresh coconut meat, the thin, hard shell still attached, split from one of the fallen coconuts that littered the moss-covered floor. We'd toss the baited traps into pools up and down the streams. Some traps had a rope that we'd tie to the base of a palm tree or big rock that hugged the pool; other traps had no rope, and we'd just dive in and scout the bottom with our bare feet until we felt wire, the rapid waterfalls making it impossible to see. While we waited for the traps to fill, we'd make drinks and laugh as we danced with the girls beneath the lush canopy. And while the shrimp attached themselves to the bait, we'd attach ourselves to the girl of our choice. We'd hike on separate trails all the way to the top of the rainforest, where, at the end of one such trail, is a stone tower. Stairs lead out to a parapet that allows the eye to dance on treetops, out into and through clouds. But on this particular day, there is nothing to see because of the weather, and all that's really to do once there is make love. We communicate this mutual desire through touch, as my hand and fingertips invite her to walk in front—"after you, mi querida"—up the steep, stone stairs. When she sees that nobody is around and that nobody can see because of the mist and fog, and that my cousin and his girl are somewhere else, likewise unseen, she is willingly seduced. Here, "Way up in the clouds," as she tells you, she answers your suggestion by removing what little clothes she wears so that you can love her in the great outdoors.

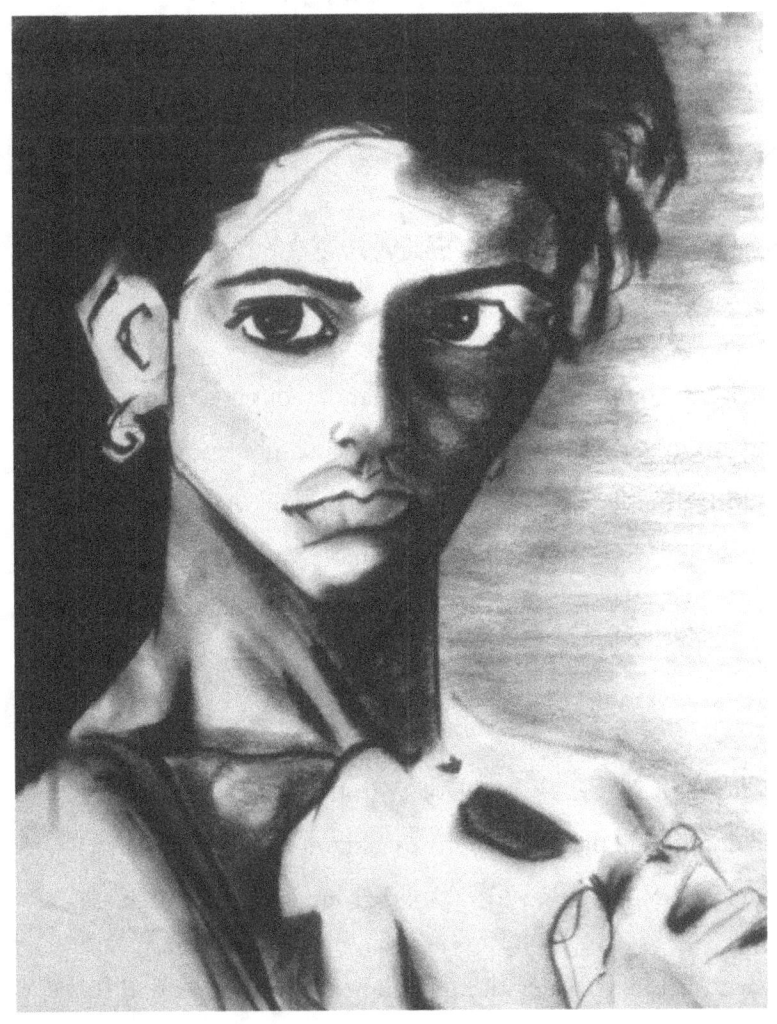

Afterwards, on the descent from the clouds, from the top of El Yunque, before retrieving the traps filled with camarones, we'd rip from low-lying plants massive green leaves, place them beneath our backsides, and slide down glacial rocks made smooth and slippery by the constant rainfall, toward camp. This was Puerto Rico on the first leg of the journey-as-artist. It was how I thought artists were supposed to live. As a teenager, I had read one too many books on Paris—Toulouse Lautrec in the brothels, and, on Montmartre, Picasso's early struggle and the joy he took with new lovers. It all seemed worth it; everything about it grand and romantic. In the safety and warmth of a home in Queens, to an overly enchanted teenager intoxicated by immortality and wishing for greatness in art and in life, reading about the lives of famous artists all seemed both unreal and alluring. Puerto Rico, in the beginning, was like what I imagined for Toulouse and PIcasso, only, I forgot to bring the sketchpad.

Teresa: "I don't like this part."

"I know baby, but it's a part of my vitae and it needs to go in here."

Teresa: "What was her name?"

"Her name? I don't even remember her face."

Teresa: "You're horrible."

HIGHER EDUCATION: PART TWO

Is he not sacred, even to the gods, the wandering man who comes in weariness?
—Homer, The Iliad

Javier told me about Artes Plasticas, the only art school on the island, thought it'd be a good idea to attend, but they wouldn't take me mid-year, so I enrolled in a few art classes at Sacrado Corazon, an old university built up on a hill, attended by relatives past and present. And, as it were, family back in New York and in Puerto Rico kept pushing, insisting almost, on getting a proper education, especially mom:

"You'll be better off with it than without it."

That haunted me. Especially when she'd say, "Oh, Gregory," in front of those words, or before any advice offered over the phone or gifted in person, as if my own name, when given life via her voice, became a warning, a rallying cry to do right, to stay on solid ground, to stay in school.

I couldn't bring myself to not heed her siren-like call for a higher education, a call that irritated and stirred a distrust I had towards my art faculties, my poor skill set. Maybe there was more to learn and get from a higher education. But my heart wasn't in school, nor was my head: I somehow missed the fact that I had enrolled in Figure Drawing 1 and handed in, for the final project, a portfolio of drawings depicting New York City in winter. I guess the heat was getting the better of me, and was, as Hemingway would say, attempting to transplant myself back to where I had come from, a cold city replete with snow. The good thing was that school wasn't far from the beach and where I had lived in Ocean Park, a tony enclave nestled between Condado and Isla Verde, where the de la Haba family had lived for well over a hundred years. I stayed with my Tia Carmen Luisa, a lady of grace and elegance, whose hair remained as jet-black in her Golden Years as it was the day she was born; and with a pair of matching black eyes, she turned heads wherever we went. That summer, she drove me back and forth to Artes Plasticas in Old San Juan so I could take the preliminary drawing tests for admissions: a stairwell, a portrait, an imaginary landscape, a real one.

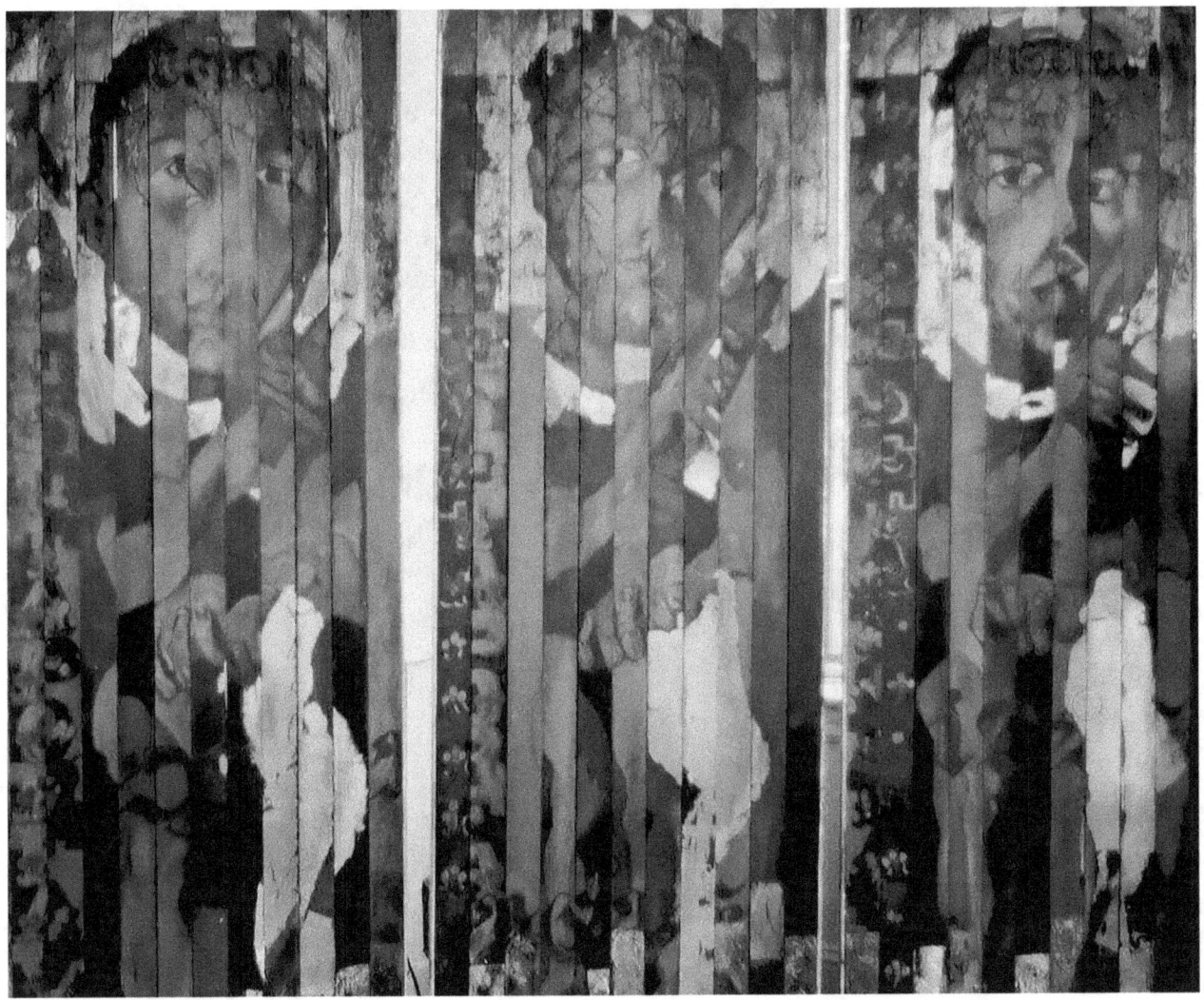

Over the course of a week or two, I passed and was accepted, and I began school in the fall. I sometimes rode my bike but mostly took the public bus, which lacked air conditioning but offered much in the way of Catholic-school girls in white shirts and pleated skirts or pressed slacks, who would laugh as they took turns describing the red-headed gringo with his large portfolio and his maricon baby-blue Miami Vice pants or green Cavarrici's with matching Guyabera shirt. As they left the bus, I'd reply in perfect Spanish, "You know you like it." Traveling to school was always lively and fun, and being in school, in the tropics, in Old San Juan, was an absolute joy. All that was missing was a sound academic drawing foundation. I just couldn't get past the notion that I needed one before I could really begin life as an artist. Not having it made me uncertain—uncomfortable, as it were, in my own white patent-leather island shoes.

But during a lunch break from Artes Plasticas, as I strolled through Old San Juan, I met Paul, homeless and down on his luck, who had ended up in Puerto Rico on accident. Or so he said. An alcoholic. He didn't have to say. He was a veteran who had served our country in Vietnam.

Originally from Minnesota, he'd headed to Florida once back from the War to kill his sister for stealing their dead father's coin collection. Without this asset, claimed Paul, he was desolate, no inheritance. His anger had blinded him because somehow his flight didn't take him to Florida, as planned, but to Puerto Rico, by accident, and there he was—stranded in the old city, unaccompanied, begging on street corners for nothing more than drink money, because saving for a plane ticket is beyond reach for a desolate man with drinking disease. In broken Spanish, he would recite to every passerby, "Una peseta por favor." During that first encounter, outside a McDonald's on Calle de la Fortaleza, I ordered a Fillet O' Fish for him, figuring it'd do him better than a measly quarter, una peseta.

"God, thank you, I wanted one of these for a long time."

I'd be proven wrong, though. Paul couldn't hold down food. At all. Once, for my birthday, I took him and other homeless men out to lunch at a T.G.I. Fridays. They refused to seat us. Didn't want to seat them, not one of the rotting, stinking bunch. I threatened to sue. Made a commotion. I shouldn't have. Within minutes of eating some of the bread that came before the meal, one of them regurgitated it onto the table. And Paul, poor Paul, crapped his pants after the first bite of his burger. With tears in his eyes, he asked to excuse himself from the table. I looked over at him, my insides wrenched, and replied, "Yes, please." We watched as he left a track all the way out the door. The other five couldn't finish their meals, not because of what they saw, but because what they ordered was too much. I asked for another round of drinks, both out of habit and guilt, which they did finish, and requested all remaining food in doggy bags. Party favors, of a sort.

It's curious and ridiculous how much the gaze of a prudish and painfully chaste man touched by love can sometimes express and that precisely at a moment when the man would of course sooner be glad to fall through the earth than to express anything with a word or a look.

— Fyodor Dostoyevsky, The Gambler

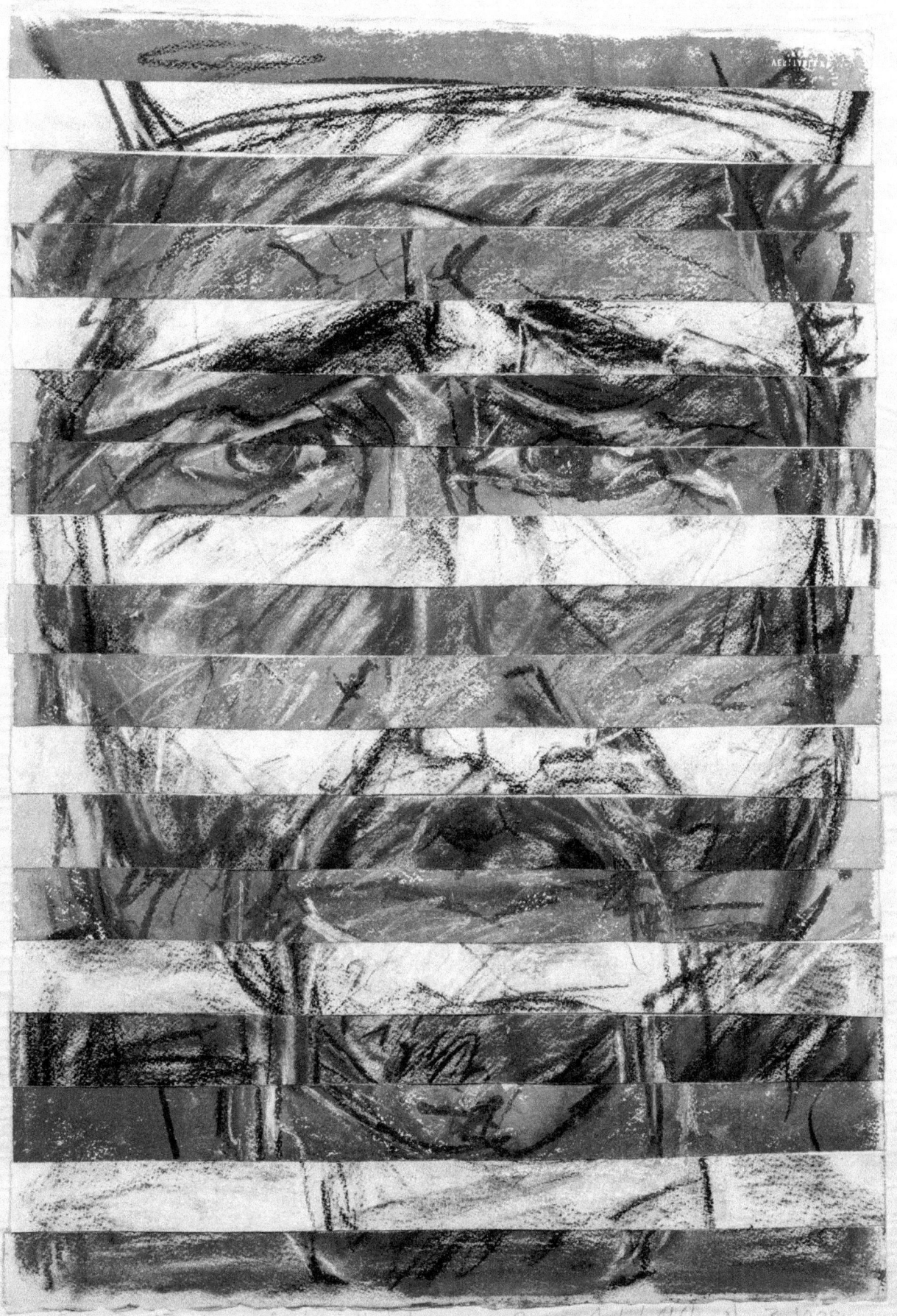

My Grandma but the Cost of War & Alcohol ——— Nov 3, 1989
Paul Durbin

The next night I searched all around the Plaza de Armas, the main plaza of Old San Juan, in the hopes of finding Paul. It was where we usually sat and talked and where he first let me draw him, on a bench, in front of the fountain that children, lovers, and tourist tossed coins into. Standing guard around the fountain were four larger-than-life statues of The Four Seasons. Each figure looked away from its post, paying no attention to the homeless men who scoured the shallow water in the middle of the night. Paul was nowhere to be found. I walked up San Jose Street to the Plaza that ran along Calle San Sebastian, past bars I'd drink in with friends from Artes Plasticas, and all very kind people.

One of those people was a young, gifted kid who painted better than anyone I had met up until then and whose work most resembled an Old Master's, only he worked in colors like those of the buildings of Old San Juan—pastel pinks and yellows—and in blues and greens of the turquoise waters surrounding the fortified city. But he had no money and had to leave because his family, who lived in the country outside San Juan, couldn't afford the three-dollar-a-credit tuition. Instead of an education in fine arts, he went straight into the world of social services; full-time employment in order to support his family.

I remember him standing in the courtyard of the school saying goodbye, beautifully colored paintings clasped under his youthful, brown arms. All I did was join the other students in shaking his hand. Some patted his back, wishing him well as he walked out of la Antigua Casa de Locos, the 19th century building that originally housed an insane asylum—and how crazy was it that the most gifted amongst us was the one leaving the old cuckoo's nest? How did I let that happen? Because it was more important to support homeless models who roamed the narrow adoquin streets? I was spending more each day on booze alone than the cost of all his credits combined. I should've offered to pay his way. I actually may have. Not certain; can't remember. I choose to recollect that I made the offer and that his Boricua pride prevented him from accepting, and to remember that I wasn't feigning regard when I bid him, "Adios amigo." More certain is this: I missed an opportunity for honest-to-goodness talent to rub off on me. And I was livid about it. A rage was building-up inside over the unfairness of it all. The one kid in the school who clearly possessed some god-given talent had to leave the school because of financial reasons beyond his control. Yet somehow, he still managed to hold his chin up high and smile as he walked off the school's grounds, a smile as full his arms carting away his art.

Later that day in Old San Juan, down Calle Del Cristo, on the right side of the street, beneath a bench out front of the Hotel El Convento, I found Paul sleeping. I roused him with a nudge.

"Indiana, is that you?"

He called me Indiana because I always wore a fedora hat like the one in Raiders of the Lost Ark. Except mine was white.

"It is, Paul. How are you? I brought you this." I handed him a bottle of Don Q.

"I'm sorry 'bout yesterday, Indiana. I didn't mean to make such a mess."

I told him I didn't care about that and added, "That's what they get for refusing to seat us right away."

He laughed. "Do you want to draw me?"

In exchange for the booze, I was allowed to draw him. A bottle of Don Q cost three bucks. I had his complete attention. A perfect model until he needed to put his head down, which he did without warning or request. It was like watching a helium balloon slowly make its way to the floor. After drawing him, he would often say how honored he was. I always told him how honored I was that he'd sit for me and thanked him for his service to our country. With honor, another bottle of Don Q, for us both. People were always around as I drew Paul, San Juan is busy day and night and if tourists weren't packing the streets at high noon there'd be plenty of others walking about, to work or school. I sketched Paul mostly in the town square, seated on one of the many benches and where I often found him sleeping beneath one.

After several days of sketches, though there were many and I'm not sure which, I asked him to please sign his name at the bottom of the drawing, next to mine. This, an attempt at something unique, my first art collaboration. He smiled at the idea, took a deep breath in, exhaled, and looked me in the eyes as his own welled-up. His look—of desperation, anguish, and joy—made time stop for me. In the two magnifying glasses that were his eyes, there it was, my life, passing before me with a big question mark over the future. "What are you doing here, Gregory?" I wanted so badly to capture in drawing the way he looked at me that day, the two of us stationed in front of the steps leading into the 500-year-old Cathedral of Saint John, where one day the Bishop of Puerto Rico, draped in silk robes, would marry me to someone special. That marriage would prove brief, even though God, according to the Bishop, was in attendance. That would all come later, though. Witnessing Paul in the yellow glare of the lamppost, his salted eyes hanging in front of me, now sending back alternately dull and then gleaming shapes of light, there was no divine. It was all human, and terribly so. I felt utterly incompetent and frozen. How does one render humility? Humanity stranded and broken? I was unable to.

The drawings I made of Paul Durbin were expressionistic in style and nothing like those scrawled by the Old Masters I so revered. No, mine were improvised and rudimentary, with heavy-handed lines, unrefined, a face unlike any existing in nature, in reality. The subject had become purely non-objective in the drawing, with features both exaggerated and distorted. Drawings so far gone from the touch of an Old Master's hand that I subsequently abandoned, for the remaining stay in Puerto Rico, any hope of drawing like one, becoming one, and, instead, let myself separate, in mind and in action, further away from them. I allowed myself to act outside the old-world-traditionalist mentality that I had boxed myself into and tried, without much preliminary or conscious efforts, to become a modern artist, a contemporary doing contemporary-minded things, like cutting three drawings into strips and gluing them back together in new arrangements, alternating strips from drawing one with drawings two and three.

The approach seemed child's play, and Picasso's quote, "It took 90 years to paint like a child," crossed my mind, and I wondered why it took 90 years and figured he was just being cute, as a bravado-stuffed Spaniard braggart would. But no bragging rights would come with these drawings, only apologetic feelings towards them and Paul, for falling short of doing justice to the loftiest of subjects, during this, my first true life-drawing lesson. It was 1989, and at 19 years of age, I was stuck, natura-morta.

Stuck, though, only in the head: In my back pocket, an American Express card was stashed. I could bolt out of there at any moment, leave Puerto Rico in a flash. Too hot? I could buy an air conditioner. Too cold from the air conditioner? I could buy a down blanket. No food? No such thing. Ever. I wasn't rich by any means, but I was far removed from so many of those impoverished artists living up on Montmartre in Paris, in the late 19th and early 20th centuries, so far from Paul's situation, that mine, alongside it, seemed a childish exercise in extended mockery. It seemed a lie. Like the one I told American Express as a sophomore in High School, penning in a $200,000 a year salary while sitting in a pizzeria at lunchtime. Artists atop Montmartre resorted to burning what they could to stay warm. I was burning through money I didn't have—to be cool, to fit in on the streets of Old San Juan as artist-in-residence. When a teacher on lunchbreak from Artes Plasticas passed the two of us sharing swills of rum from a bottle of Don Q, she looked disapprovingly and said: If you were an actor, I might understand your method some. Are we an actor now, Gregorio? Que estas haciendo?

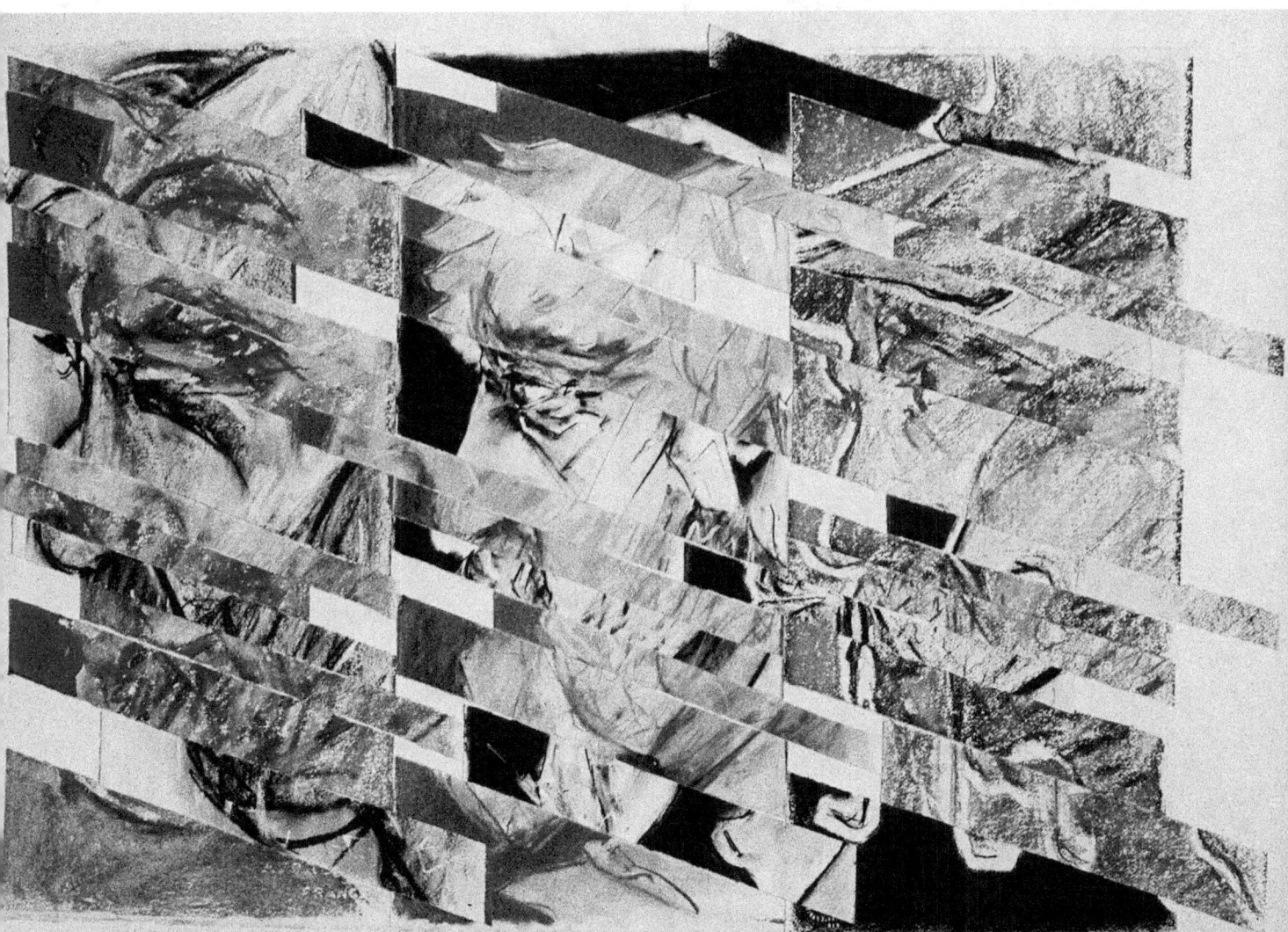

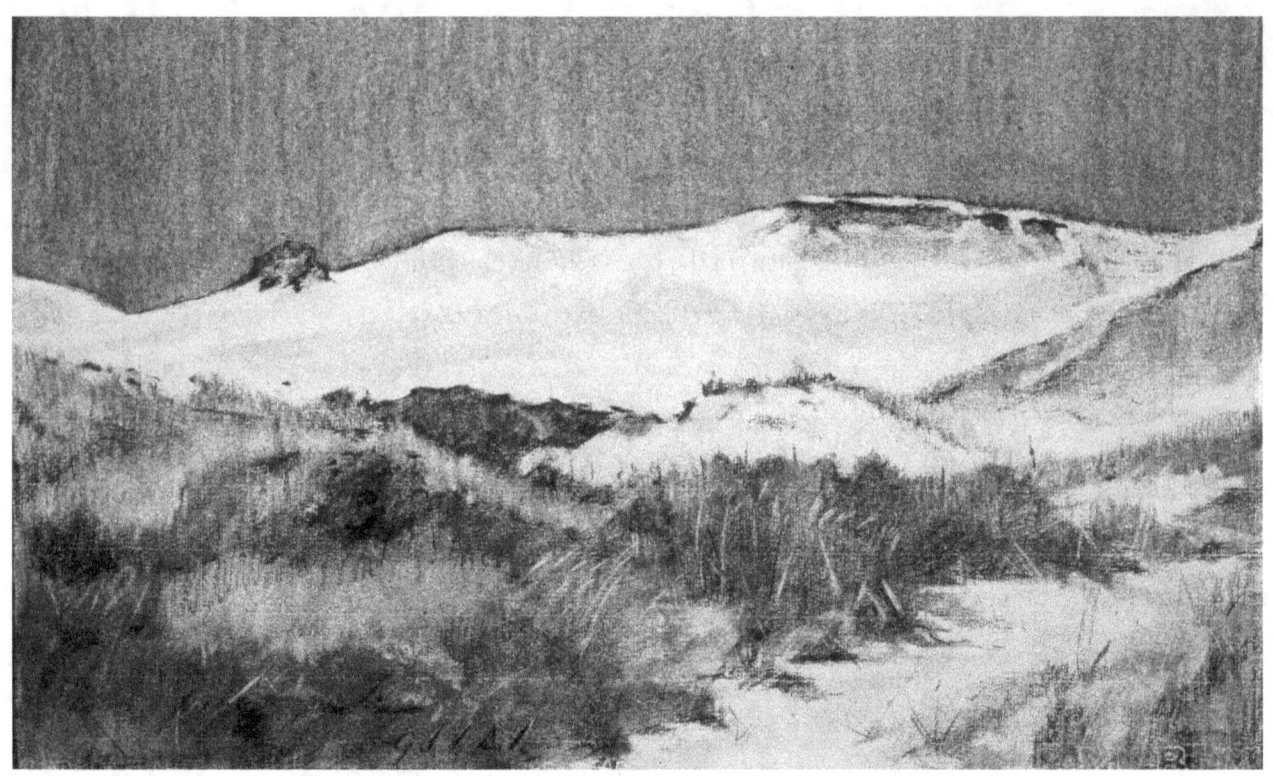

REFERENCES

I've always jotted down notes. On napkins, scraps of paper. Idea sketches to work with and contemplate at a later date. Reminders to remember.

"Sooner or later, everything disappears. My nineteenth year for instance. It vanished ten years ago. I still haven't a clue as to where the hell it went. Yesterday is already gone, a memory now. Distorted at best, forgotten at worst. This is why I love art and set out so many years ago to become a painter. Art, for me, is the clearest reminder, the closest resemblance to all that once stood; to all that was, to all that once could have been or shouldn't have. Each painting I create is an attempt to capture a certain truth from the moment or subject at hand. A visual remembrance, a token, they become individual capsules filled with the essence of that time, place, and subject. Art can therefore become, or translate into, a testament to all that we believe or don't believe; a further reminder to cherish, care, and love all that we hold dear—before it all disappears, forever."

In early May of 2001, I wrote a note to Teresa:

Gone to Montauk. Will call you later….

Montauk, for me, is difficult to predict, and that's part of the draw. When might I go? Who might I find? How might the cliffs and beaches look after a storm? I like that it's predictably unpredictable. Montauk was also an annual fishing trip with family from birth to teenage years, and later, sporadically, I'd sometimes drive solo, not even getting out of the car—drive to the lighthouse, do a u-turn, and drive straight back to Queens. The journey of it always was, and is, calming. The same stops for coffee, the same long way to avoid traffic, the same slowing of the breath once out of the city, and the same return to a quick pace. But this napkin-referenced trip east was meant as a head-clearing, soul-searching creative rendezvous. A mid-week getaway to work some, think a lot, and pay more attention to the needs and cares of the creative spirit within. Sounds fucking corny, I know. But it's the truth. The path to artistic discovery doesn't come with a roadmap. And with mistakes made and bad turns taken what else is there to do but run far away from them for a while and try fighting them out in isolation, in solace. But "the path" gets lonely, dizzy, too, sniffing mineral spirits all day in the studio with nothing but a bunch of portraits looking back at you. And then, every painting is forever telling you what you did wrong and what could be improved upon. It's an art unto itself to know when to stop painting. Another art to sell it and yet another to commence once again. It's really no wonder artists go mad, drink too much, or outright kill themselves. And this despair is when things are going relatively well. Unlike the last two years spent floundering, waiting for things to happen and when they didn't.

Sometimes all it takes to escape this creative claustrophobia is a night out with fellow artists, sharing in libations and laughter, discussing each other's work, true camaraderie. Other times, a stroll inside a museum or a gallery will do. But when the hustle and bustle of the business side of art, of selling it, or selling the idea of it, and the convincing that takes, trumps the making of it, relief requires a larger gesture. When the studio becomes a confounding nuisance—one corner filled with paintings calling out for a fresh face, another stacked with drawings waiting to be framed or rendered immortal in paint; an easel in a third, holding an unfinished portrait whose sitter hasn't shown up in weeks let alone paid the latest installment, and a mirror in the fourth corner that screams back at you, "Get. The. Fuck. Out!" because things didn't go the way you wished and patrons didn't patronize as expected—then you know escape must surely come or going out of one's mind becomes inevitable.

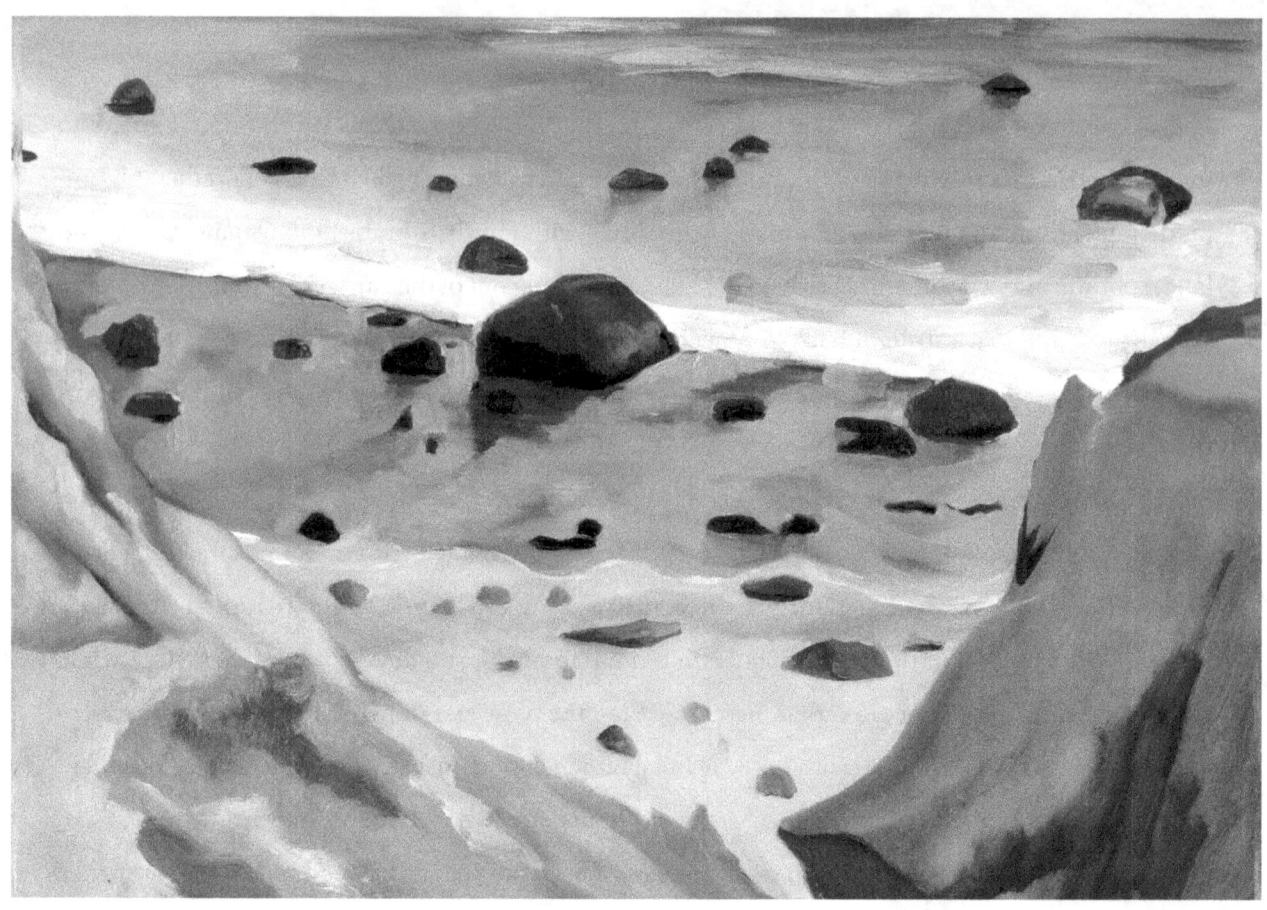

Once, when still a child, and while watching the movie Lust For Life, starring Kirk Douglas as Vincent Van Gogh, I clearly remember laughing with my father. He cracked, "Look at that dope!" when Vincent lost his painting to the wind, his canvas swept off his easel and thrown out into the field. I was around ten years of age at the time. Now, at 30, the early spring afternoon found me mid-measure on the Montauk cliffs trying to capture in paint the dramatic, rugged landscape and laughing not so readily as my French easel, along with the work in progress on it, collapsed and took flight from the 80-foot-high bluff—crashing down upon the very rocks and boulders being painted.

A matter of practice and belief, I always make a point to put a work in process alongside the actual object or portrait that I'm working from. I step as far back from the canvas as possible and view the work from every perspective. This way, my eyes are able to jump back and forth—from object to painting, painting to object—and back again, in order to check the rendering of form, line, proportion, color, and values. The decisive gust responsible for the easel's demise was unrelenting, the northwest winds dispersing the canvas as casual as a whip, and the momentum knocking-loose

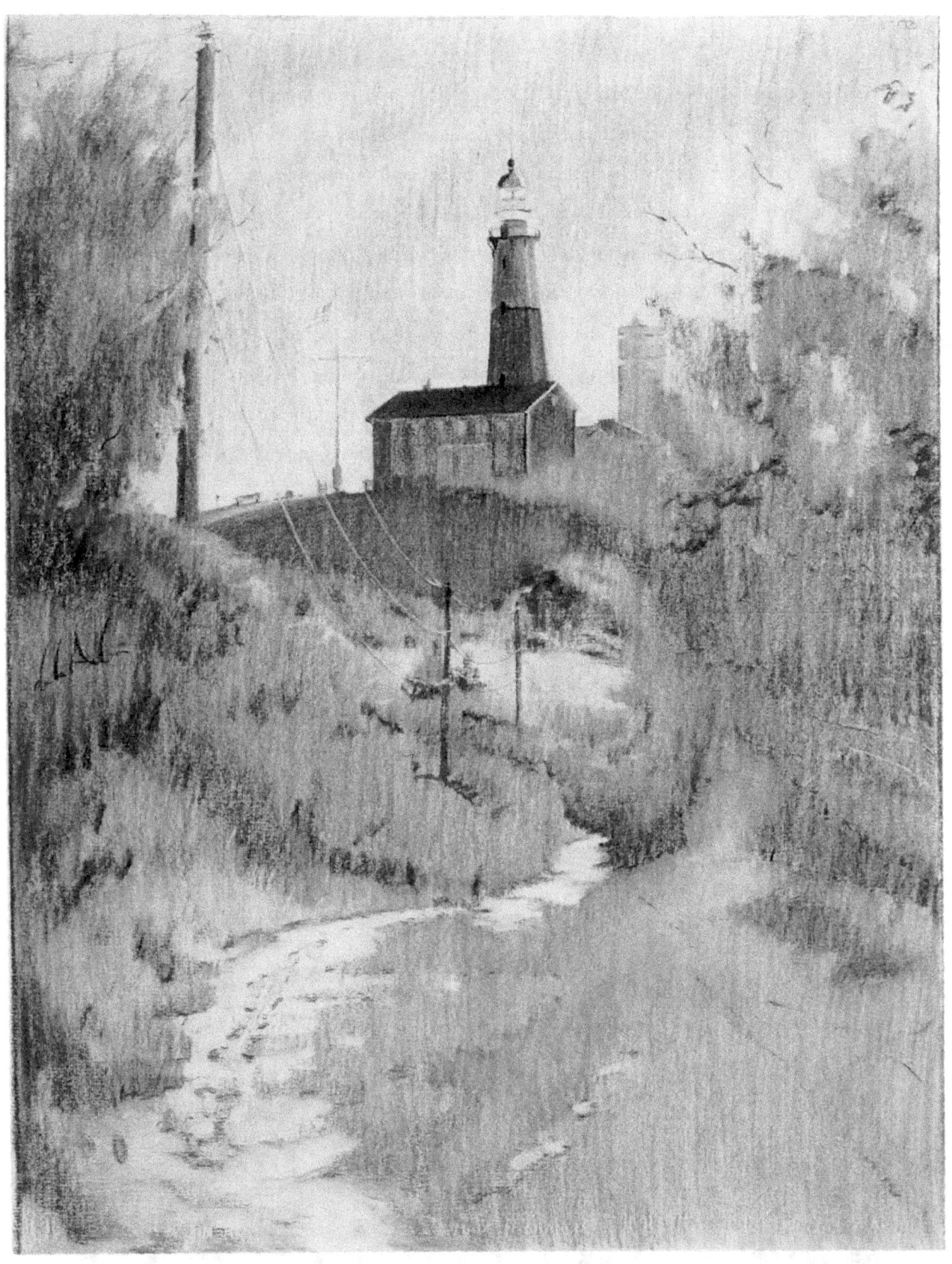

my well-stationed easel. I stood firmly at the edge of my perch and watched as the French easel and the painting it held took a sudden and violent beating on an unwanted journey down the jagged bluff's face. As it hit the rocky beach below, one of the easel's three wooden legs broke off, landing atop an outgoing wave. The paints and brushes held in its confines were thrown across the beach, some even popping up and out before hitting bottom, landing within the crevices of the bluff's face. Amazingly, the painting itself, after escaping the easel's grasp, landed face-up alongside the very grouping of boulders depicted on the canvas. I stood still, bewildered, but full of good humor at this "new perspective." I cautiously approached the edge and peered down as my eyes (by rote) and the painting (by jetty) jumped back and forth from the boulders to the ocean. I had done a rather good job at "hitting" the color notes! My $200 easel was shattered, but my earth tones were on the money. A smile of satisfaction crossed my face until I noticed a fisherman on the beach laughing, inspecting my situation from below. I was almost sure the wind whispered a refrain: "What a dope."

...P.S. Might stay a while.

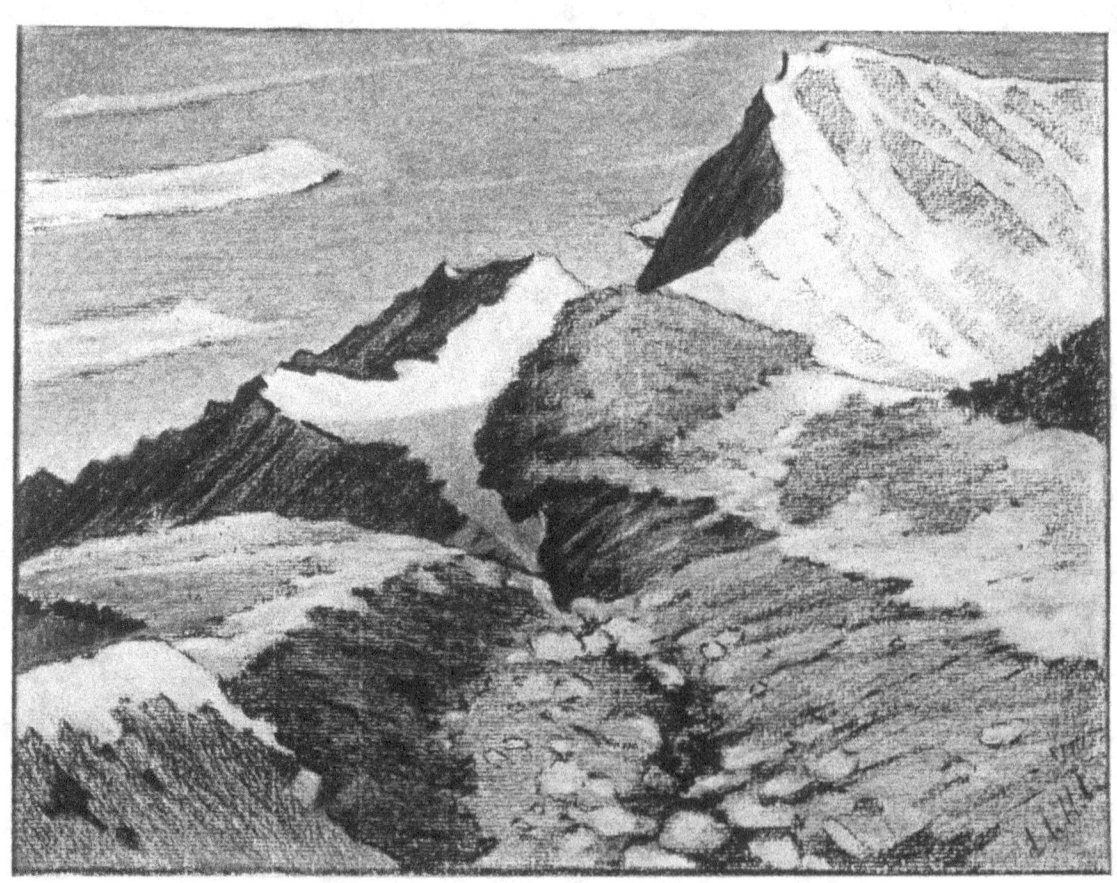

May of 2001

One hopes never to upset one's wife, and when I finally called later in the day, all I could do was assure her that everything was OK and that I wouldn't be gone long. I needed to clear my head, I explained, and when I returned, we'd have a nice dinner at our favorite place.

Her main concern: "Where are you going to stay?"

Followed by a characteristic pang of caution: "Don't drink too much!"

But a week turned into six months because one week wasn't enough and each week thereafter brought about a stronger urge to stay and figure it out. Whatever that was. And to draw and paint to my heart's content—a heart that, on the drive out, wasn't content at all, with my art.

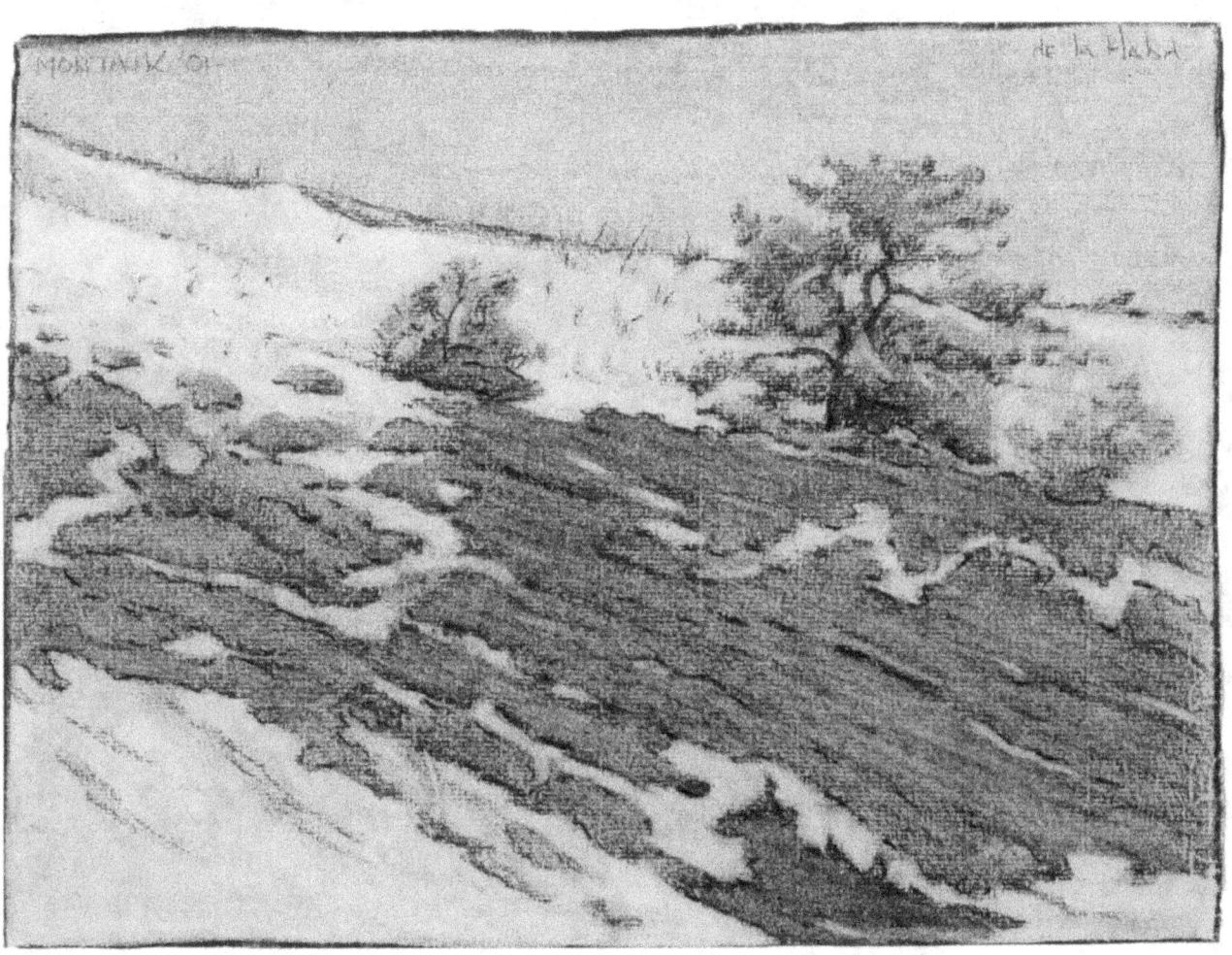

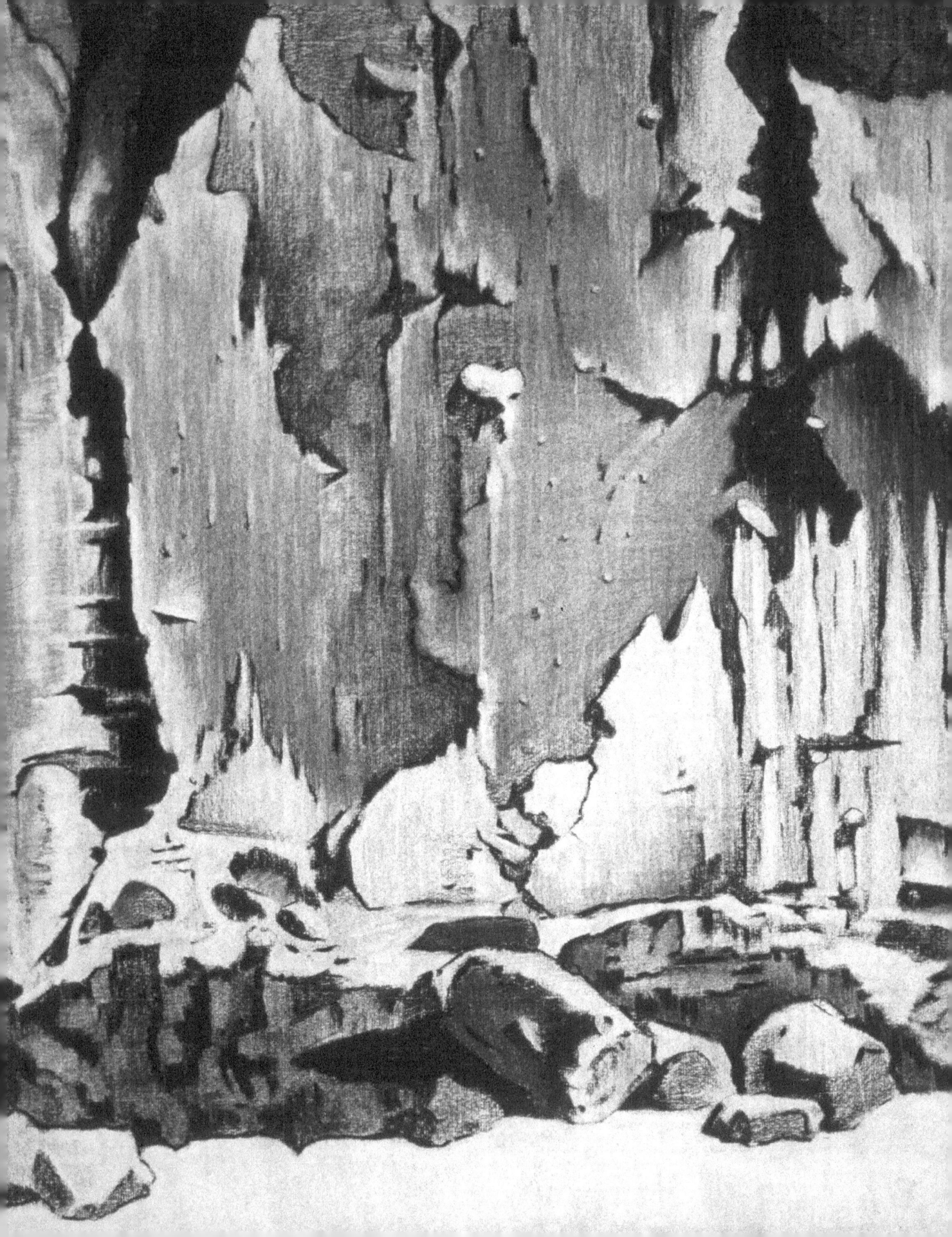

EXPERIENCE

Keep trying. Keep failing. Keep closing your eyes, so that you can open them.
   -Note to self

Montauk, July, 2001

When I returned home from Montauk on Friday nights, it was her enthusiastic questions that reinforced how amazing she was—and is. When I arrived, her request was always the same: "Show me your work before we go for dinner!"

"You're not hungry?"

"I can wait…did you do any more drawings of the horses? I love them, Gregory. Will you do one like that again just for me?"

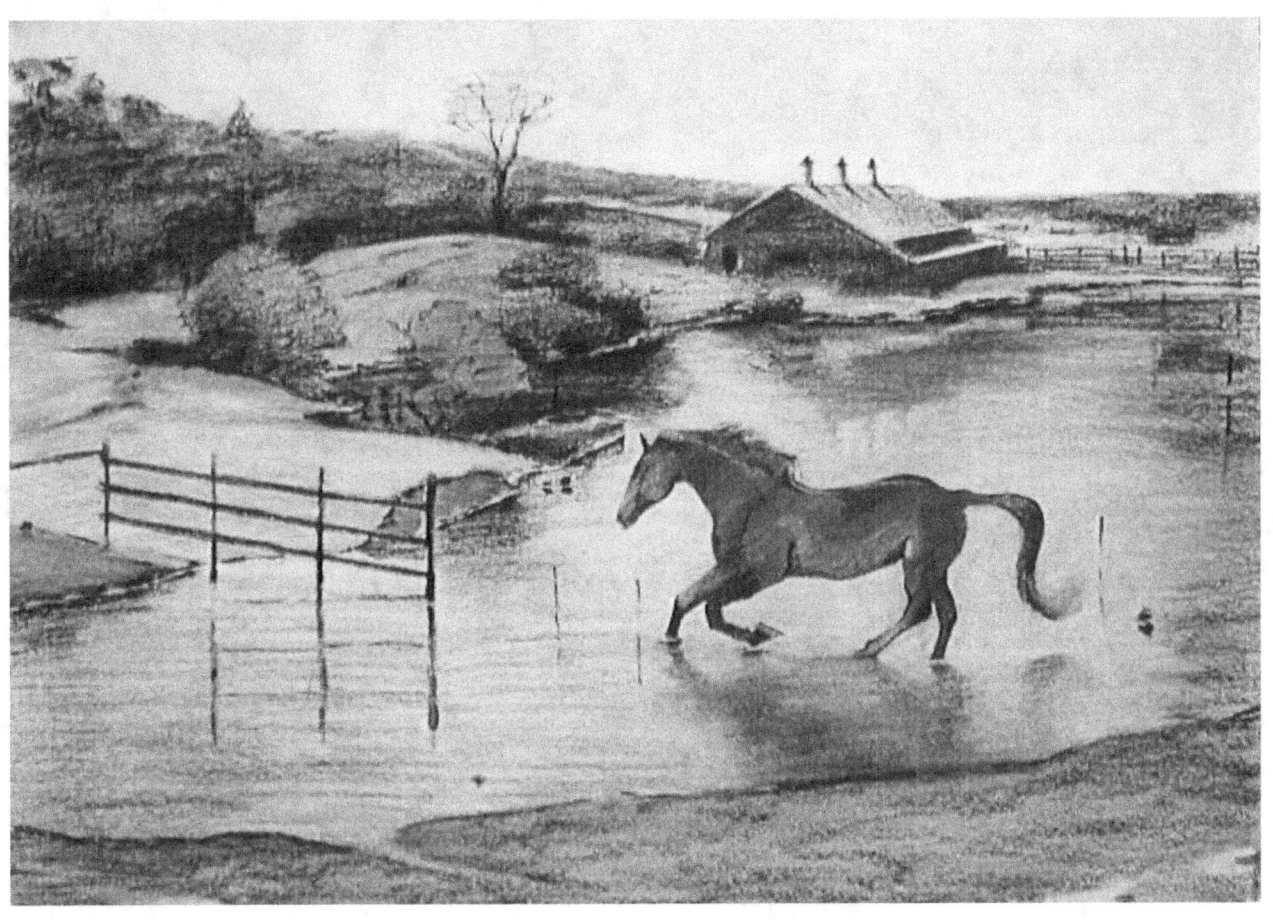

MONTAUK

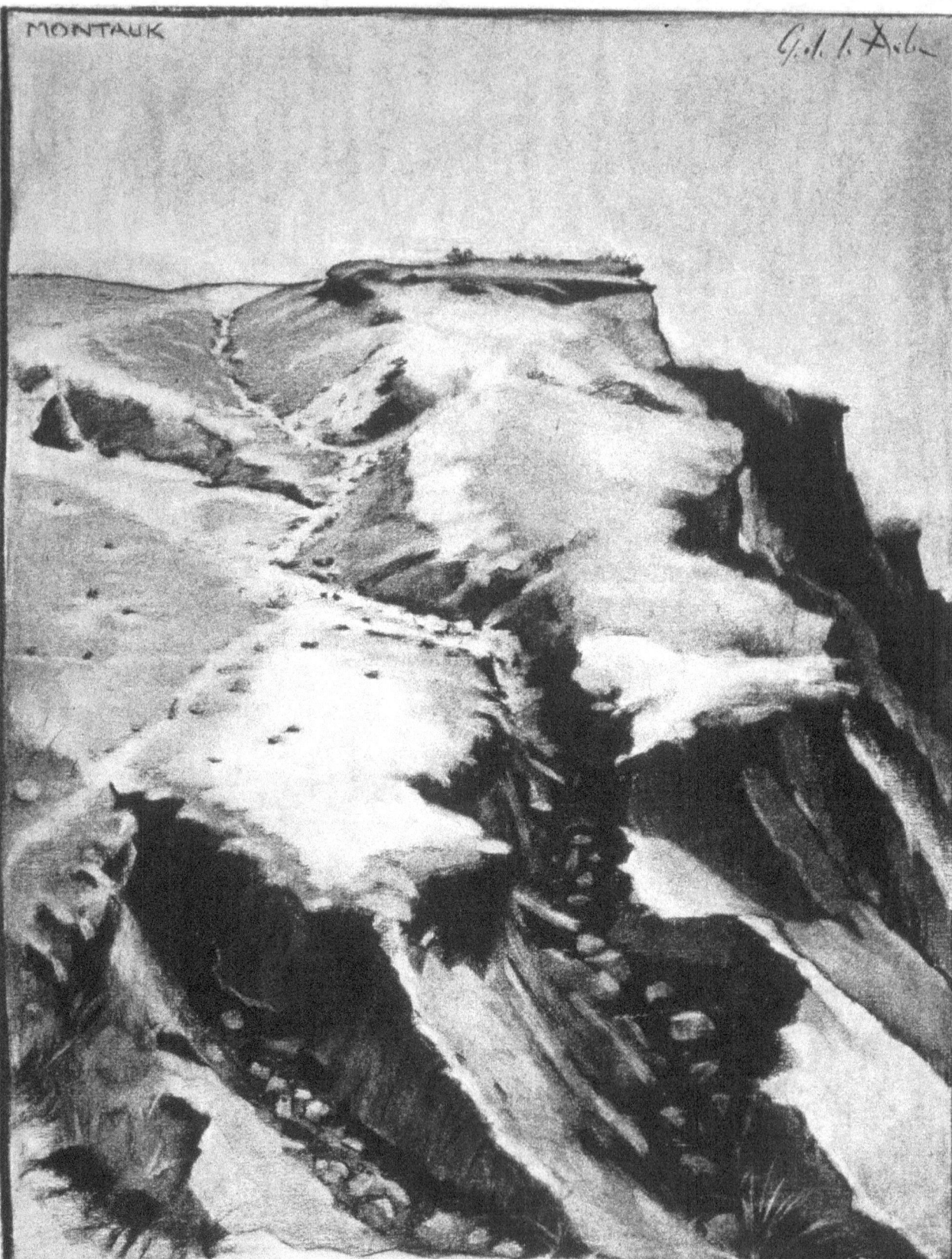

In some ways, experiencing love—just love—doesn't get old. Other things do, but not that. In the beginning of the Montauk sojourn, the passage of time was measured by the days spent away from Teresa with Fridays always being a return to her. It was easy to remember when Friday was approaching; the bars would get crowded, marking the arrival of Thursday night. They filled up with city people looking for that longer weekend. But by mid summer, after a few months of work, my body was more in sync with the tides than the days of the week. At that point, more people were staying in Montauk, and staying for longer stretches; and the bars became as busy on Tuesday as they were on Thursday. Sometimes I forgot to keep my promise to Teresa that I'd return home on Fridays. A phone call to her work on Friday afternoon was a telltale sign that I'd be a no-show. "It's okay, Gregory. I'm kind of tired tonight anyway. You take your time and don't rush back. Come tomorrow if you'd like and we'll go for dinner then." Whether I showed up Saturday evening or Sunday morning, Teresa was always eager to see the work I returned with.

Teresa: "Oh, I love this one, baby. But what is it?"

Me: "Erosion on the cliffs, over by Ditch. I cropped it just so, close-up."

"It's very different from the rest."

"You're very different from the rest."

"Oh really? Up close or from afar?"

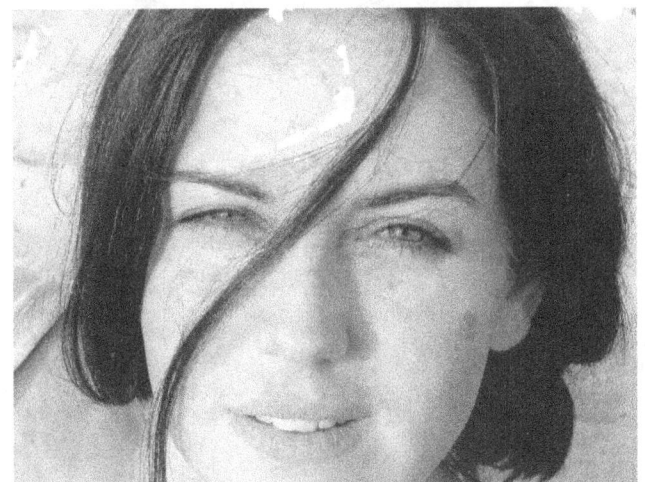

There is no erosion problem until a structure is built on a shoreline. Beach erosion is a common, expected event, not a natural disaster.

—Living With Long Island's South Shore by Larry McCormick.

That quote stuck. People get caught up on the "because" in life, wondering why something completely foreseeable occurred, ascribing intent where none exists, or invoking and then lamenting tragedy, when what the world is really doing is just turning. The last three month's work outdoors bears witness to the natural progression of erosion, unfolding slowly and steadily along Montauk's coast. Every day, consistent as the tide, there was my neighbor, Walter, clipboard in hand, translating this erosion into figures and layman's data. In pencil, he'd jot down what he saw

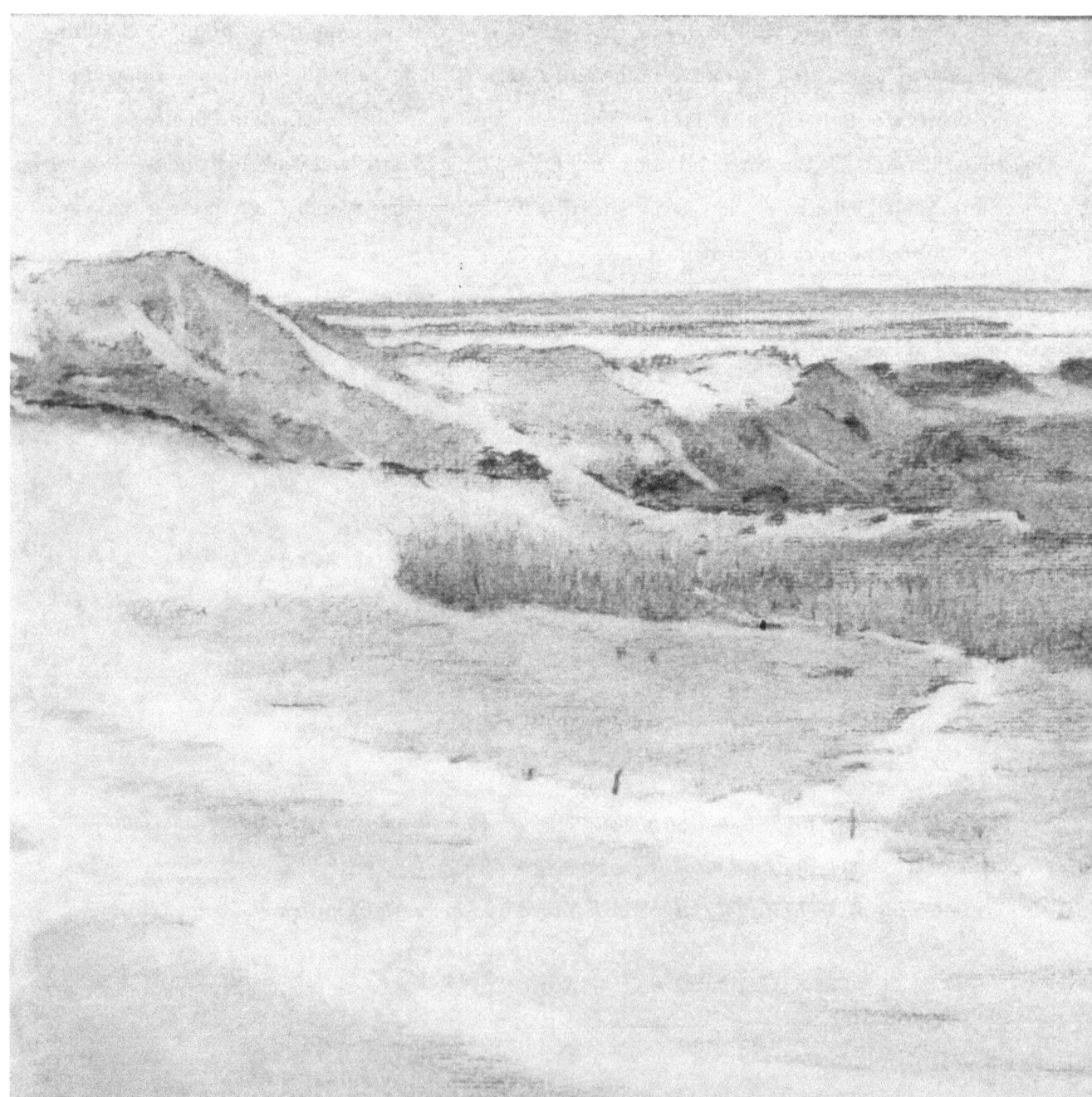

in relation to the sand on the beach and the high-tide mark the ocean had left behind and the exact time and precise location all this had occurred, and during the course of his morning routine, he'd go up and down Ditch Plains, sharing stories with anyone who'd listen. A concerned citizen, he did this for the town, all the while embittered by the vulnerability of the place he loved—by its weakness—by how much sand was forever being carried up island away from his home. All he could do was note its disappearance on a clipboard. His little dogs, meanwhile, dug happily, getting lost in all the sand that still remained.

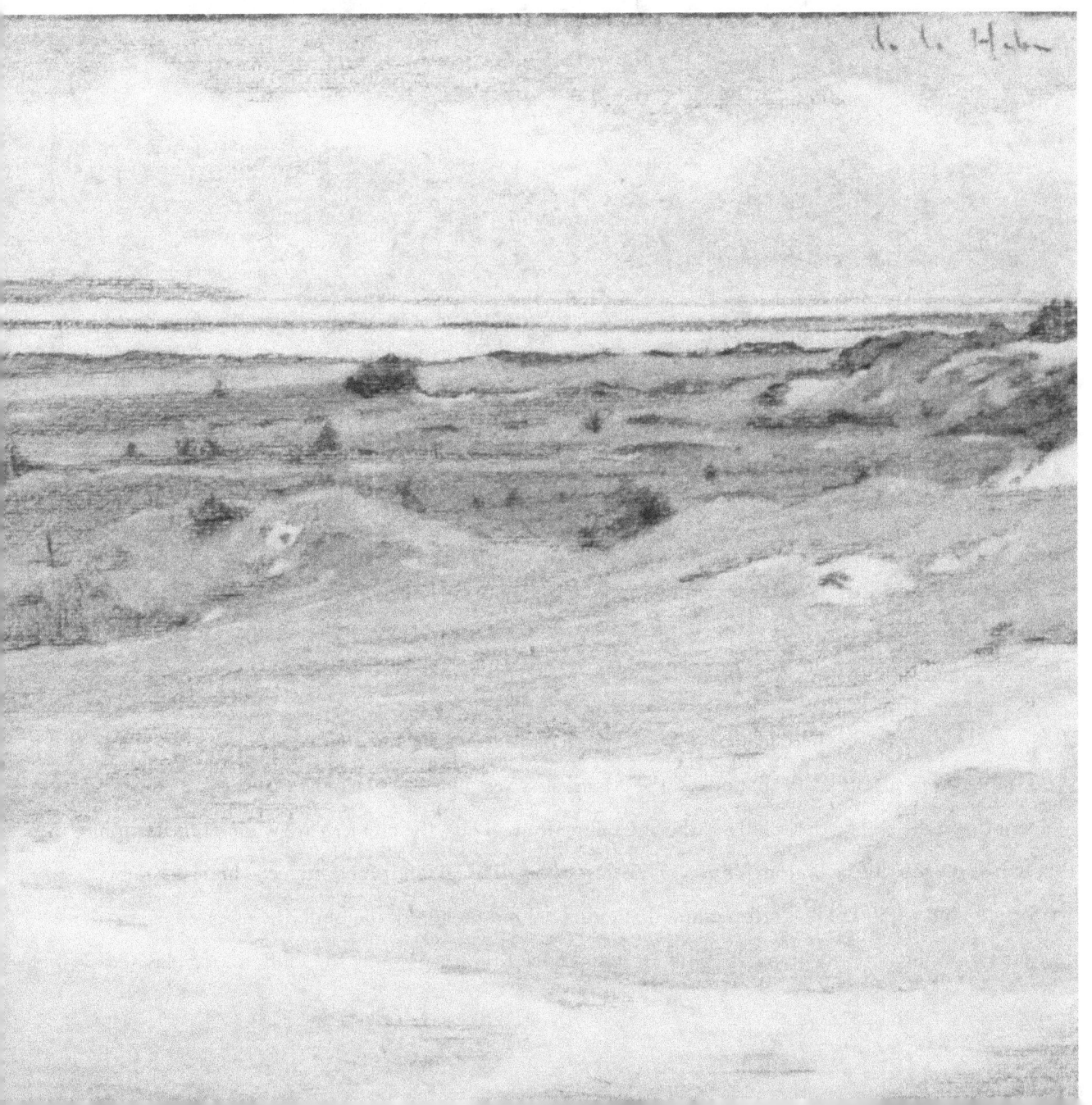

VISUAL LANGUAGES (SPOKEN AND UNHEARD)

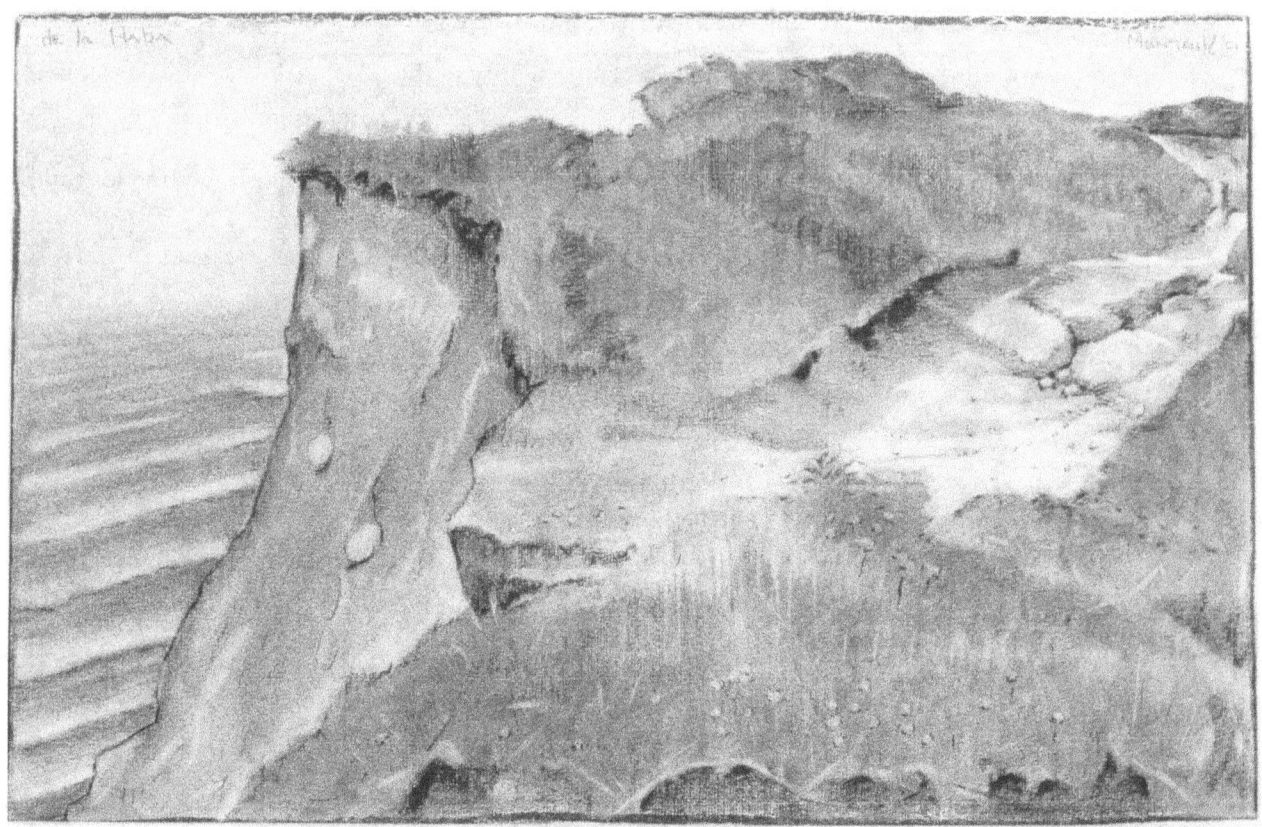

One day, I went looking for someone to tell me a little more about the formations I was drawing along the coast, especially over by Shadmoore State Park and Camp Hero farther east. I rolled up a few drawings and brought them to Larry Penny of Natural Resources in East Hampton.

Everyone said he was the one to see.

"The crevices here in your drawings, which are very good by the way, are called 'hoodoos,' a name given to similar formations in the American West by early geologist explorers. The water runs down the cliff face as it falls, gathering momentum. Thus, the crevices are wider at the bottom than at the top. At the bottom, or toe, of the formation, alluvial fans of soft material and rock debris form a kind of talus. The flattish plane that exists behind the top of the bluff line owes its origin to water running laterally along the bluff crest and back from the edge of the bluff, taking clay sedi-

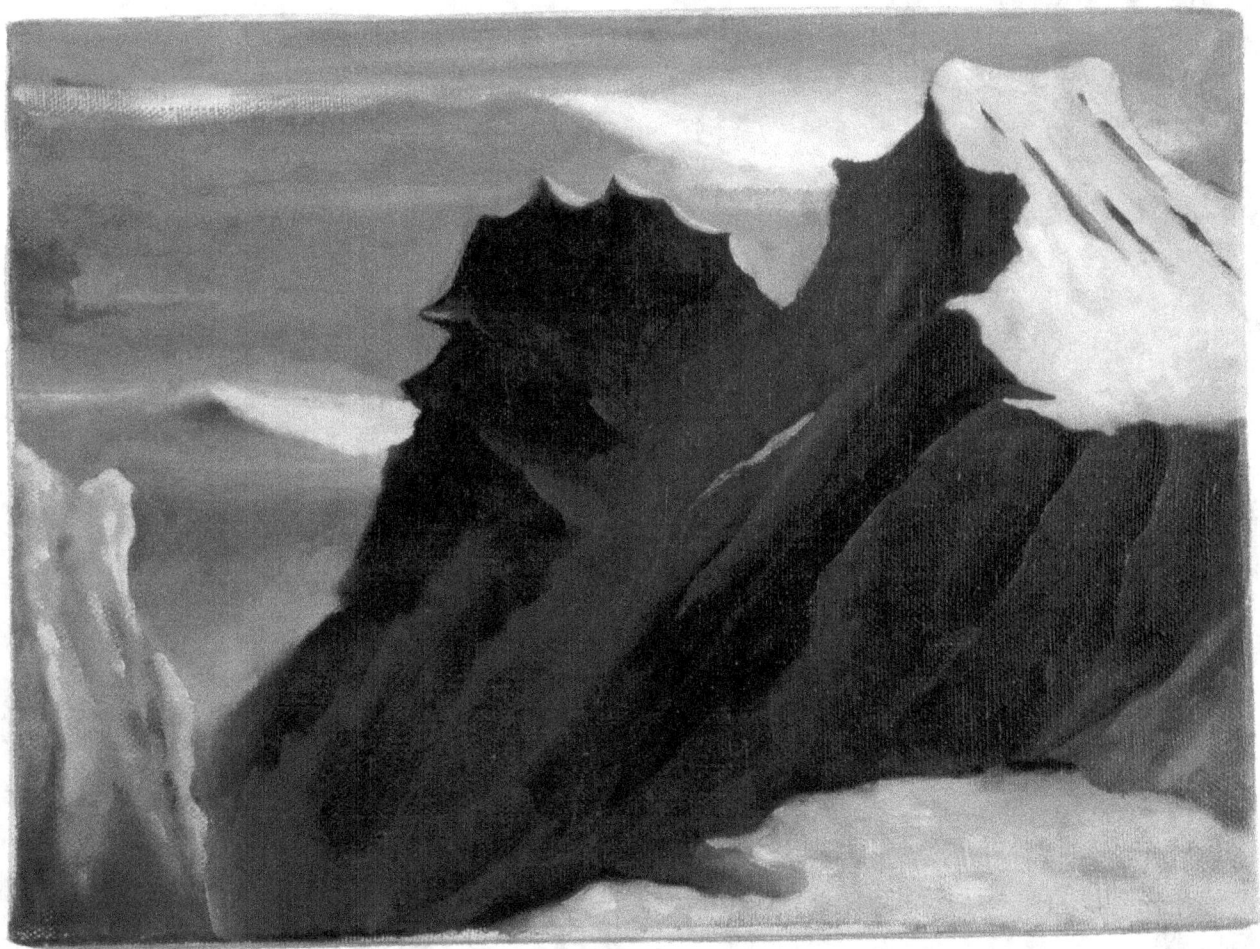

ments with it and spreading them out. These crevices will ultimately widen into bigger ones. They will then become ravines or arroyos that empty onto the floor of the beach and will ultimately serve to funnel water from the top of the bluff to the beach."

"I see. Would you like to buy one?"

"Unfortunately, they don't pay me enough to collect art, thank you."

"I understand. I barely get paid enough to keep making it."

With deadpan delivery, he added, "Well, I'm sure you didn't set out to be an artist because you heard the money was good?"

I rolled up the drawings, thanked him for his time, and headed to the car to make the return trip east, back to Montauk. I drove past the village of Amagansett, with its quaint tack shop for the few horse-set folks who live on the still-fewer horse farms not yet sold into development; past the

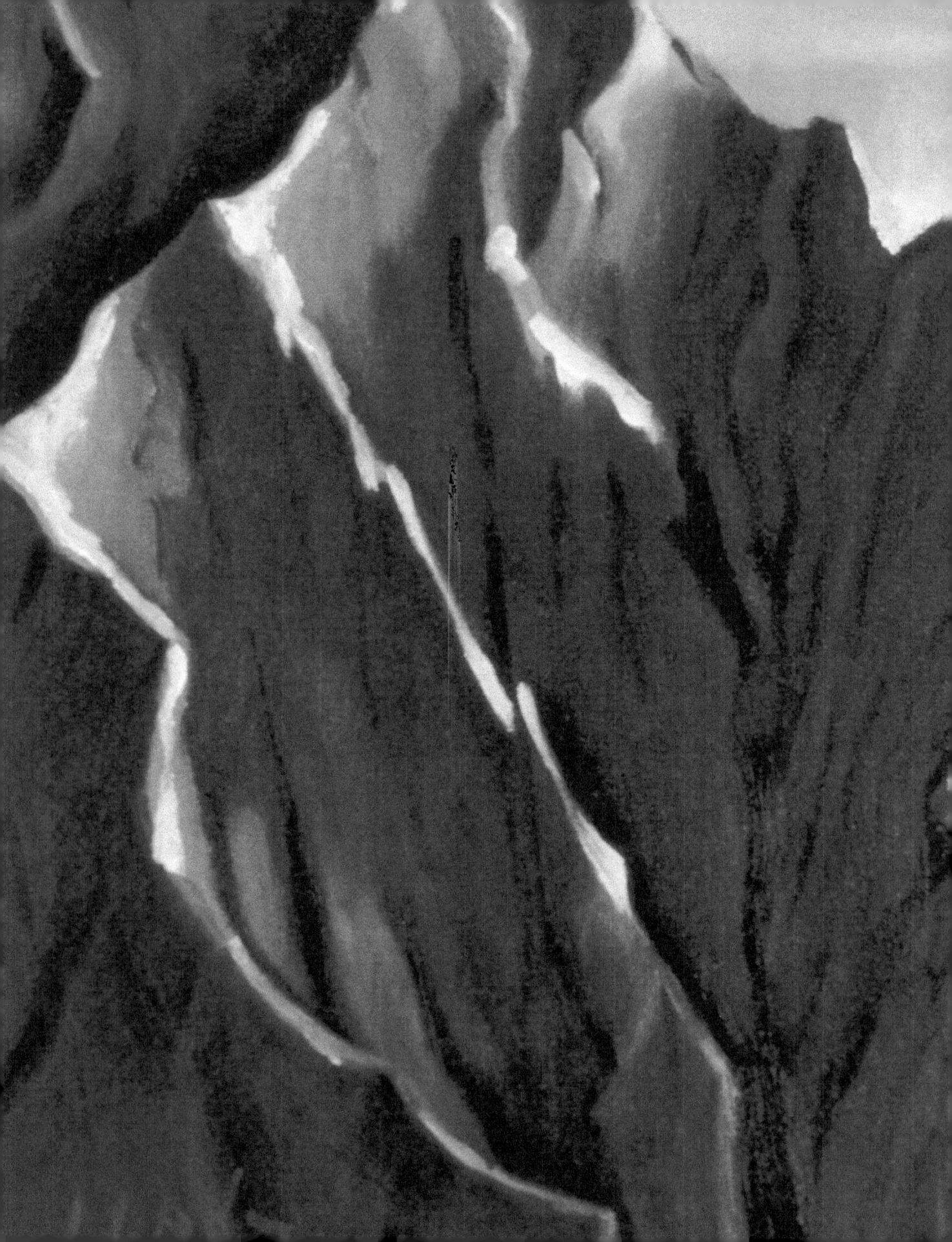

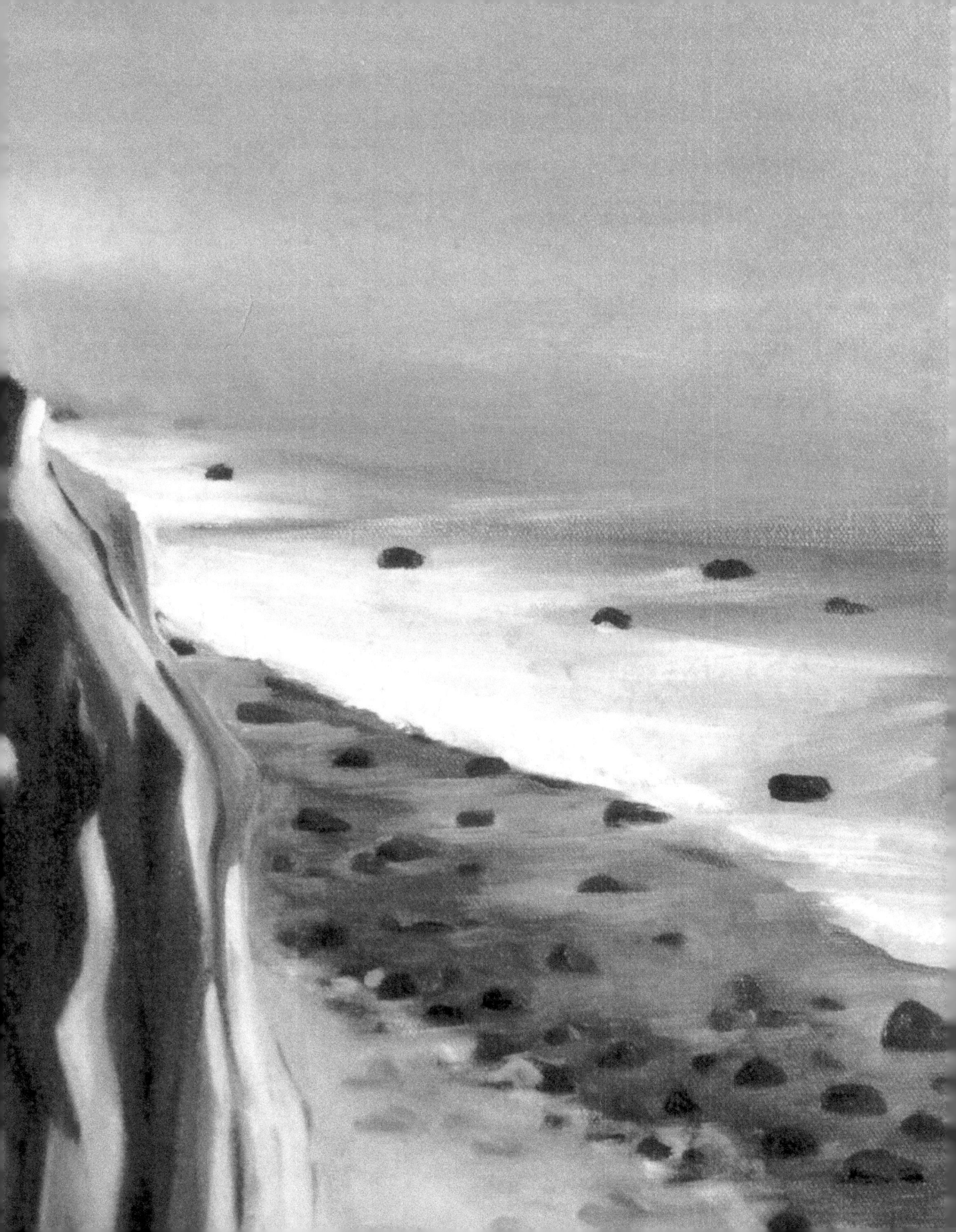

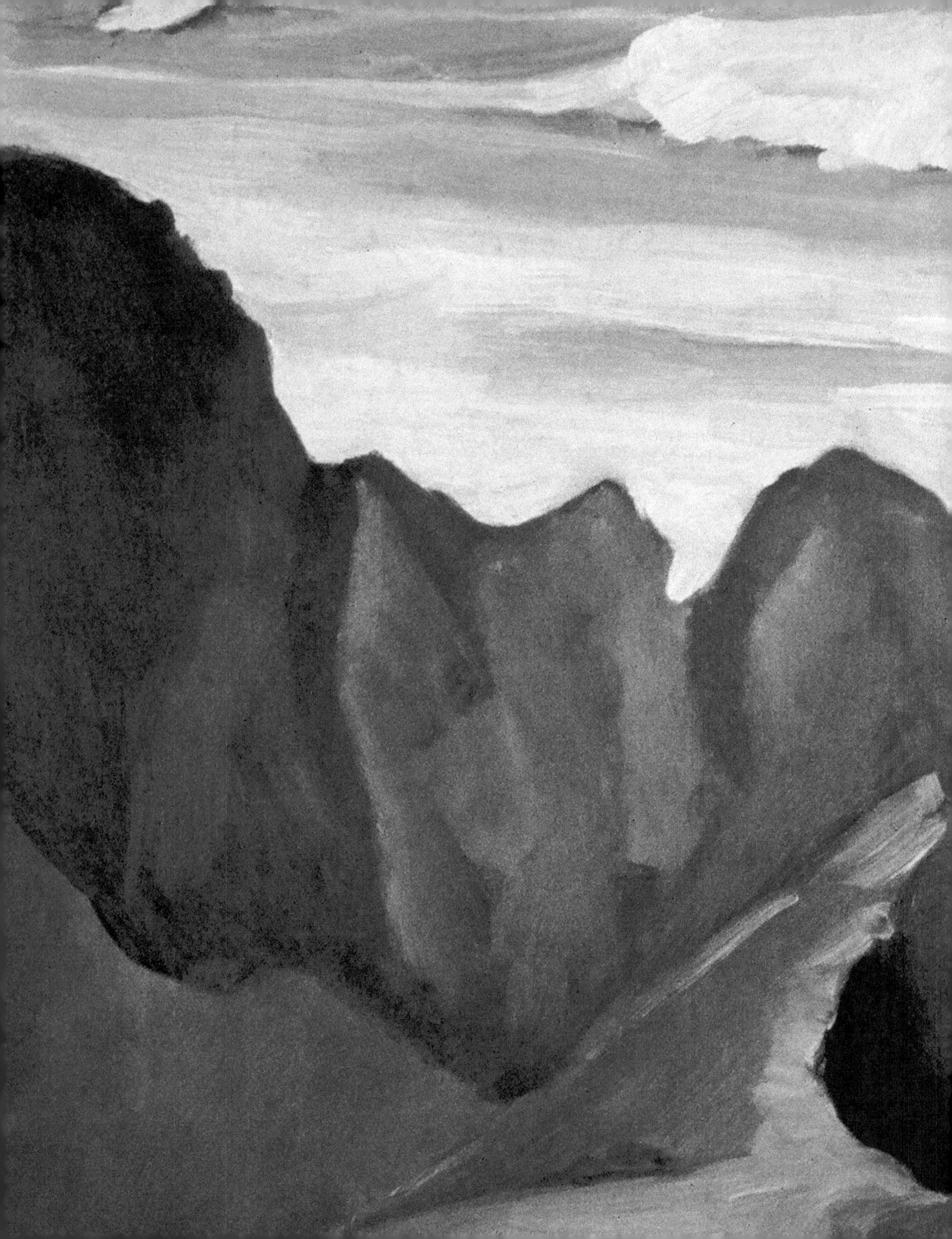

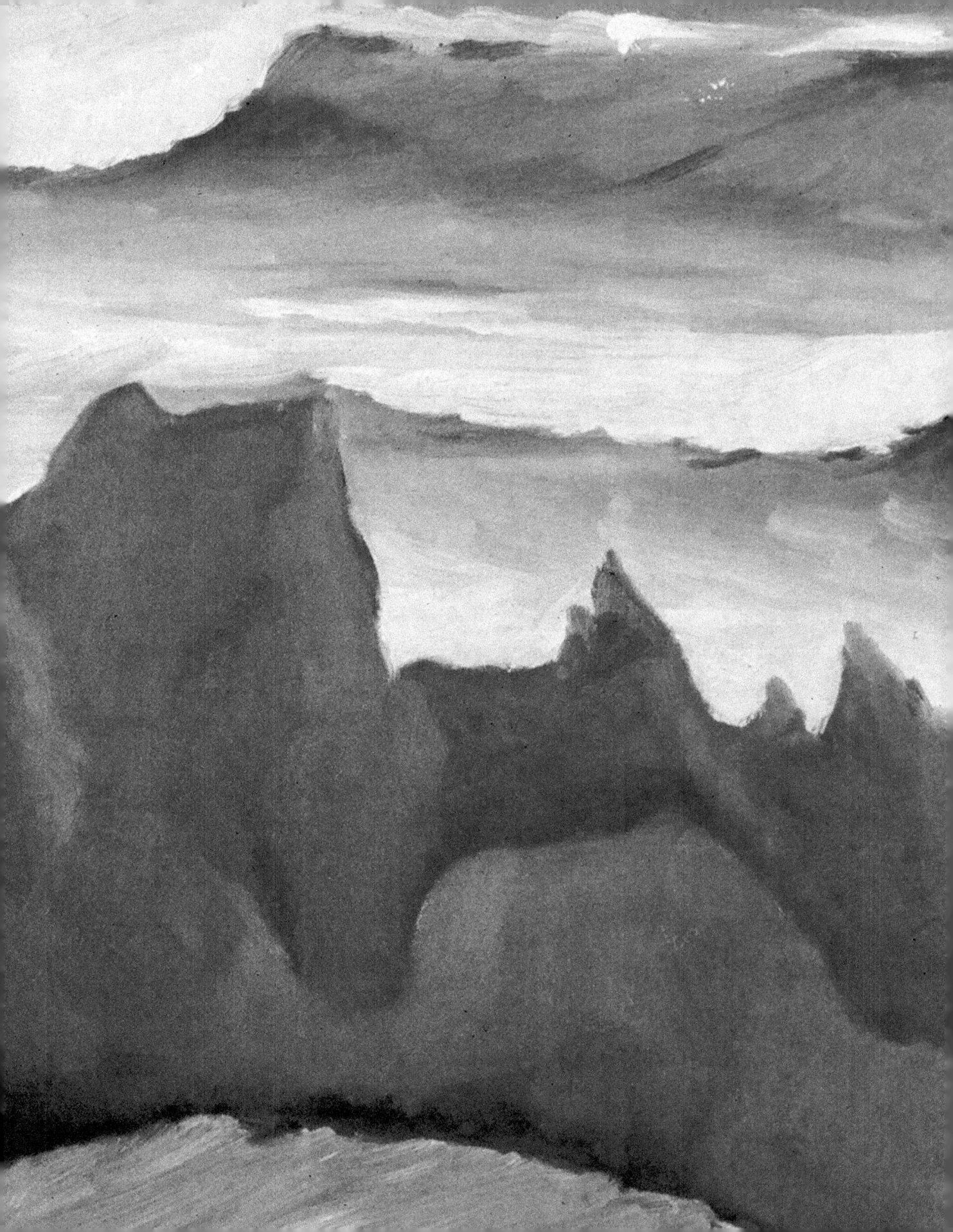

summer galleries with their summer art displays set out like lobster traps, hoping to bag a collector or designer (with matching client sofa); past the seasonal eateries stocked with young Mexican and Irish migrant workers; past the little old wooden church painted in heavenly colors of soft pastel cream and baby blue, its royal blue trim anchoring God's house to Earth; and the Farmers Market opposite that, where the Jitney Express line is bloated with Manhattanites who've accessorized with designer suitcases and recyclable bags bulging with local corn, strawberries, peaches, and asparagus. Farther still, past the flat stretch cutting through Napeague State Park, where the Long Island Rail Road's track ballasts run parallel to the road, visible, for most of the trip back, off to the left.

To the right, due south, skimpy, low-lying dunes—molded by tide and wind—break up the otherwise flat terrain. Although unseen, the beach is there, awaiting the next storm, when it will rise over the dunes and cover the road entirely. But not now. Now's the time to look up: once out from beneath the stately American Elms of town and the windswept pines that mark the transition from man to nature, the sky breaks open into a mass of translucent, limpid blue—a captured sea, locked and floating in the hemisphere above. This is Napeague Stretch. It cuts across 1,364 acres of protected Earth, most of it wetland, spanning Amagansett to Montauk. It reaches from the Atlantic Ocean across the entire narrow width of this section of the South Fork, to Gardiners Bay and Block Island Sound, where ospreys and sea hawks nest and hunt. It is where the winding road through

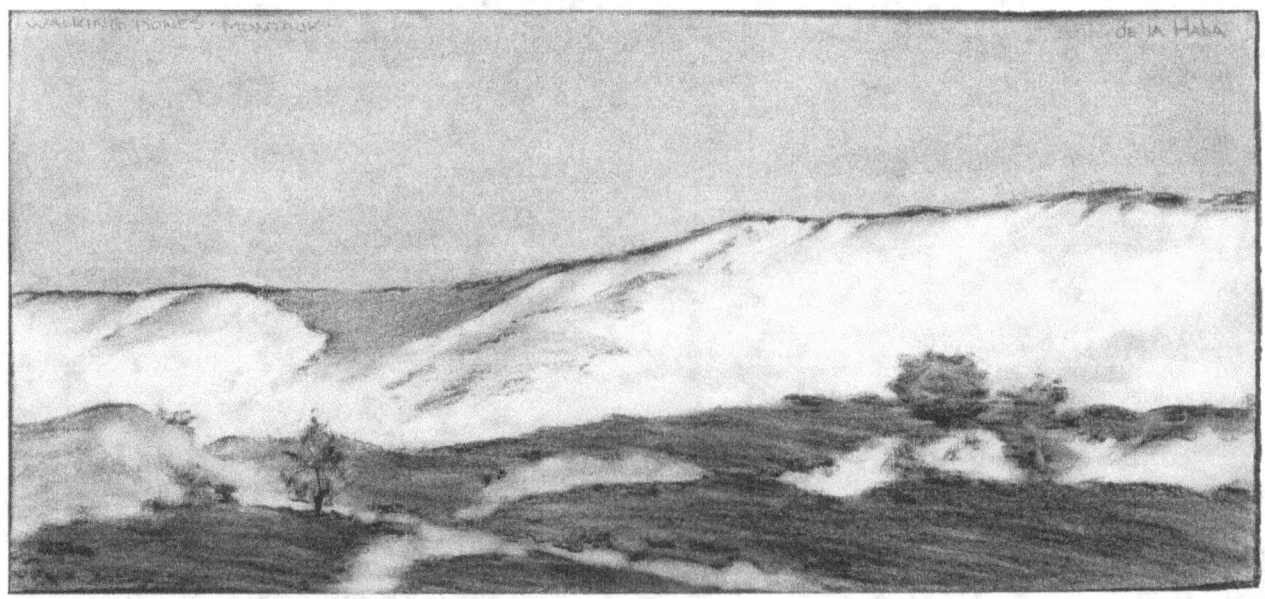

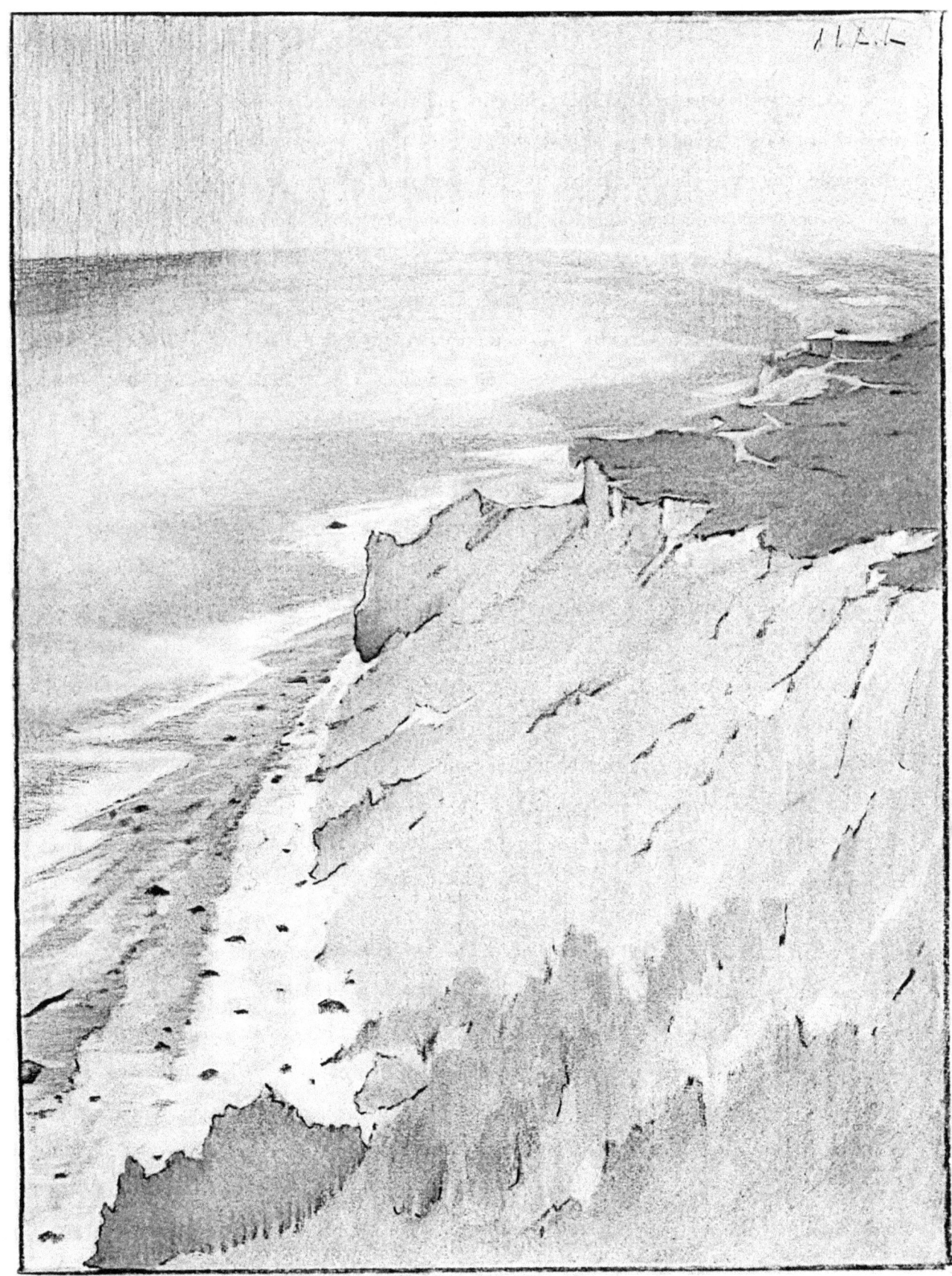

town suddenly straightens, and the solid yellow line splits into hyphens, which launch themselves at the car's grille and, through the rearview, exit out the tailpipe. It is here that the road offers itself up to speed demons. It is here that impatience finds sympathy: you can push the pedal and tear free of all slowpokes and Sunday Drivers. On this day, clouds don't exist, and the sky seems to sparkle and reflect light even though it shouldn't. Everything is clear, more noticeable. The sand littered with dried-out pine cones and browned needles. The telephone poles, ones that carry giant and heavy braids of cable to the end of the island, stand at perpetual slant. Farther back from the road, beyond the railroad tracks, osprey nests rest atop even taller poles. Water is near, lots of it. Vision clarifies and my senses come alive. High speed awakens the mind, rejuvenates the body, and it all revs up the art-spirit to live, to keep pushing on and not look back.

At the end of the Napeague Stretch, the road forks and offers motorists two distinct drives into the town of Montauk: Old Montauk Highway, hilly, with limited vision, and loved by kids as the roller coaster option. The second is a newer, faster, well-paved, more direct route: Montauk Highway. Before making a choice, I decide to hit the last commercial structure, Cyril's Fish Shack. A cocktail and a visit with the always personable man whose namesake bar I frequent feels like the right call. Cyril's portrait, which I drew earlier in the season, now hangs behind the bar, framing the adorable bartender who's currently dropping soft bananas into a blender with Myers's Rum, Bailey's and Kahlua. Cyril likes telling me how great his weekend was and how much money he pulled in or how much he lost because of the rain, and I inform him that I lose, too, when it rains, and we make a toast and hope for sun in the coming days.

Cyril enjoys his rum. When his drink gets to the quarter mark on the plastic cup, he tosses the remaining rum and ice into the shrubs next to his table in front of the outdoor restaurant. I like to watch the waitresses, who, on constant alert for this flourish of his, rush to fetch him a new one. After many drinks, Cyril leaves me sitting alone at his table up front, and I reflect on the hoodoos at Shadmoore State Park. They look like solidified sand castles, some reaching 90 feet high. And like sand castles, not much is needed to tear them down. If it weren't for their cement-like clay foundations, they would have been washed away years ago. I think about foundations, that notion of what holds something together, roots it to its spot, and finish the last of what's in my cup.

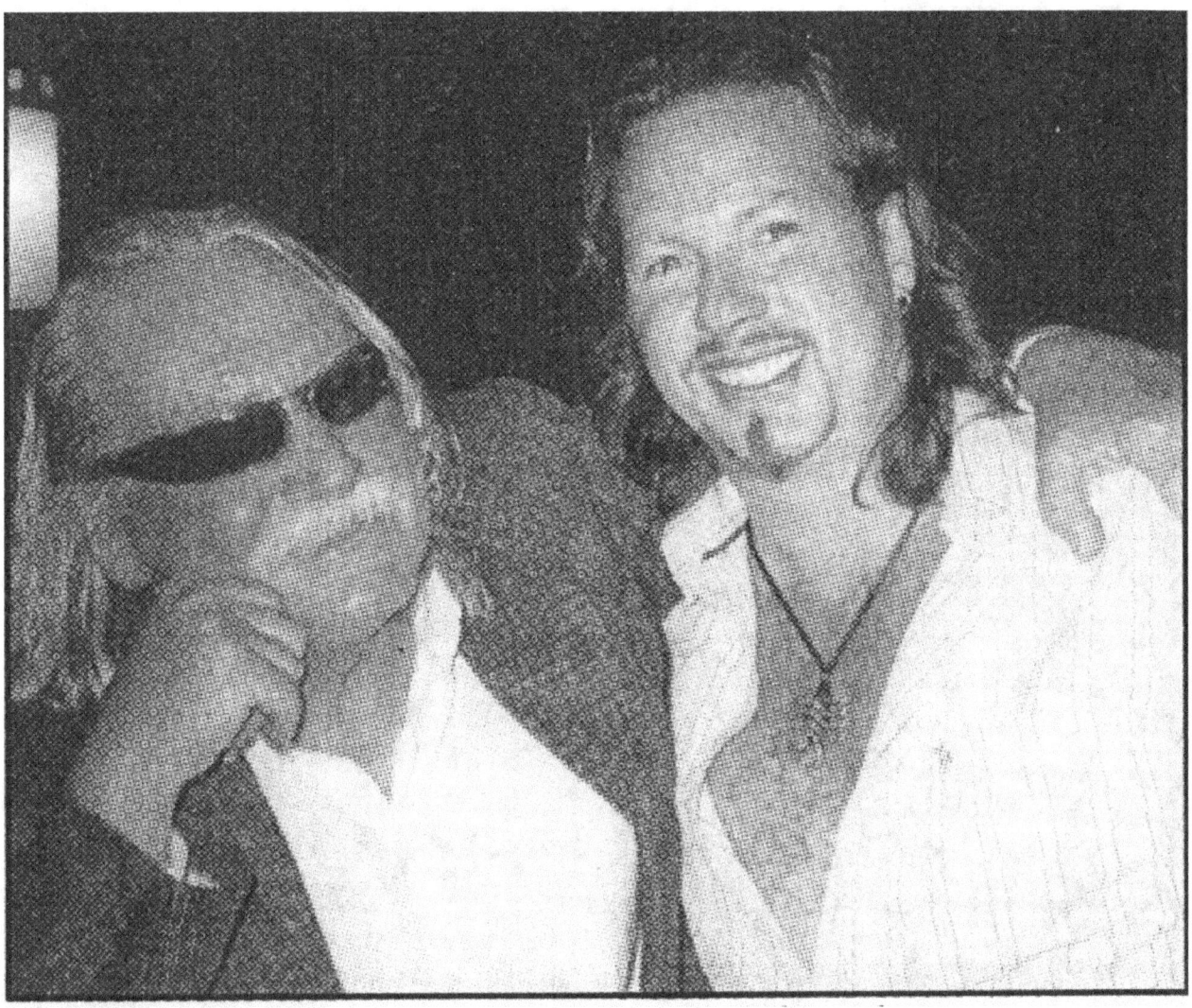

The Hoodoos perfectly describe how time and nature are fragile and fleeting, incapable of standing still or remaining unchanged for long. As with a portrait sitter in the studio for the first time, there is an urgency to capture all the big shapes and forms before things are altogether different at the next sitting. Too much immediate focus on the details instead of the "bigger picture" will yield an image that is piecemeal instead of cohesive. Homes built upon sand ignore the bigger picture. The foundation is everything.

Many days have ended with a feeling of accomplishment. Days spent doing, rather than thinking about doing. Days when the analytical mind stepped aside, allowing a purely visual one to drive the painting process. When the landscape, the sea, the cliffs, the dunes sparked creative energy, took hold of the eyes and, like a pendulum, put them in motion—a full, synchronized,

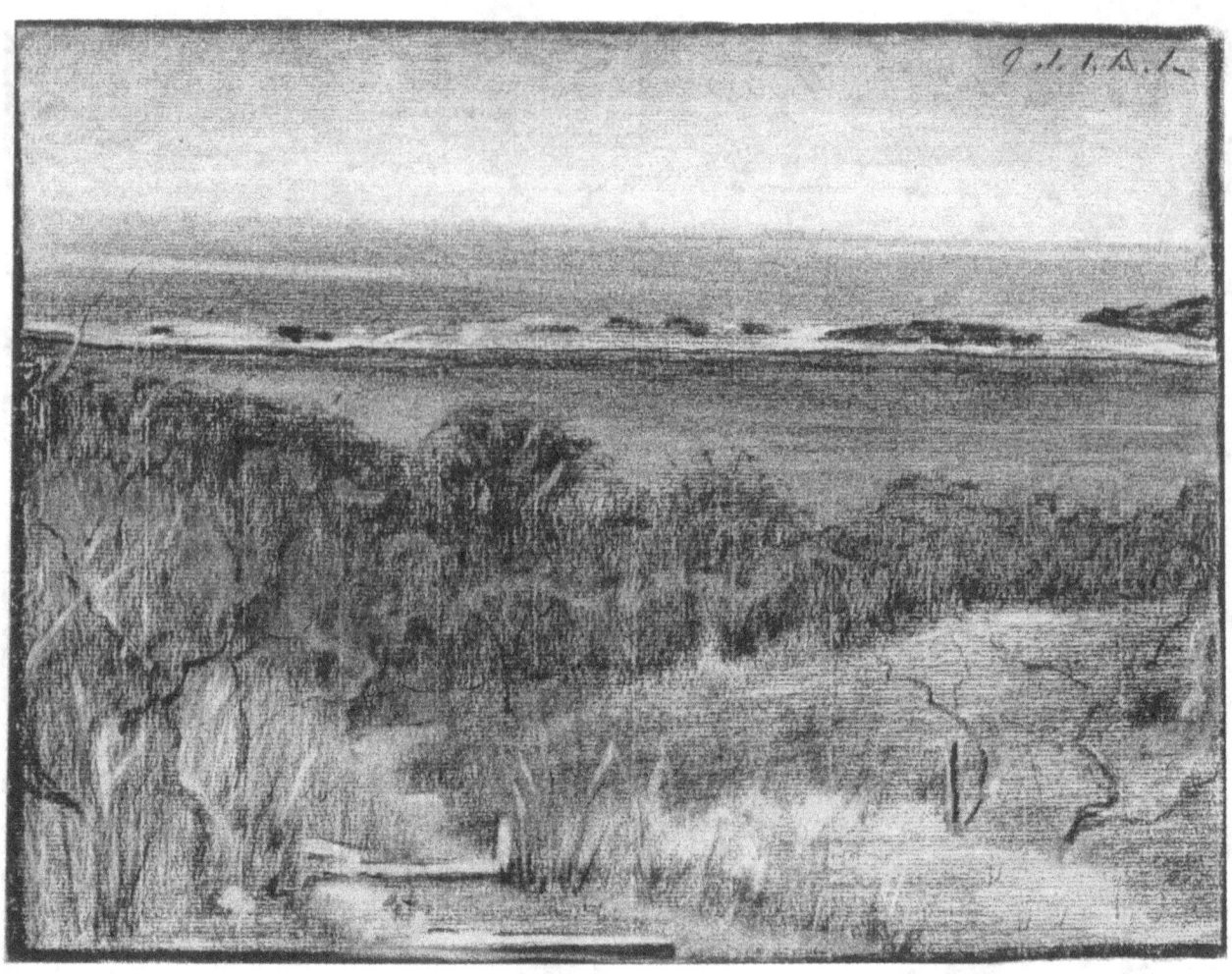

and coordinated connection with my drawing hand, which swept swiftly and confidently across the paper or canvas until all of that energy appeared in the work. When my hand no longer knew what mark would come next, the eyes, on cue, led the way—looking off the paper and out to sea, or over the dunes, up the bluff's face, or down the beach for more signs, more energy, more lights and shadows. The image was always there, waiting for the eyes to take, to memorize, to seize and hold tight, or tight enough, so that nothing was forgotten. With accuracy and precision, the hand glided easily through the work in progress, rendering it continually better until completed. All that was left to do then was rest and allow the mind to leisurely wander back into the picture, the mind thinking what it may. On most days, it was pleased and only thought about the next drawing, the next day. The following days, however, only brought more rain. They left me idle, in bed, thinking about the past.

EXPERIENCE

Life is the art of drawing without an eraser.
    —John W. Gardner

I first learned of John Tunney when visiting a restaurant he owned in Eisenhower State Park, called The Carlton. A fancy place with a private cigar bar on the second floor, entered by way of a sliding bookshelf. Tunney is sharp, brilliant, and knows how to get things done; a "hospitality expert," as he often labeled himself. He also knows how to get people to get things done for him. That's how we eventually met, back in early 1998. While scouting out The Carlton as a venue for my wedding to Teresa, David Tunney, John's younger brother, informed me that his brother collected art and was in need of an artist for his next big project. The Carlton joint provided enough evidence that this guy Tunney was the real thing and that I simply had to get my work in his hands. I assured Teresa that this was the place to marry, and the next day, I drove back out and left a deposit of five thousand dollars, in twenties, along with a small portfolio of my work, John Tunney's name marked on both, figuring one would definitely help focus his attention on the other. At the

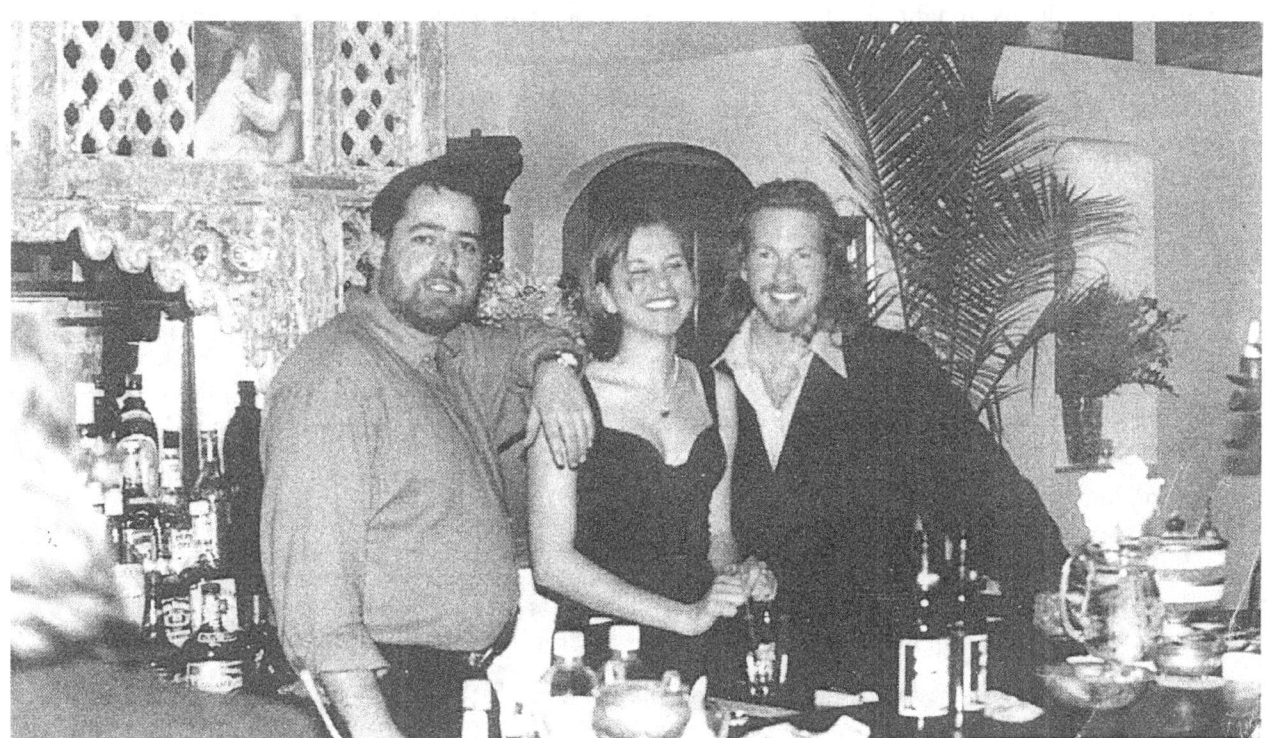

time, I was riding high: I owned a racehorse that was winning and a club in Queens that was gaining popularity. As much popularity as an illegal club could gain, that is.

Club Vertigo was in full swing when Mr. John Tunney called. "It looks like you're the guy for the job," he said over the phone.

I invited him to Queens that night to discuss. He arrived at 11PM. The scene couldn't have been more compelling: live music, packed with patrons, dancing and mingling bodies accented by candlelight and blue haze strobe lights, giant palm plants in massive cement urns positioned at either side of the stage. The band played a mix of rock and funk, and the heavyset, powerful black female back-up vocalist paired perfectly with the lead singer, a shaggy-haired, thin-as-a-rail type who possessed such a unique style and banter you were sure he was going to hit it big, except he didn't because he was always too drugged and too stoned and last I heard, had moved to LA without so much as a whisper voiced over his arrival.

John loved the band and wished to bring them out to his place and thanked me for having him over. He confessed later that he was a little intimidated by the Greek bouncers downstairs, who worked the old freight elevator needed to get to the fourth floor, and the even bigger bouncer stationed outside the club's entrance. He also noted all the Greek and Italian mafia types who kept coming over and kissing me on both cheeks as we spoke. We were drinking some of the best Greek wine, which I had corked and ready at our VIP table up on the second-floor balcony. It all used to be our home—the balcony, the main floor—and big enough for my studio, too, the VIP area our former bedroom where Teresa and I used to talk until the wee hours of the morning, alone. But I turned it into a club, without consulting her, without asking her opinion, and now a hot Greek hostess in a mini skirt, heels, and low-cut blouse checks to see if we need anything. John is pleased by everything he sees and hears. At that moment, I was pleased. Things seemed to be working. Falling into place.

After a few glasses of wine and an exchange of compliments, me praising his restaurants and he my art, John sent for his briefcase. The bus boy returned promptly and John laid out before us blueprints to a new restaurant: Temple Bar and Grill inside the main lobby of Caesars Palace in

Atlantic City. The ceiling plans called for a thirty-by-sixteen-foot mural. It was my largest commission to date. The only criterion was that it be fun and exciting. After witnessing me in my element that night and seeing my work first hand, he was convinced that I was indeed the man for this job. That night, even Teresa seemed convinced that the decision to open the club was a good one. But when your future wife is one who always sees the flip side of things, it was no surprise that her first question after John left was:

"Now where are you going to paint this, baby?"

"I'll paint it here."

"You'll paint it here? You'll move all these chairs every day and move them back each night?"

"The club is only open three nights a week."

"But Gregory, you have the bar, the stage, the plants, the couches, the tables and all these chairs to fuss over each week."

She brings attention to the things I choose not to see, the pesky little details. I have no answer for her.

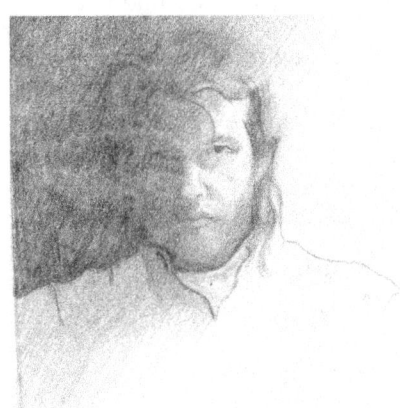

The worst of all deceptions is self-deception.
—Plato

Be wary of Greeks bearing gifts, the saying goes. It wasn't unexpected, but it did come sooner rather than later. Those fuckers who kissed me on the cheeks, owners and friends of owners from other clubs and bars in Queens, hated that I was getting lots of attention and money and had the hottest place in town (all illegally), luring away "their patrons." They knew what to do and did it. It was too easy: after enjoying a drink with me upstairs they'd pull the fire alarm on their way out; or they'd call the fire marshals and report over-crowding and illegal business activity. The cops and fire marshals eventually found their way upstairs. But as a Queens native who had attended an all-boys Catholic high school, I knew a few influential and well-liked members of New York's Finest and Bravest and was, initially, able to hold them off. But after the third attempted shutdown, during the fourth month in business, the fire marshals put it to me: "De la Haba, we don't give a shit who you know anymore, you can't do this."

I begged them for just one more week. I had, after all, booked a short, fat Greek guy's wedding. His relatives from Cyprus were already in New York hanging out at the club. He would've fed me to the dogs had I canceled. The marshals looked at each other and made their way out with a stern warning: "The last time!" That following Sunday, as this surprisingly gorgeous bride cut her cake, the friendly and courteous fire marshals returned and came on in without knocking. I assured the guests that they were friends who were just there for some cake. "Opa!" an old Greek man cried out, raising his hands and clapping. "Opa!" I shouted back. Gold badges dangling from their necks, all five marshals sat at the bar, faces plastered with huge grins as the bride brought them frosted layer cake, on that, the last day of Club Vertigo.

But it was one of those blessings in disguise. Teresa was right; I had to commence work on a thirty-by-sixteen-foot painting, oil on canvas, which was then to be glued to a ceiling, and where was I to do it if not in my loft, my studio? So the closing of Club Vertigo couldn't have come at a better time; in the three weeks following John's visit, while I was still open for business, I had been researching flame retardant materials per the hotel's safety demands, sketching pictorial elements of the picture, inquiring about prop rentals for the photo shoot, scheduling models and so forth. I was nearly finished with that stage and ready to begin the next, and I needed to begin it right because it had to be right—lives were at stake here. I had never painted on "flame-retardant" canvas. Plus, the exposure would be tremendous, John assured. My space was returned to me, to us, as a studio and a proper home for a new bride. This made Teresa feel better. But it also made me realize that this—painting—was what I should be doing, not running a club until the wee hours of the morning. And the sum paid by the commission covered the rent for over a year, relieving some of the stress of making a living as an artist. I immediately began work on two separate canvases, both measuring slightly more than sixteen feet wide and exactly sixteen feet high.

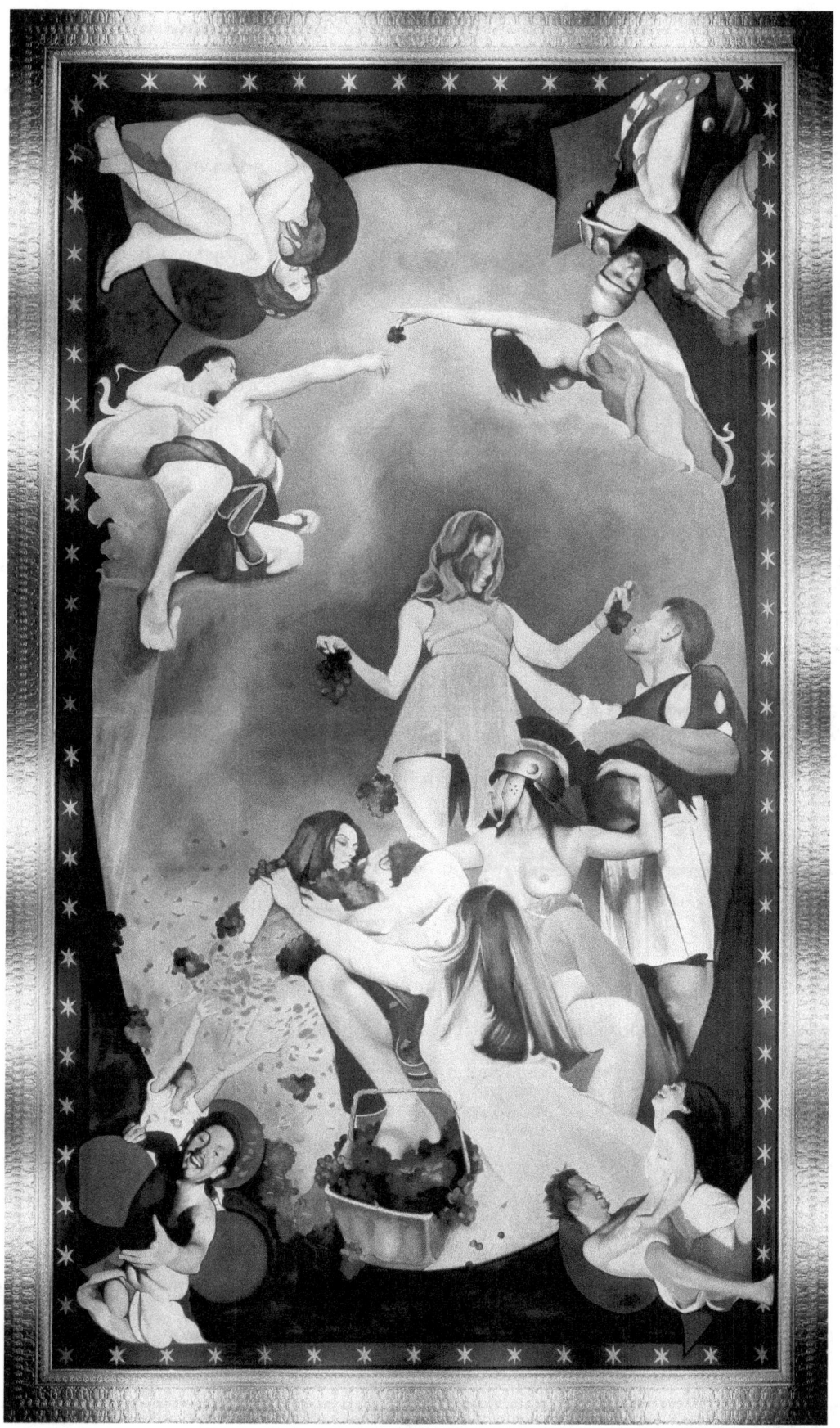

61

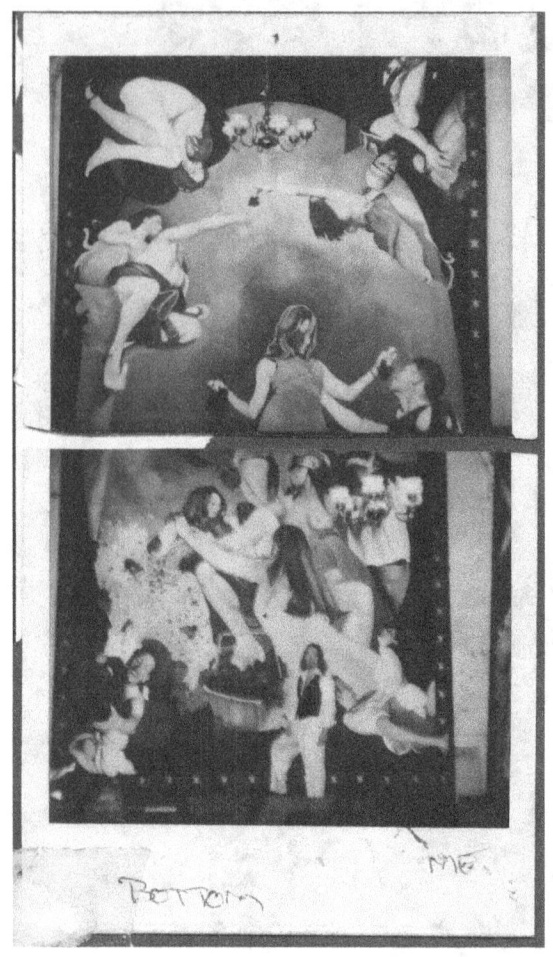

My only concerns were that the center seam align just right, and, more importantly, that the installation be expert. It had to be perfect, otherwise, the figures in my chosen subject, a Bacchanalia, would look distorted. Ruining it. Ruining me. Bernini was run out of Rome in the 1600s for fucking up on a big project. I couldn't afford that. I amused myself a little by thinking that maybe, just maybe, a painting of a drunken, Roman-themed orgy, with myself as Bacchus, god of wine, drink and revelry, would look even better distorted. But who was I kidding? I thought of artists who intentionally distort their drawings, their figures, their portrait heads, some painted with big heads and small bodies, others with elongated bodies, like the work of El Greco, and rounded heads with little rounded and delicate features like those of John Currin, all for effect and style. These people are lauded in the contemporary art world. And of these painters, what came first, the style or the artist?

Tastes are forever changing and styles that seem forced and contrived change even faster and can look as dated as 18th century paintings by Fragonard or Watteau, as an Elvis on velvet. And of artists who embraced mistakes, what about them? Artists who prized errors, like the abstract and expressionist painters of the 1940s and 1950s; artists whose frantic gestures, executed with such "gusto and bravura" that the critics named it, and wrongly so, I believed, raw genius: I didn't get then. I wasn't there yet. I believed it all had to be perfect. Exactly the way I wished, the way nature looked. Figures placed exactly as composed, their revelry and gestures expressed as envisioned, intentionally, on purpose, with meaning achieved only through an understanding of form, line, and color all learned through years of doing and undoing, not brought about by accident.

There is a reason why grand figurative painting was held to such high esteem amongst the Old Masters: very few ever did it really well. Mistakes cannot be tolerated. The head belongs on the shoulders, the hips must align, the laugh has to be real and placed just right on the face; the grapes must be edible. The "fun and excitement" that Mr. Tunney demanded must be real and ever present. Picasso advised, "If you want to paint a portrait, paint a chair." Yes. Silly. Funny. It worked for him. What came first, the silly paintings or the silly thoughts trying to validate the silly paintings? That sort of thing would not work here. Mine was picture-making with rules, measurements, and proportion…with a patron watching over the shoulder to make sure it was so.

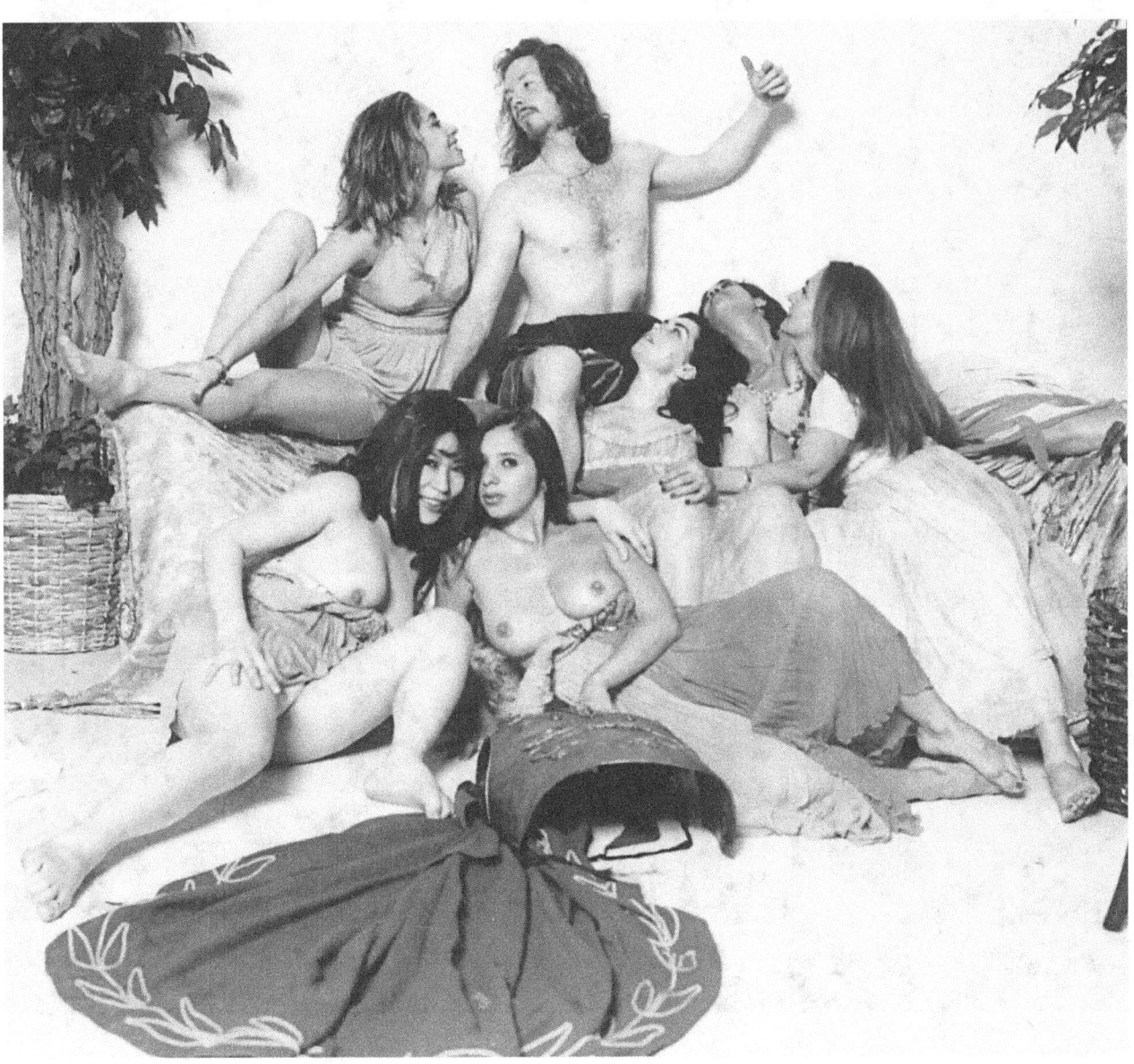

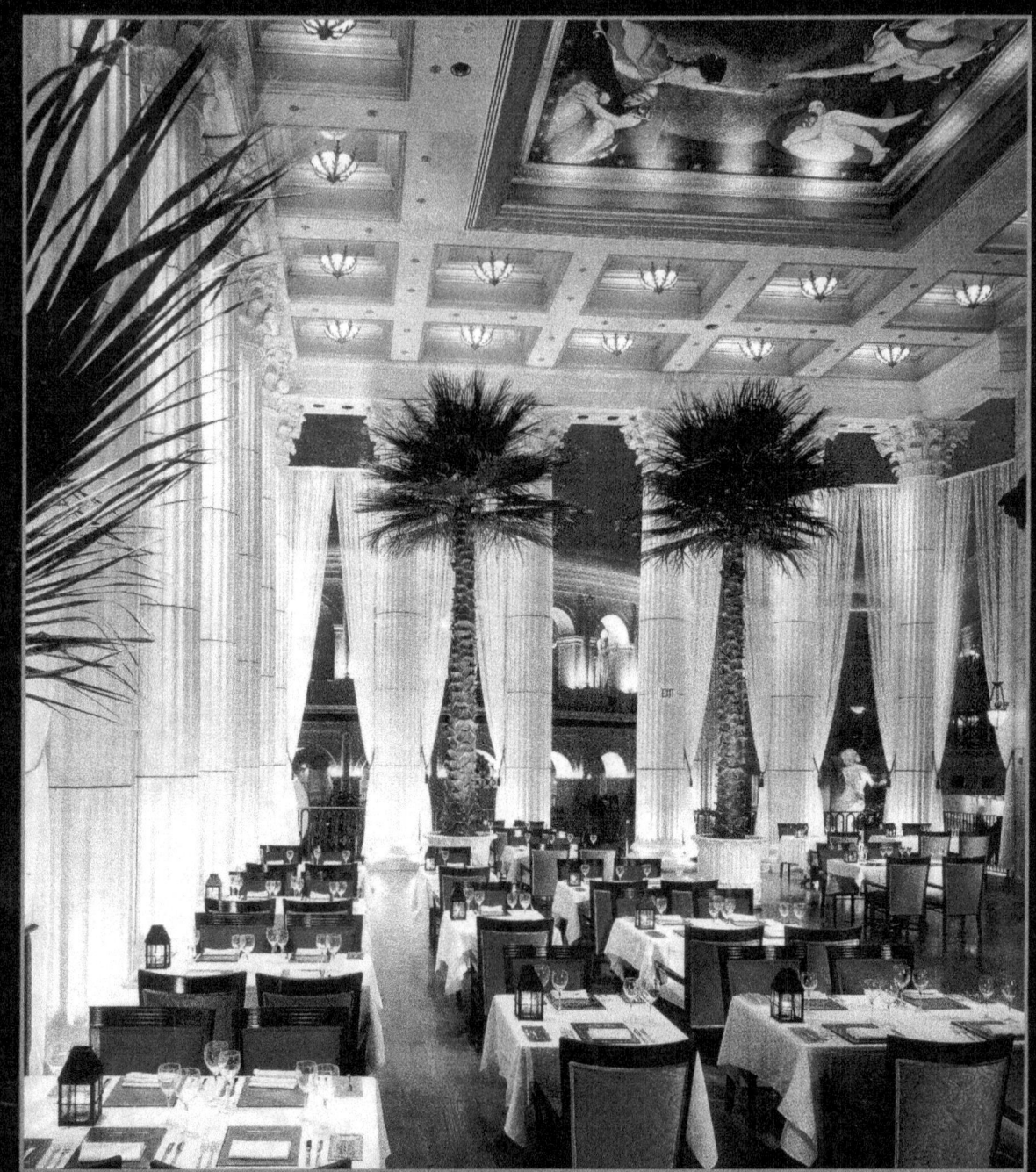

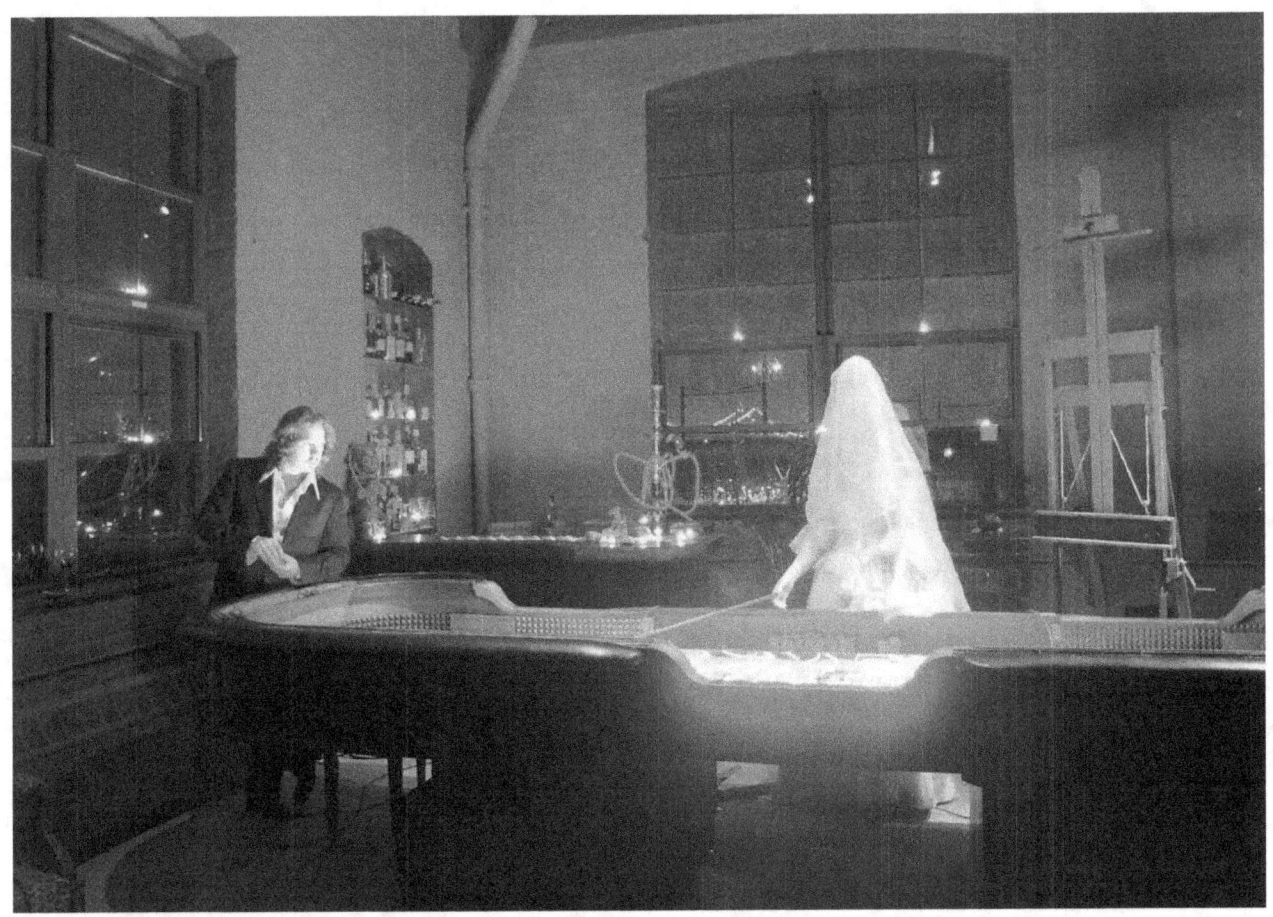

SPECIALIZED CERTIFICATION

The Medici created and destroyed me.
   —Leonardo Da Vinci

In late 1999, I had a routine as artist—staying up all night to work; squeezing lots of paint from tubes; methodically cleaning brushes with Turpenoid, shampoo, and then hair conditioner (because sable-haired brushes from Europe required the utmost care); gently pressing excess water out from those hairs to help ensure that they retained their original shape (round, square or filbert-shaped edges); waiting impatiently for models to show but painting them desirously when they finally did arrive; stretching canvases the old-fashioned way, by hand and with tacks, not staples, because that was the tradition; grinding pigment and oil on a thick glass plate with a Muller because store-bought tubes and the colors inside them weren't rich enough; going to the Egyptian cafe on Steinway Street for mint tea and a hookah of apple-flavored tobacco at three-thirty in the morning because that's when a needed break was loved, and it was an inexpensive spot, and the sight of hot coals the owner Faoud fired-up for the bubbly and his fresh mint leaves made going to bed undesirable and getting back to work fun—rejuvenated and ready for round two—like beginning an entirely new day without ever having to fall asleep to wait for it to come. This was how I spent my days as a fully budding artist: on my complete and own accord. It was before grand commissions presented themselves as being grander than they were, or turned out to be; before all the rituals and habits of being an artist virtually ground to a halt.

My own hubris was the roadblock. See, John Tunney revealed his big dreams to me in the form of ceiling paintings five times the size of the ones we'd mounted in Caesar's Palace, and those dreams almost instantly became mine more than his. The daily, inglorious grind as artist lost its luster as the prospects of art-world notoriety took hold. For months on end, beginning in the fall of '98—after the Atlantic City mural commission was completed and received favorably—straight through to the Fall of '99, I thought of only one thing: getting the green light from Mr. Tunney for this next big project. How could I do much else when he said, "Get your brushes ready"? It was all I needed to hear from John. Heck, I've made faster dashes to the betting window on less information.

This was going to be massive, huge, slated for Las Vegas no less. Mr. Tunney was looking like my very own Lorenzo de' Medici, a patron saint of the highest order. I couldn't believe it: a ceiling worthy of Michelangelo, except this commission was for me, not the Florentine, and it was Sin City calling, not Rome. To put focus or concentration towards anything other than this project was as absurd as the ceiling was grandiose. This was not a case of counting chickens before they hatched but of leveraging the farm to buy each chicken its own coup. It was my wet dream, something of this scale. I was finally set to leave behind portraits of children and dogs, work that for years prior put bread and butter on the table when the horses didn't win or didn't run, work I could now turn down once and for all. In fact, I was already passing up such commissions, knowing that the phone would ring any day. "All eggs must go in one basket!" I told myself, the same way I placed all bets on Some Irish Legend and Imagineer and any other horse I fancied.

All-in or nothing was the code to live by. "If you're going to fail, fail big," da Vinci said. And by God, I was "all-in" for Las Vegas. Grand, creative things like composition and color scheme consumed the entire right side of my brain while glory took hold of the left. From here on out, paintings were to be measured by the yard, not the inch, I assured myself. My art would finally rise above the mundane and receive the attention it rightly deserved. It had to. Not only were the brushes ready but the paints were purchased and the sketches made. Which way for my close-up? Eventually, my faith and bombast convinced even Teresa.

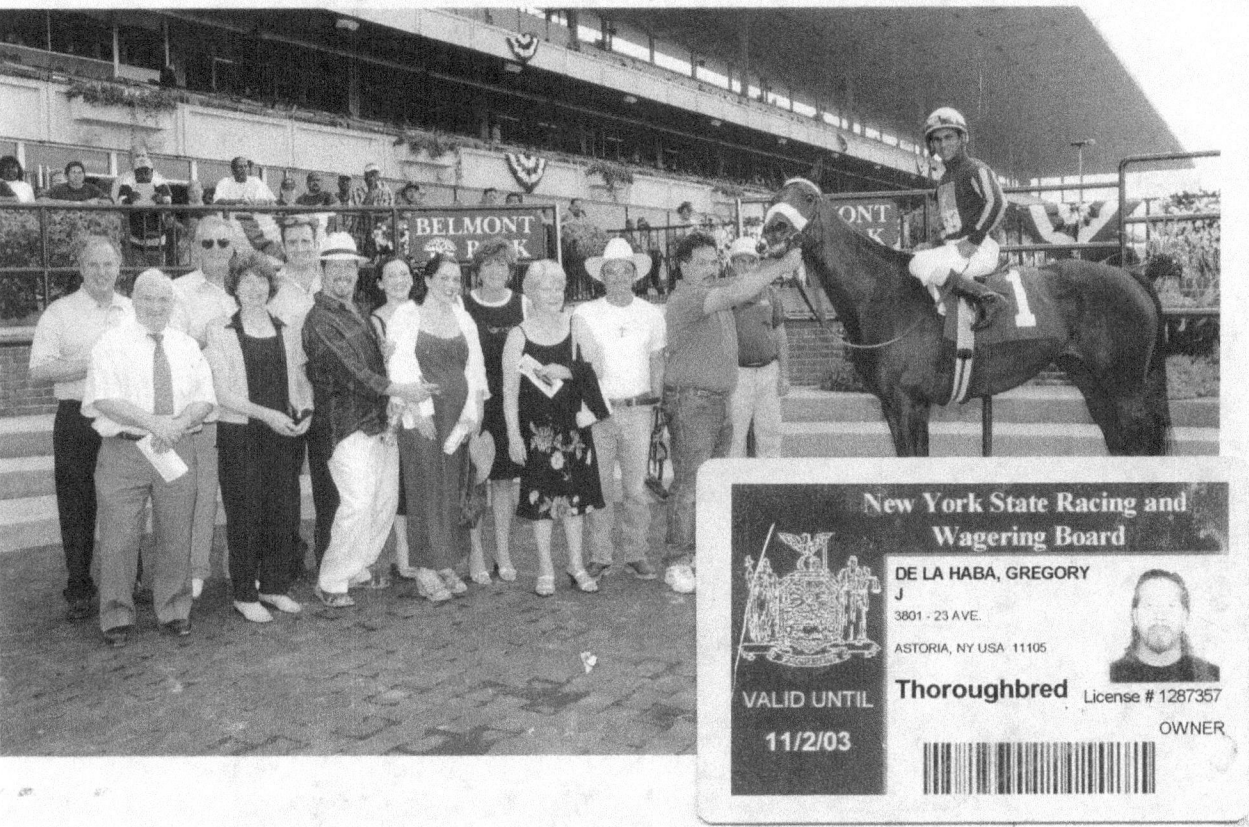

Gregory de la Haba & Theresa de la Haba owners **SOME IRISH LEGEND** Shaun Bridgmohan up 1 1/16 miles time 1:42:2
Belongs Fast 2nd-Leo O' Brien trainer-Bo Bo's Thunder 3rd

Me: "We need to go to Vegas ASAP."

Teresa: "Why? You didn't even get the commission yet, Gregory."

"Teresa, I will. And when I do, I'll need to know what I'm in for, what I'm up against. Tunney told me this ceiling is tremendous, bigger than Michelangelo's Sistine Chapel ceiling. The potential here is huge. Do you realize how big this thing could be?"

Teresa: "What I realize is that John hasn't given you any money yet but only shared with you his ideas. And then when we get out there, you'll find a craps table sending you 'lucky signals' or a roulette wheel 'that's bound to hit black.' No, thanks. How about we take a nice drive to the Hamptons and spend a night or two out there?"

Me: "You're being irrational about this. This is my art we're talking about here. And of course I'll play a little while we're in Vegas, why wouldn't we make the most of it?"

Teresa: "I see."

My headstrong, "dream-big" attitude always got the better of me. It dictated our course together even though both of us weren't always enjoying the ride, let alone agreeing to go on it at all. I was so fucking superfluously ready, I was not only ahead of myself and the proposed project, but also two steps ahead of Mr. Tunney, his vision, his budget, and his timetable, so much so that I didn't see the changes-that-life-brings coming down the pike. We worked great together before so why wouldn't we in Vegas?

And so it was with shock that I one day found myself asking, "What do you mean, John, that you're not putting a ceiling painting on the ceiling?" As Tunney explained—in matter-of-fact, businessman's terms—that my dreams were dashed, Teresa's words beat a nurturing told-you-so rhythm in my head: "Learn to listen, Gregory, to those who've already made it."

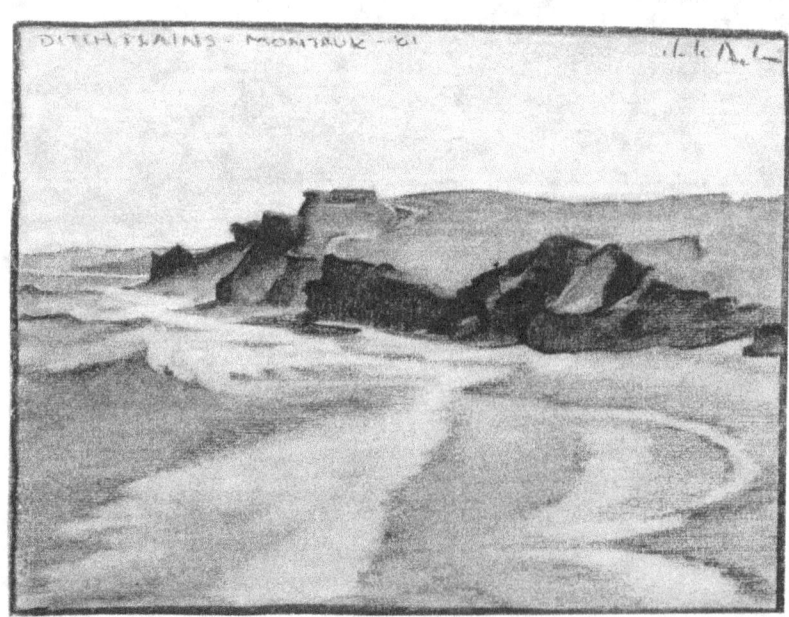

THE LOST YEAR (AND THE WASTED ONE)

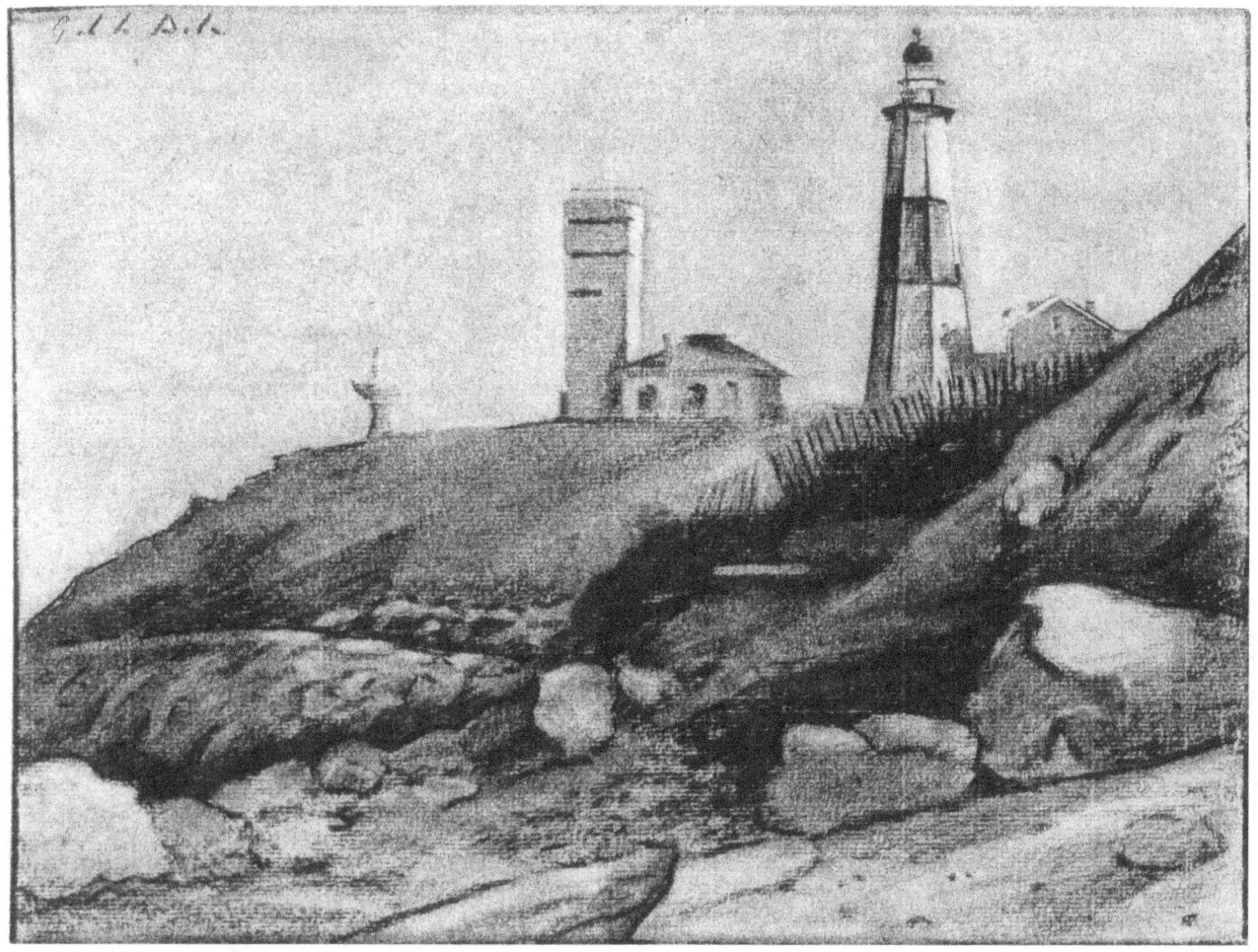

Ah! well a-day! what evil looks
Had I from old and young!
Instead of the cross, the Albatross
About my neck was hung.

—Samuel Taylor Coleridge, "The Rime of the Ancient Mariner"

The daily ritual of making art and the gradual falling in love with craft that had, over the years, followed, were both gone. Back in Boston, during my student days, it was the passion to be an artist—to paint pictures in oil on canvas—plain and simple, that got me out of bed early in the morning. There was so much to do, so much still to learn. But then I went on to acquire craft and understand technique and the next step, I believed, was establishing oneself as a successful seller. And when you're in your twenties, with a horse that's banking bucks and a major commission in Caesar's banking some more, and the prospect of something far greater than both coming into reach, the idea—the reality—of another level of success became very appealing. Fame, even, seemed plausible.

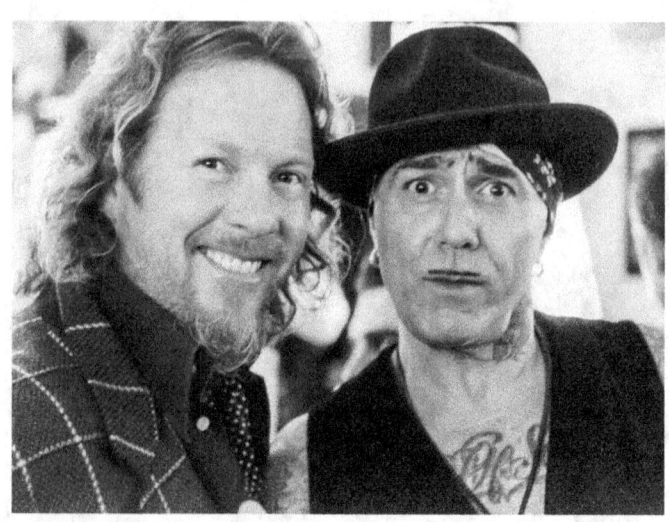

It no longer, or not entirely, was about the art, but about future payoffs, revenues from posters and prints, press coverage, branding, and the custom suits Savoia The Tailor would make so I could wear them at the craps table and in the winner's circle. Becoming a successful man took precedence over everything else, squelched, especially, the far humbler aspirations of the romantic day-dreaming artist-kid with something honest to say, one day, in paint. I became the artist on the make, hell bent on proving myself successful, to others and especially to my wife. I should have, while awaiting the commission, painted some worthwhile pictures, such as landscapes of Montauk or Manhattan cityscapes (the studio's roof access in Queens provided that), things people will always enjoy and purchase. And with a reasonable asking price attached, one based more on an hourly rate like that say of a school teacher—instead of pulling high prices out of my ass which I usually did; prices based on my feelings of the work's value—I could have sold the paintings, too; the point, more importantly, would have been to just keep going, to keep painting, to keep the mind as properly conditioned as the brushes.

There was a flaw in my character, apparently, which my oldest brother, Lawrence, pointed out early on, much before this, in a letter he wrote: "You should stop trying to hit Grand Slams all the time and focus on making it to First Base and be satisfied with that." I remember folding the letter back up, sliding it in the envelope, and placing it in the dresser drawer for safe keeping, then losing it somehow during the move from Boston to New York and feeling low about it. Advice from an older brother in the form of a hand-written letter that I once held on the edge of a bed in a temporary room. Words neither ever forgotten nor ever heeded.

Rather than nothing at all, something could've come from this time, I'm certain of it. Maybe the discovery of a cool new brush from Spain that improves paint application or a new color like Courbet Green from Williamsburg Paint for the morning's squeeze-out, anything, no matter how small or insignificant, but no. Gone was the simple olfactory pleasure when fresh oils are squeezed

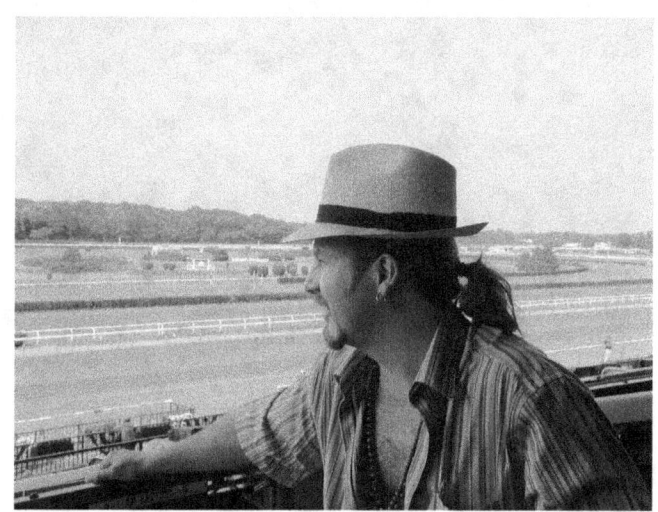

onto a palette, gone was the ocular joy in those colors laid out, watching the extra linseed run off the sides before patting it up with paper towel because too much oil in a picture causes an unbearable sheen, which is an unpleasant surface to behold. Much like what the studio mirror reflected after Vegas fell through. I wish I could say that that was the lost year, but it wasn't, it was the wasted one.

The lost year came after that, in 2000, a time when the sound of racing hooves pounding past the finish line was the only thing that got me up and out of bed. The horses breathed life from their flared nostrils which seeded the track with their essence, and made me feel alive. And as the weight of the wasted year became borderline unbearable, everything about them grew more exciting. Playing the horses was something that I was good at, enjoyed too much, and because I possessed a history of making some serious money with it, why not? Besides, bringing donuts and coffee to the boys on the backstretch made me happy, genuinely so. But, trust me, it really bites a man in the ass when his horse makes more money than he, when handicapping ponies—doing so devoid of all emotion—proves more fruitful than a work of art to which that same man gave all his heart. It's bittersweet and turns the mind up on itself, questioning everything, when leaving a racetrack

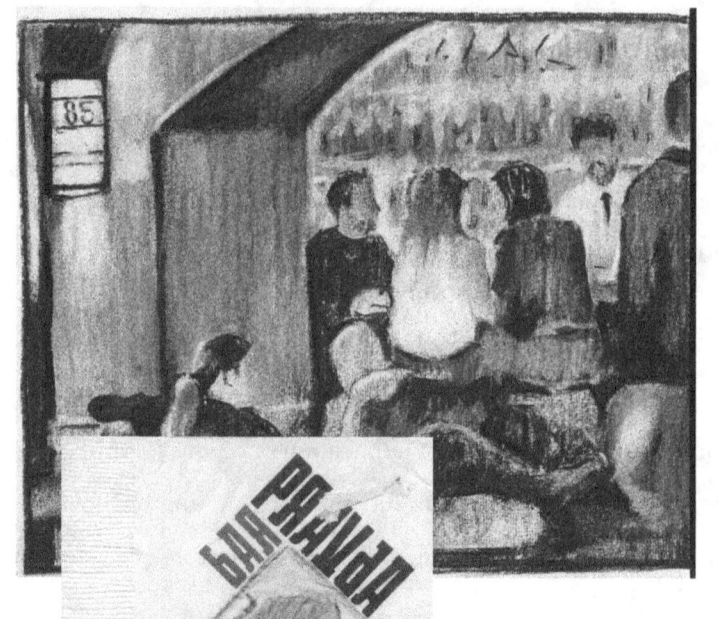

with over 20g's in cash for two minutes work (on the horse's part) while a painting that cost three months of agony and sweat can't find a buyer (in years) for ten thousand. What about five? Do I hear three? Feelings about one's value dissipates as the painting's price gets slashed.

My scope of vision had narrowed tremendously, focused squarely and solely on horses and quarter poles instead of easels and subjects. The shock of not getting that Vegas gig near paralyzed me, but it was the realization of having wasted an entire year waiting for it that set me back for another year: one year of sickness, one year to recoup. Yet I didn't recoup. In part, because I wasn't sure what the fuck the diagnosis was. Instead of taking well-deserved breaks in the middle of the night from painting, the evenings turned into excuses to drink at Balthazar, Pravda, or Pastis. Sure, the sketchpad was in hand, but intention, love, and passion weren't. No, paper and pencil became withered, dead things, props to position myself as artist, to show Teresa that I was going out for inspiration, to gather ideas. And sure, I even sold some pieces and made a few good drawings, but if an art historian looked back, there'd be no "period" or "body of work." Little, really, to note.

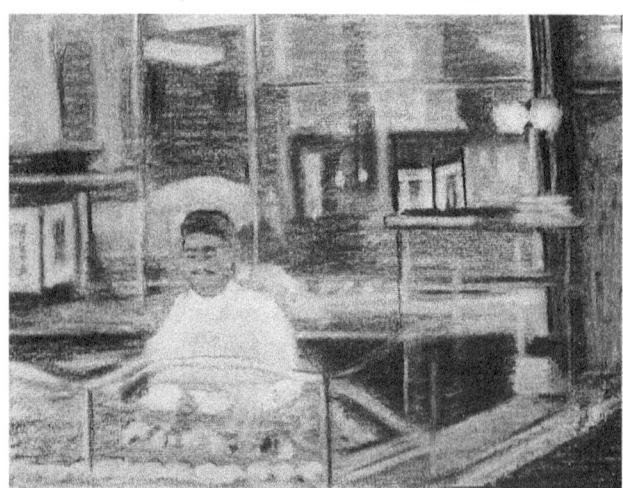

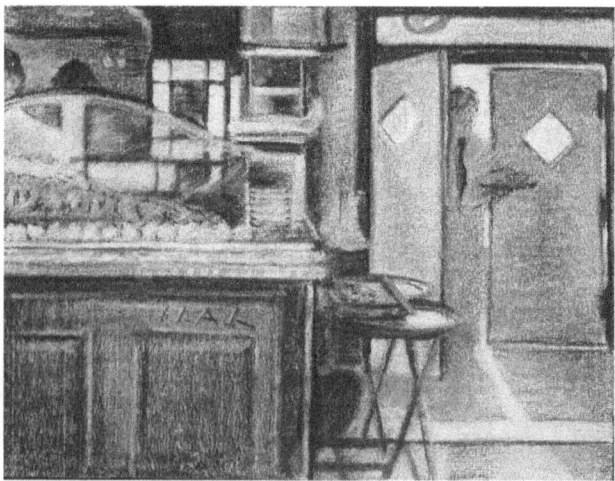

In April of 2001, Teresa and I made-off on a little getaway to celebrate our third-year wedding anniversary. I remember walking along a quiet back road on Long Island's North Fork wine country, telling her I needed to get away. That I had to take some time off and disappear for a while.

May, 6th, 2001 (Gone To Montauk... continued)

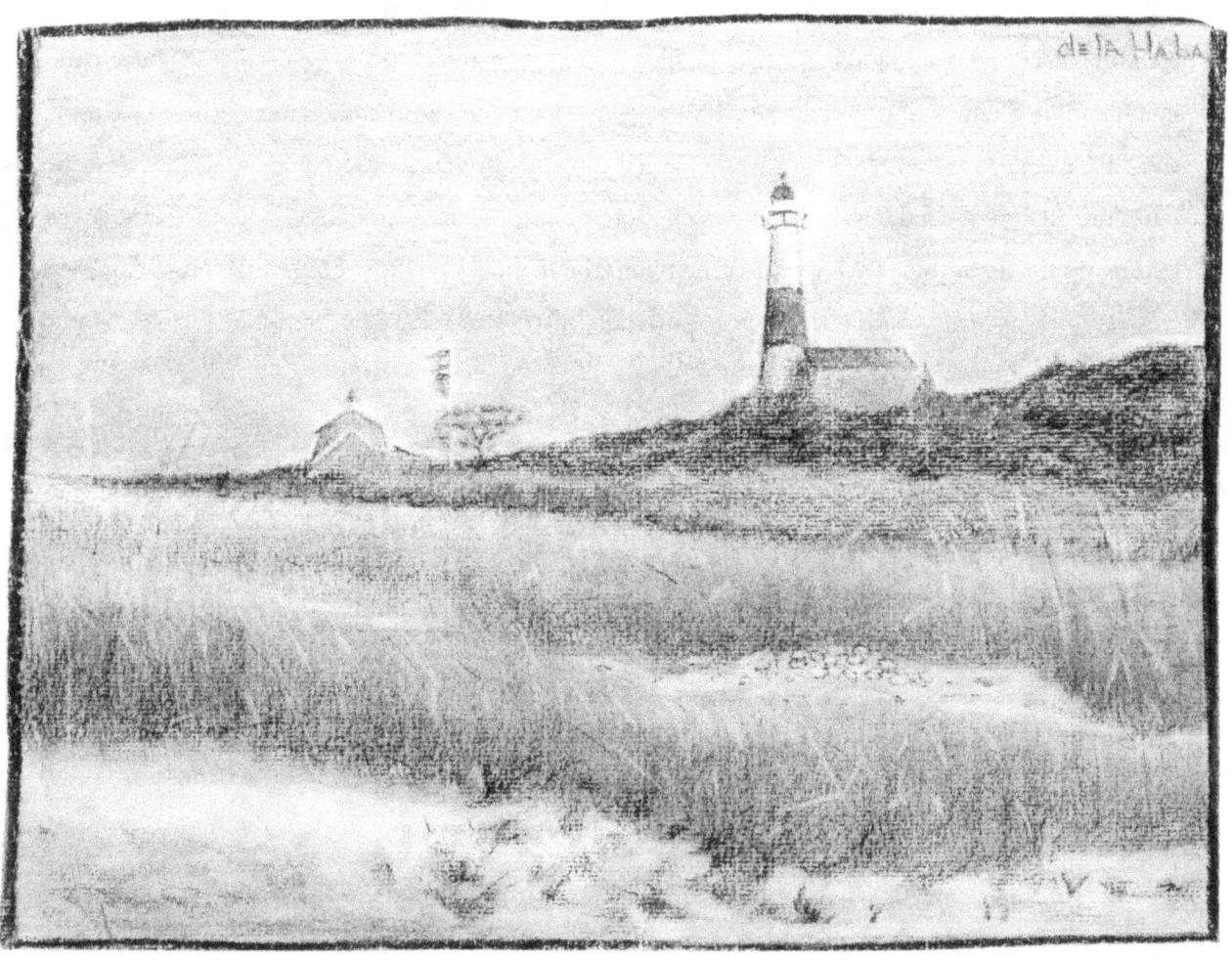

I packed some extra clothes, a French portable easel, two sketchpads of different sizes, some new canvases, paint, brushes, and charcoal. Had I still a fishing pole, I would've packed that, too. Then again, maybe not: my purpose was work. A cup of coffee from Astoria Diner and a full tank of gas were all else I needed. Ready. It is 114 miles from Astoria, Queens to Montauk. Set. Go.

At the hour of 5AM, the trip took one hour and thirty minutes—closer than when dad drove. Time flies when you're on a mission and with no traffic. I bypass the two-block town of Montauk barely slowing down and head straight for the lighthouse. I accelerate once again, feeling safe that no cop cruisers are on the road at this hour, this time of year. My only concern is hitting a deer, so I slow the fuck down after spotting two feeding right out front St. Teresa's church, (yes, St.Teresa keeping an eye on St. Gregory) just up a bit from the tackle shop where dad and I would buy worms. It's also where dad would have to circle the block because mom needed to go inside the church and light candles. She was always lighting candles—any chance she got. And on any vacation we took, there we were—dad, my older brothers, me—circling, waiting for her to come out feeling as if she had done her good deed for the day or week. Sometimes, I went in to light candles, too. I enjoyed folding up the dollar bills and dropping them into the metal moneybox. I once asked if our prayers wouldn't be answered without the money, and mom instructed me to "just light the fucking candle and be quiet about it."

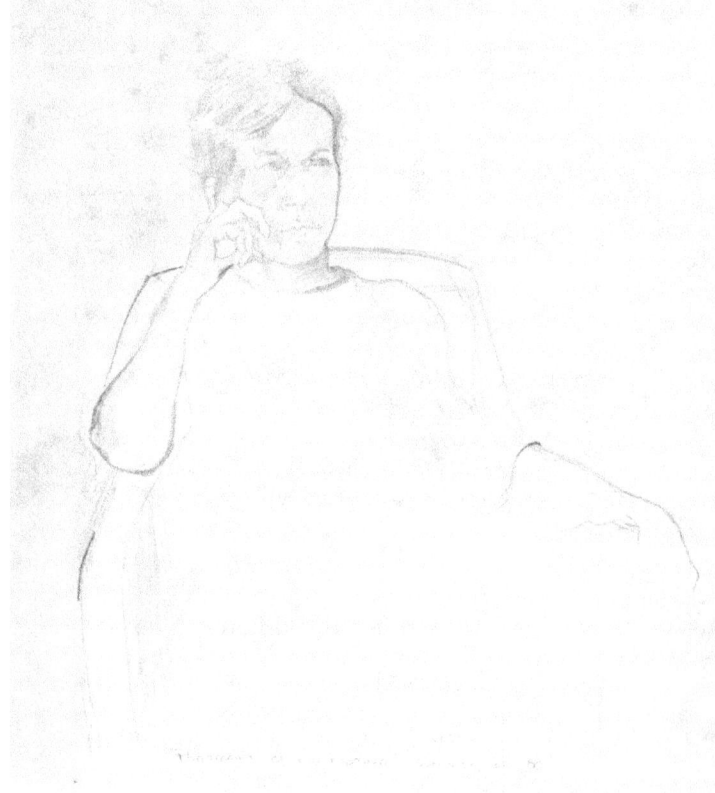

Raised in Corona, Queens and once a member of an all-girl, leather-biker-jacket-wearing gang (with the facial scars to prove it), mom never quite rid herself of 1950s gang speak and possesses, to this day, an endearing way of getting across any message.

Did Kerouac ever kill anything speeding cross-country with Moriarty? At 100 miles per hour, a deer would crash straight through the windshield and cut your fucking head off. I reached the lighthouse doing no more than 60 mph and coasted into the parking lot. The little attendant booth was empty. Mine was the only car. No one in sight. Remarkable, I mused, considering there's 9 million people in motion where I started off. I grabbed the smaller sketchpad and some charcoal, threw the portable French easel over my back, and quickly made my way southwest of the lighthouse, looking for a narrow path I recalled from long ago, which shuttles anglers back and forth from the Atlantic Ocean. Was it still there?

I walk along the grass on the side of the single-lane road, climb over the low wooden barrier, and spot what appears to be a tiny clearing. Beneath a canopy of browned, leafless trees and vines, a sandy foot-trail emerges. Memory recalls the same giddy excitement experienced as a kid, walking through woods with two older brothers, in search of mischief. It is quiet. Misty. Fifteen feet out, a deer stands still in the brush.

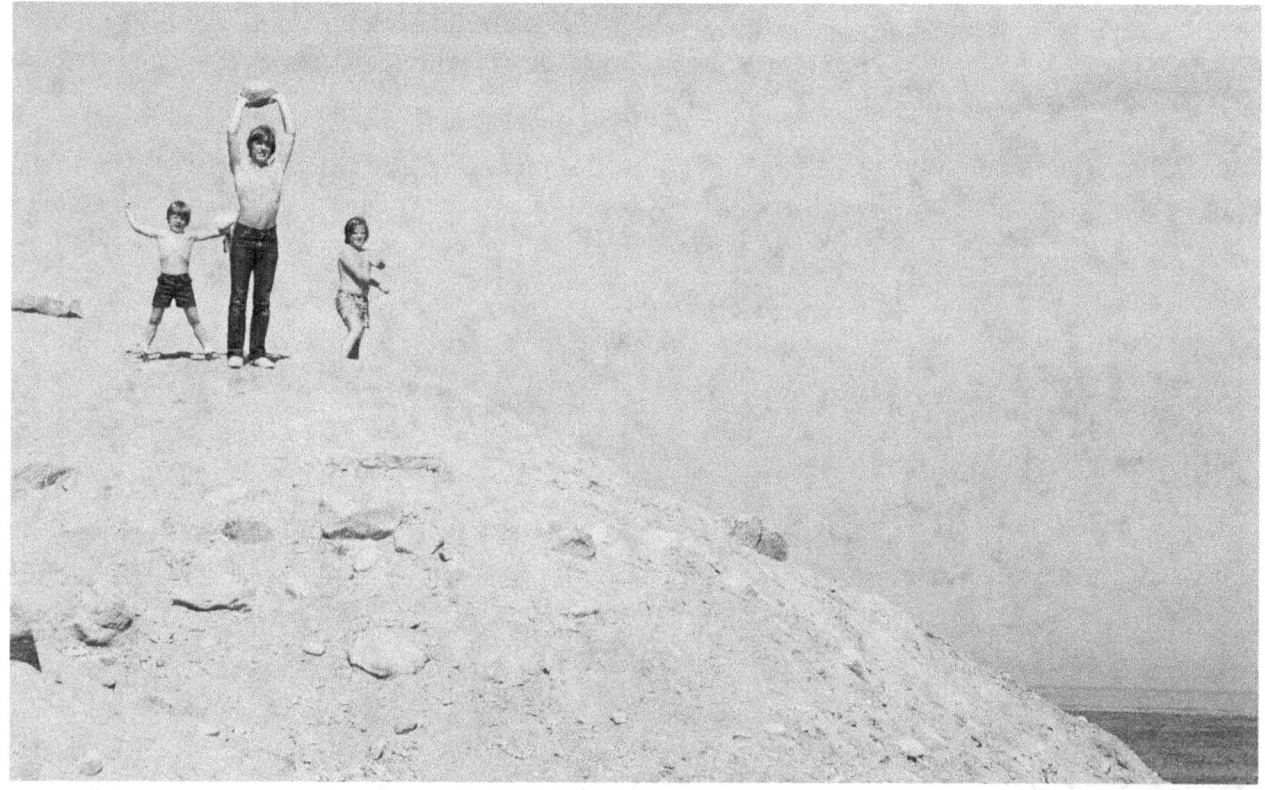

The smell and sound of the Atlantic is near. The path opens to a low clearing with the lighthouse on the left, up high on Turtle Hill, named years ago by locals who took notice of the bluff's profile, which resembled that of a turtle sticking its head out from beneath its shell. That was in the mid 1800s when the lighthouse stood 300 hundred feet from the water's edge. Now it is barely 80 feet away: the turtle turned to soup. The shoreline by the point is littered with rocks, tons of them, big and small. Untired by repetition, the Atlantic throws itself up against the shore, again and again, against the bluffs that rise mightily on the right side of the path, westward, some reaching over 100 feet high. Standing there, one cannot help but think of ships crashing upon this rocky shore. Or of ships having been out to sea and then guided safely home by this lighthouse, which George Washington commissioned in the latter part of the 18th century, when ships and lives were lost at sea all too frequently with God their only true beacon of hope.

A light fog drifted through the May morning, and I watched the famous Fresnel lens twirl round; it was one of the brightest parts of the picture I had started. The mist muted all of nature's

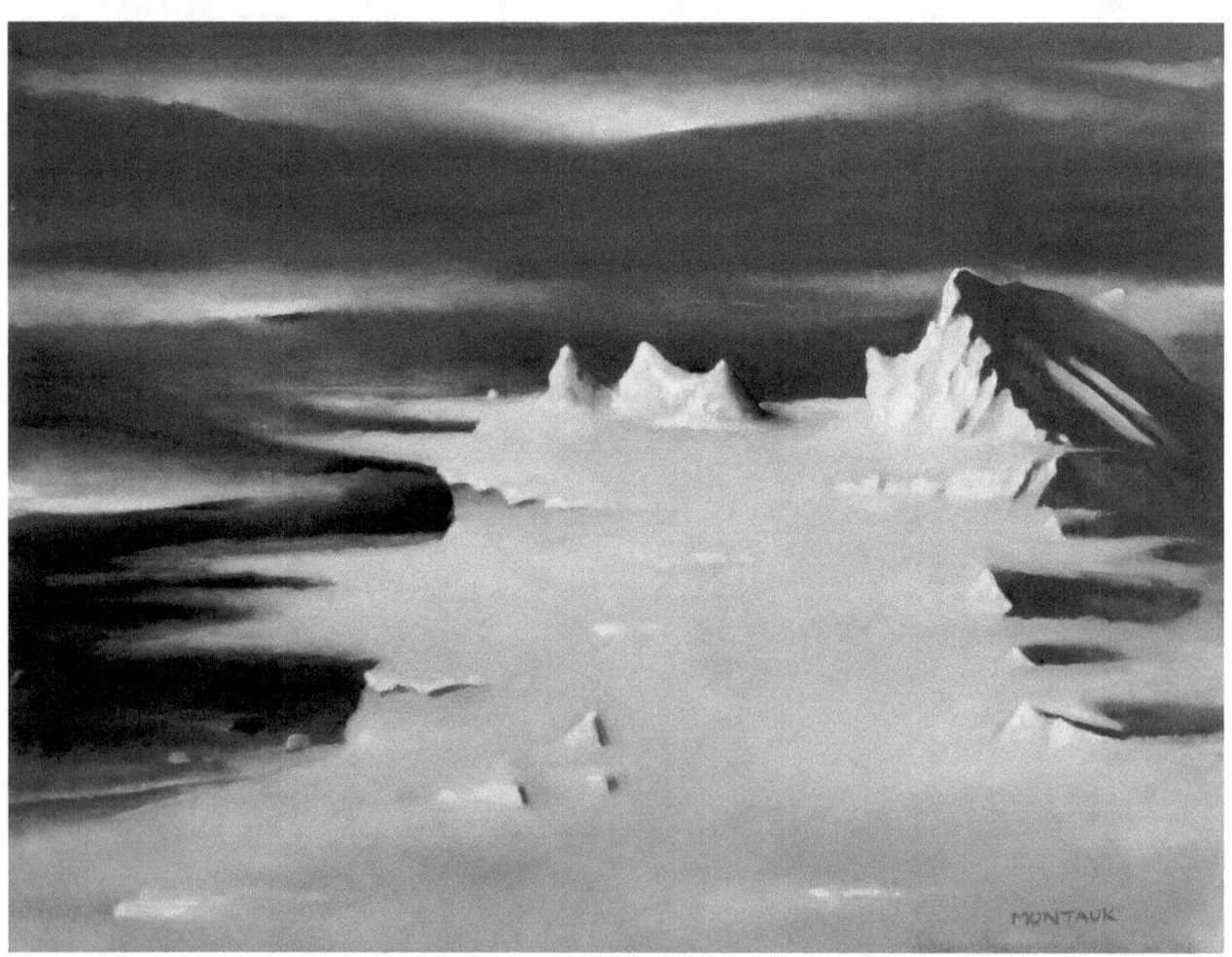

colors that day. The scene reminded me of a Whistler painting: very tonal with a dash of one, maybe two highlights, the second being the whitecap of a small wave turning slowly a few yards out, atop water otherwise smooth. The cold seemed to still the water. It was stilling me. I kept looking at the landscape, but I was no longer in the mood to draw. The excitement of getting there, the buildup on the road, was fizzling away as a thought rolled down from Turtle Hill where the lighthouse sits: could I have chosen a more cliché locale?

The steady stream of waves breaking upon the shore rolled the boulders and rocks with frightening ease. These were not even big waves. Shifting back and forth with the ebb and flow of the tide, the rocks produced a low thunder, a rumbling underfoot. I pictured them, thought of them—moving in sync yet muzzled in sound by the weight of the water and thus made ethereal. The rocks don't bother to fight this process. Over the years, they are ground smoother and smoother, smaller and smaller, rocks turning to pebbles and pebbles to sand, and sand carried off to Rockaway, Queens, perhaps, during storms, and from there, who knows?

A French portable easel was strapped to my back; years ago, I bought it only to make myself feel more in tune with those 19th century "en plain aire" artists I greatly admired. It was a cool contraption, just like the portable watercolor set, which came with a hidden brush and opened to reveal tiny, perfect blocks of pure color and which I kept inside one of the easel's holding compartments. I purchased the watercolor set after seeing a Turner show in England. It immediately began to live in a storage bin, next to stained-glass panes and lead stripping, which I acquired following a single workshop session in stained glass window making; see, I was going to elevate stained glass to a new art form. That was until I viewed the Albrecht Durer etching show—or was it Rembrandt's etchings at the Morgan Library?—and forked over a small pile of cash for an entire set of etching equipment and copper plates and signed up to study with this great printmaker, Blackburn, in midtown. How fast all those fucking things petered out, nothing made of the initial enthusiasm or the dreams of pushing some genre to a new height or depth. And now all I needed was a lady in a white dress with an umbrella to appear on the rocks surrounding the lighthouse. This spot was made for Monet or Renoir, not de la Haba. Not me.

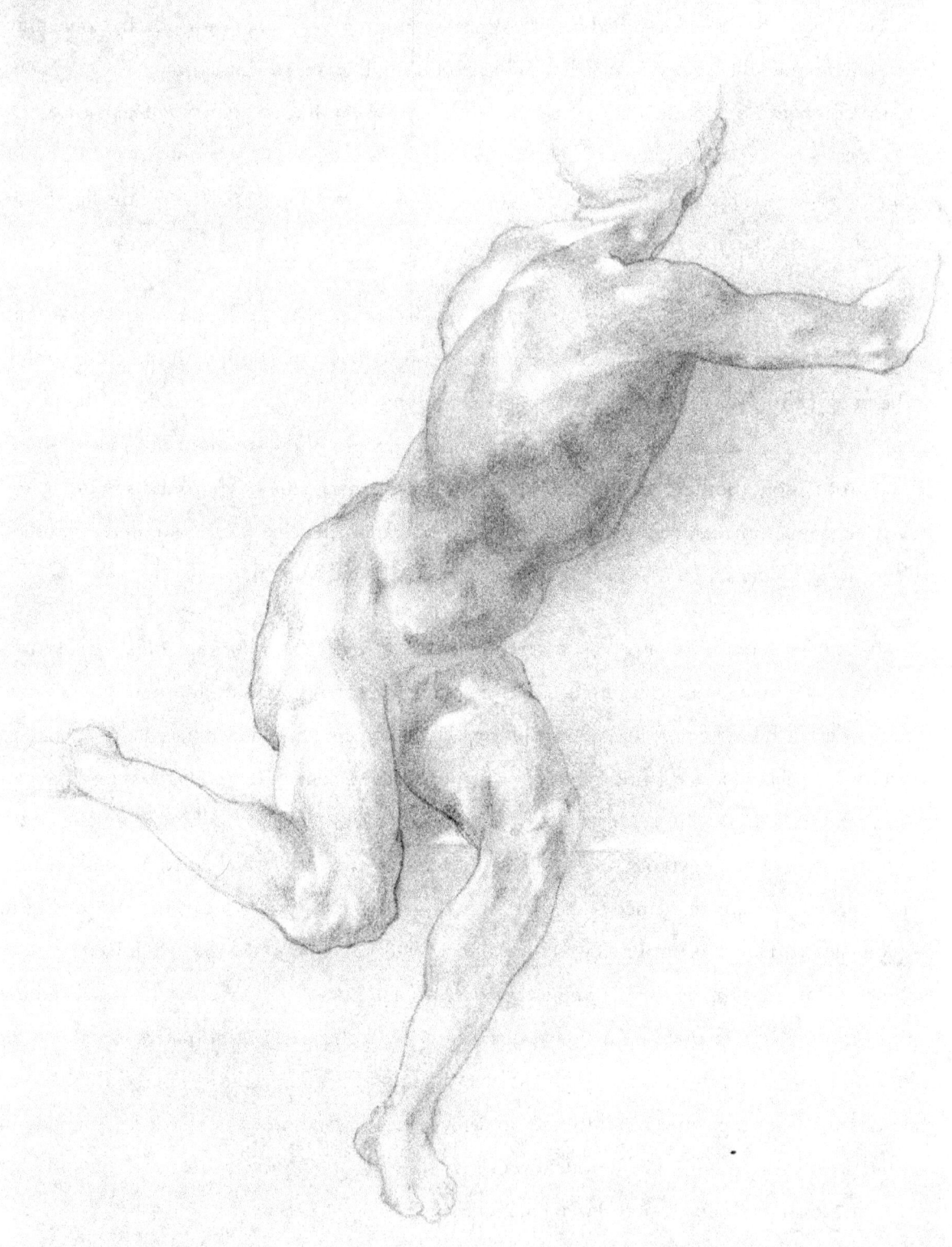

EXPERIENCE

Not choice, but habit rules the unreflecting herd.
  —William Wordsworth

While living in Boston, the local museum hosted a major show: all of Claude Monet's series paintings, landscapes where one could tell time of day, season, and temperature. Truly magnificent. Nature packaged in paint on canvas and displayed for the first time in 100 years the way the impressionist maestro intended them to be: together. I even went back to the studio and made a few copies of his work: rich impastos, the paint piled thickly and swirling. But I did them for one reason and one reason only: to sell. Everybody loves Monet. People eat up this impressionist stuff. I sold every Monet copy made. In the end, all paintings are meant to be decorative, right? That's what one of my teachers along the way said.

But I thought differently. Painting was more than just that. It had to be. I thought of Goya and his life, hardened by tragedy and Los Caprichos, his testament to horror witnessed: the famous Fifth of May painting, depicting Napoleon's troops executing his fellow Spaniards. And Manet's homage to that! And of Caravaggio and his painterly assault on Rome, and how he'd kill for his art, and did. Of Velazquez capturing Juan de Pareja's integrity, honor and glare, and with such truth conveyed in the portrait that it outright frightened half of those 17th century citizens who saw it on first exhibit inside the Roman Pantheon. While teaching myself to paint in Puerto Rico, I had begged God to allow me to possess only some of that talent. But God doesn't answer beggars, so I moved on from God, stopped praying but kept wishing, wishing to hold the figure to those greater, grander ideals, to the highest ideal in art and beauty, just as the Greeks—to whom Michelangelo measured his greatness—did 2,500 years ago. This is what enraptured me as a kid: all these great men, now immortal, remembered for their style, their visceral vernacular, their name! And yet there I was, looking at a lighthouse in the fog, painfully remembering that "landscapes are held on the low end of the picture-making hierarchy." With brush writing, I wanted to script across the canvas a story untold in a language unseen. How? I asked myself standing under the bluffs on the lee side of the peninsula, both scouting a set-up location and stalling. This is why I'm here, I answered. To consider exactly that. To relax and smell the sea.

I leaned down and gently dropped the sketchpad and box of charcoal onto the beach—these, the expensive sticks of charcoal I didn't wish to break into pieces—and before standing straight up again, I grabbed a handful of rocks, two handfuls in fact, and began tossing them out to sea, wondering just how long it would take for the ocean to spit them back to shore or grind them to sand. With each throw, a release: a breath of fresh air. My eyes started drifting out, southward, past the Bahamas and back to Puerto Rico and "mi Viejo San Juan." Moving there 12 years prior was not much different from coming to Montauk now: a change of pace, something stimulating, a search for artistry and identity. Is it best not to know what one is looking for? This way you won't be disappointed when what it is you're looking for isn't found? And instead you find joy and accept more easily the unwarranted, the unforeseen, the undesired? Like this landscape here now in front of me on Long Island's furthest point east.

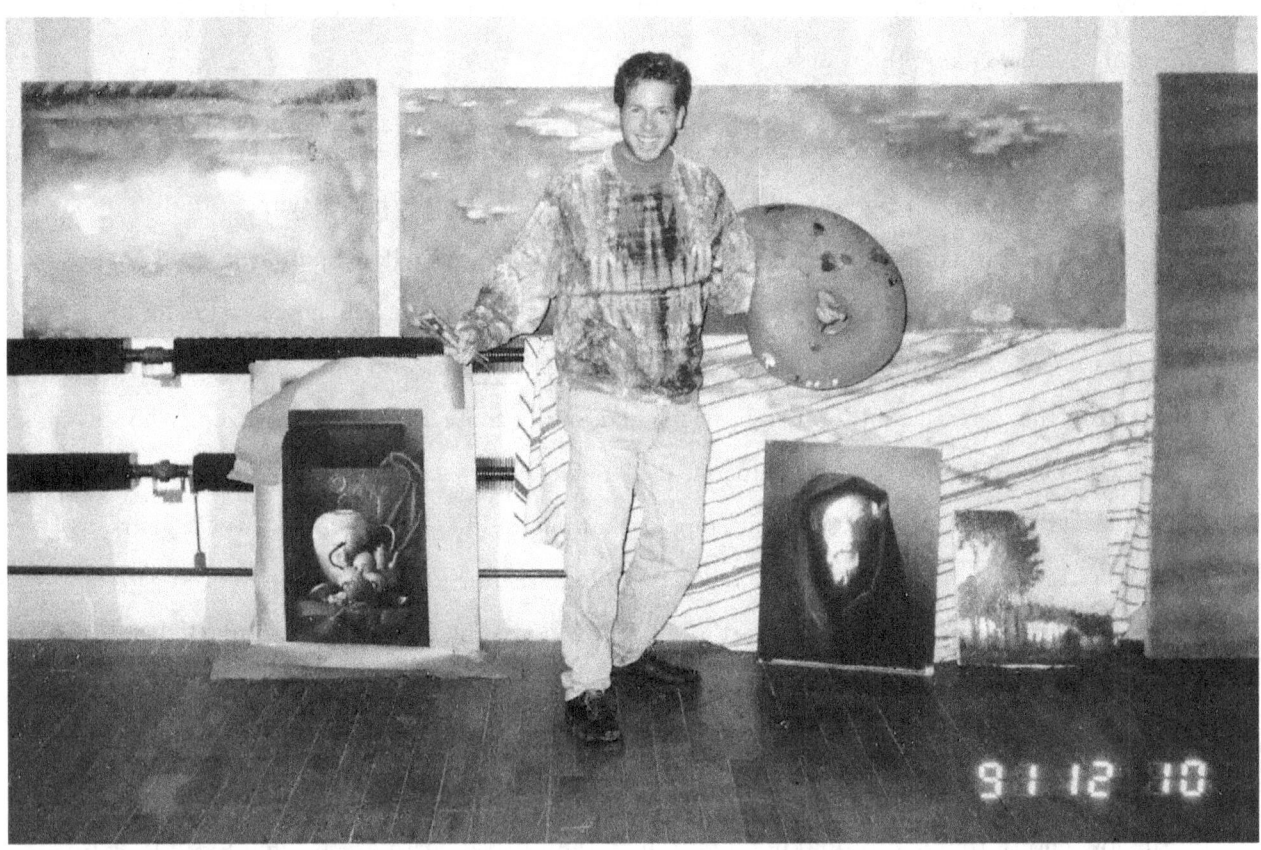

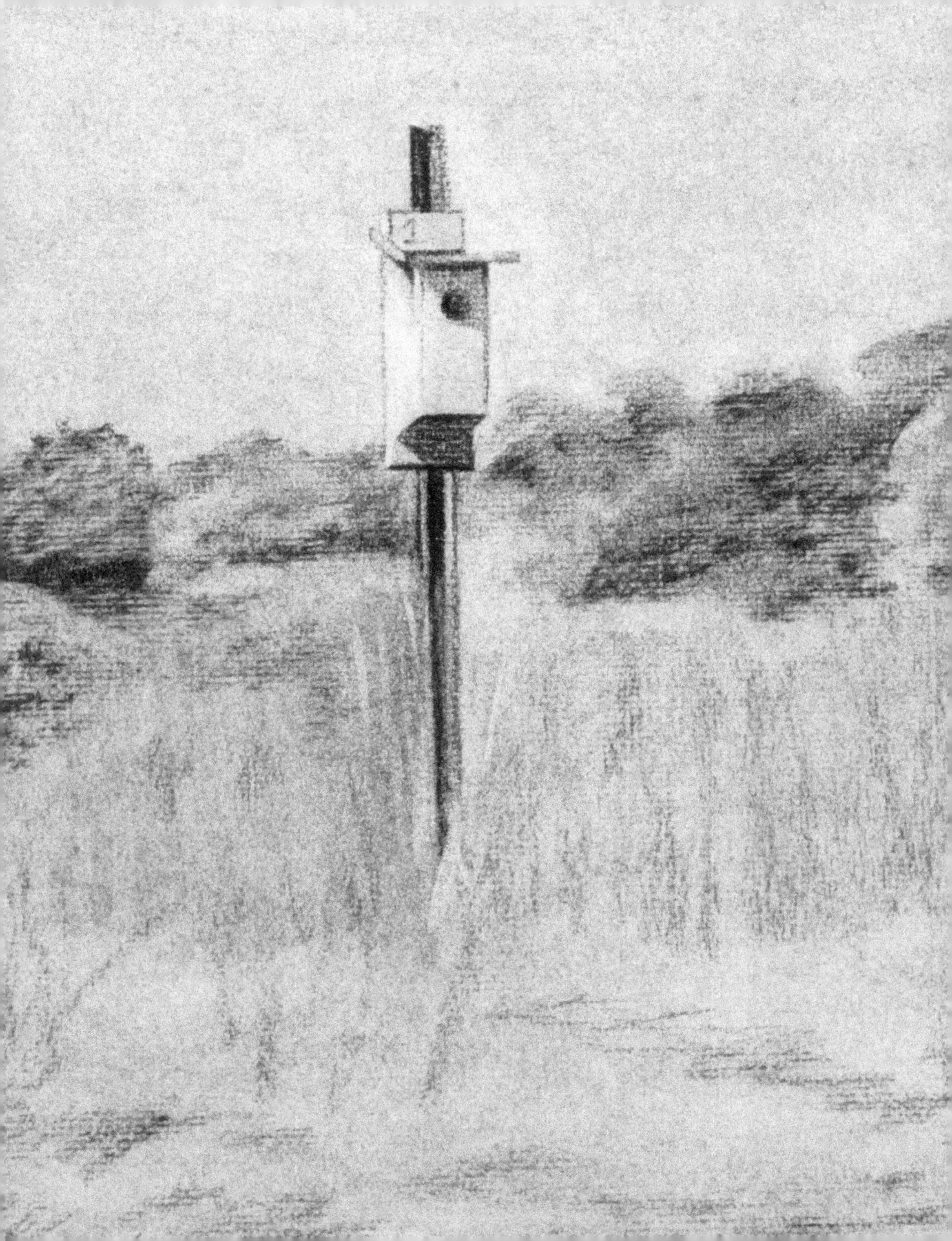

FIELD WORK (AND REEVALUATIONS)

Do not dwell in the past, do not dream of the future, concentrate the mind on the present moment.
—Buddha

But not looking back is easier said than done, especially when humanity is left behind in the dust. Stranded men, homeless. Men whom, for the most part, drink their lives away each day, and when a liter of rum in San Juan is only a few bucks, and the island an ample dealer, drunkenness is too easy to come by and homeless men too commonly drunk. I had been criticized for buying these guys bottles of Don Q. I was contributing to their problem, not helping with the solution, they told me. I wasn't so sure about that.

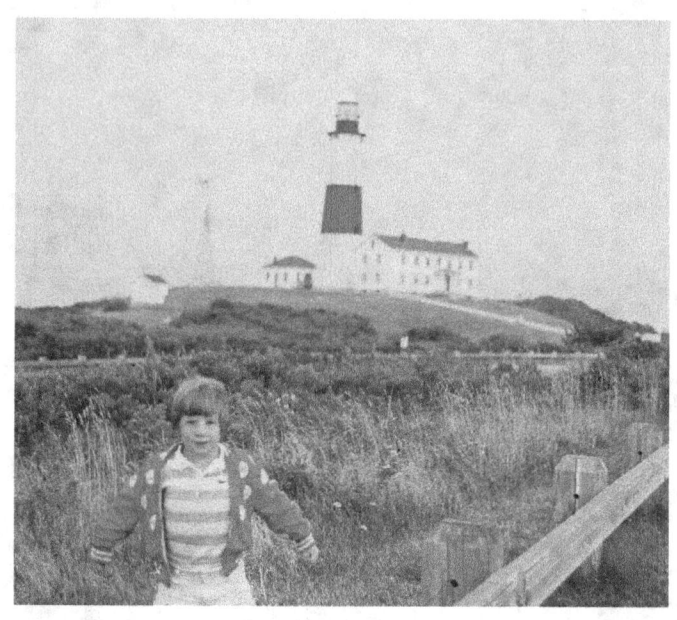

One summer day in 1989, when I was walking along a street in Old San Juan with Frankie, one of the attendees at my T.G.I. Friday birthday celebration, we passed a Baskin Robins. I asked if he'd like some ice cream.

"Really?" he replied, as if I'd offered a small gold bar. "I haven't had ice cream in years." Frankie drank rum, and he drank it straight and heavy and never on the rocks, and he turned tricks to keep the spigot on. When he ordered a peppermint cone, I heard a gentle old man speaking. It was an unblemished request. A chill shot down my back. His drunken exterior. His sunburnt, leathery skin. His dirt. Perversion. His stench. All vanished. Even his hunched back appeared to straighten. All that was left were the words, "I'll have a peppermint cone, please."

I ordered chocolate. As we walked back outside into the summer heat, he started to cry profusely. He tried in vain to lick at the melting cone while his free hand clung tightly to his chest, to his soiled Guayabera. He sputtered, "I haven't had ice cream for seven years. The last time was with my little girl." I had spoken with Frankie almost every day for two months, and he had never mentioned a daughter. He continued to gnaw at the fast-dripping cone, quietly sobbing. Green peppermint smeared his sunburnt nose and cheeks; lines of it dripped down his beard, once white now gray, dirtied and greasy. I tossed my unfinished cone into the trash, glad not to have ordered the double.

Each day thereafter, and for a total of six days, all the homeless men kept asking what happened to Frankie. He didn't mingle with the rest of them and wasn't seen in liquor stores or turning tricks with his gums down on the docks. He was spotted eating ice cream instead. Was it green ice cream? I asked myself, half joking. I saw Frankie only twice after I bought him the ice cream cone. The first time he ran away. The second time, on the fifth day, he spotted me first and came up beside me on the Plaza de Armas.

"I can't Gregorio," he said imploringly.

"You can't what, Frankie?"

He began to cry, turned his back, and shuffled away. "Frankie!", I shouted, "Come over here." But he didn't. His left hand, rising quickly from his side, made a curt gesture, as if to say, "Please don't bother me anymore!" or "Go away with your ice cream."

I watched as he made his way down the street, gradually disappearing into the crowd of tourists and lunchtime passersby, my only thought how silly he was being.

The next day, tumult ran through the homeless community. Frankie had blown his brains out. I wondered who his daughter was and what, if anything, he'd done to her. All I knew was that he was a smiling bum who liked to drink the cheapest dark rum available, the kind that buries guilt but not deeply enough. Maybe if he had preferred an expensive brandy, a cognac, something that takes years to age, it would've done a better job at washing away his sins. But when all it takes is one cone of Baskin Robins to unleash the wrath of past mistakes, then no matter what he drank or what he did, or what anyone else did or did not do, nothing could've prevented his final action.

From time to time, the remorse felt for Frankie and the fond remembrance of him and the other homeless men like Paul stir feelings of repentance for ever worrying over such a fortunate life to live as mine has been—artist searching for beauty and truth whose only dilemma, really, is in choosing what new language or alphabet to paint in, not who'll feed me next or where to sleep at night. Mine were pathetic and incidental matters not worthy of distress; my type of suffering was not worthy of salvation. See, self-inflicted wounds don't count. Or do they?

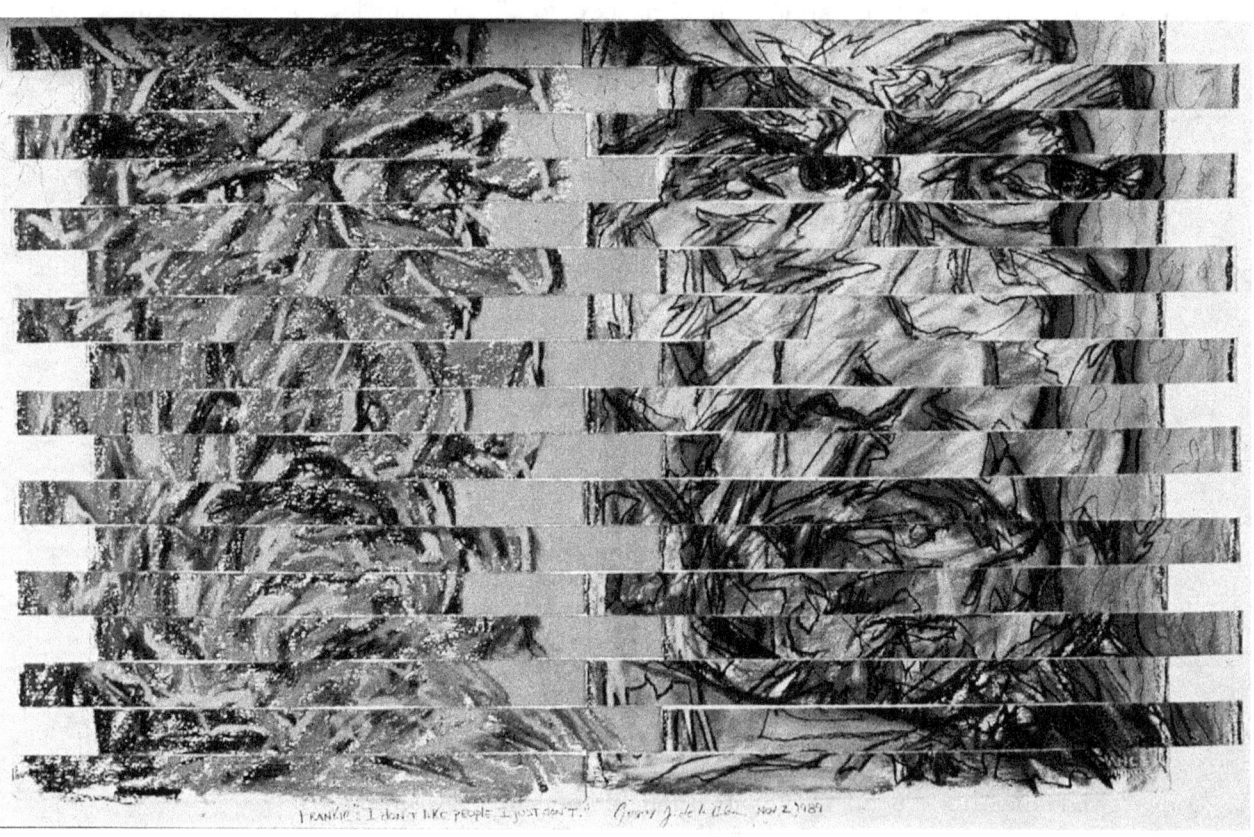

MONTAUK, MAY, 2001

Back on the beach in Montauk, a dense fog began to roll in, carried on colder air. I looked over at the beacon that pulls men in and thought of the 19th century French Barbizon master J.F. Millet who painted figures of impoverished peasants bending and sowing, gleaning and removing the bits of grain left in the fields after the harvest. Figures planted firmly and stoically in those fields, just as the lighthouse at the end of the beach was. Millet was so poor that his paintings grew mold from being left unsold on his basement's dirt floor, a home filled with nine children. Yet he somehow managed to paint, and to paint one of the most iconic and reproduced images in all art history—the farm couple praying (or mourning?) in the potato field at dusk. Millet's insight, strength, and wisdom issued forth on my warmed breath: "It is the treating of the common place with the feeling of the sublime that gives art its true power."

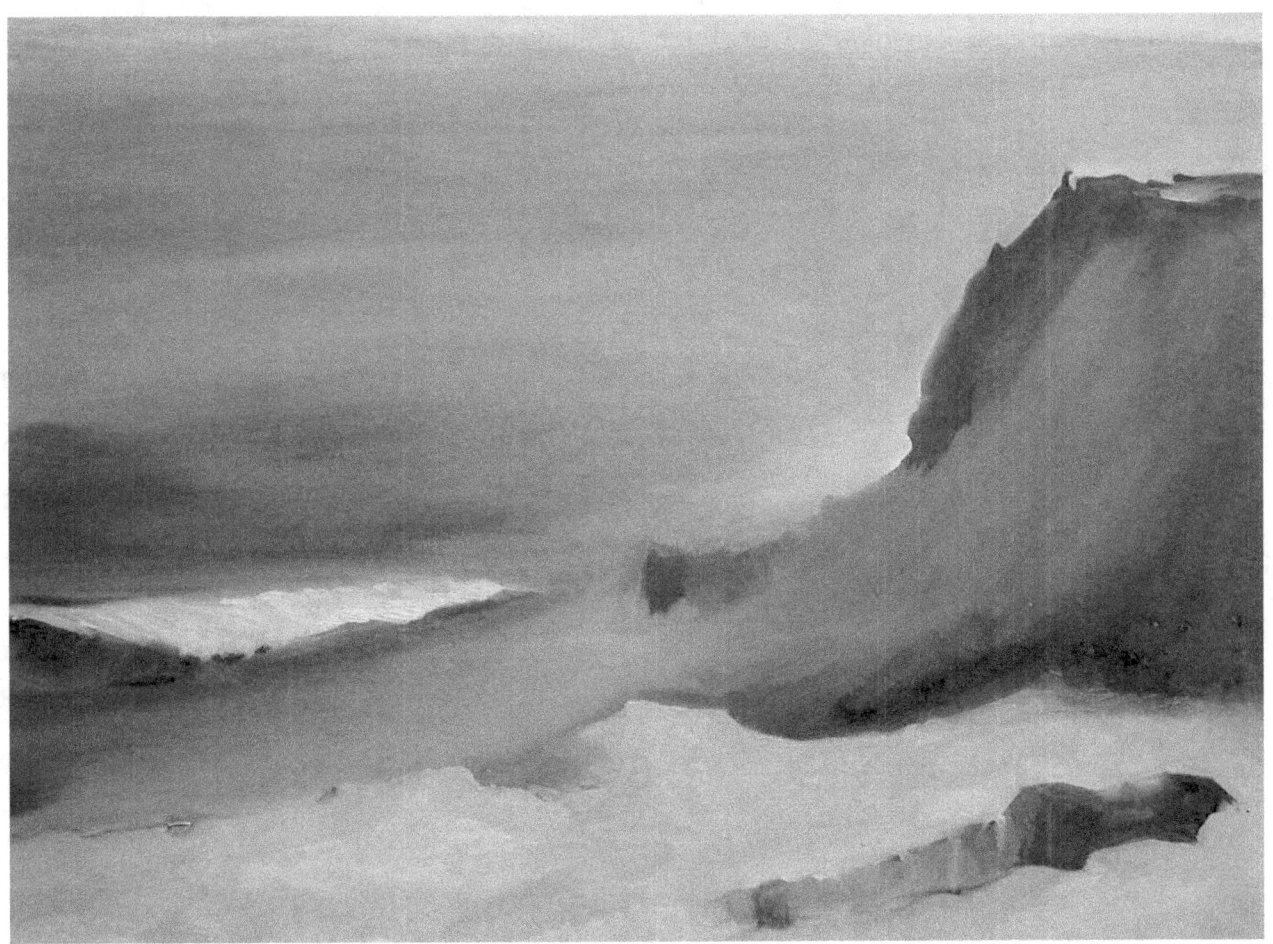

With cool air off the Atlantic sending chills down my spine, I took to throwing some rocks to stay warm. Some rocks were thrown with force to see how far from the shoreline they'd splash, others I threw at an angle parallel to the sea and with just enough precision for the rock (preferably a smooth thin one with a little weight to it) to bounce, and not sink, off the water and to do so as many times as possible until the force of the throw petered out and gravity pulled them down into the deep blue. I thought of people who came into my life for one reason or another and like the tossed rocks disappeared from the picture entirely and almost as quickly. But the rocks served a purpose that was immediate and beneficial. Memories of people and why they entered my life and why this thing or that thing happened regarding them twirled around in my skull like stinking chum thrown overboard to allure fish. What purpose and role do these encounters with others serve, what future attractions do past experiences help navigate in the future?

I vowed to return first thing the next morning. To make the first Montauk drawing of that "common place" millions know so well. Too wound up to do otherwise, I let myself wander the

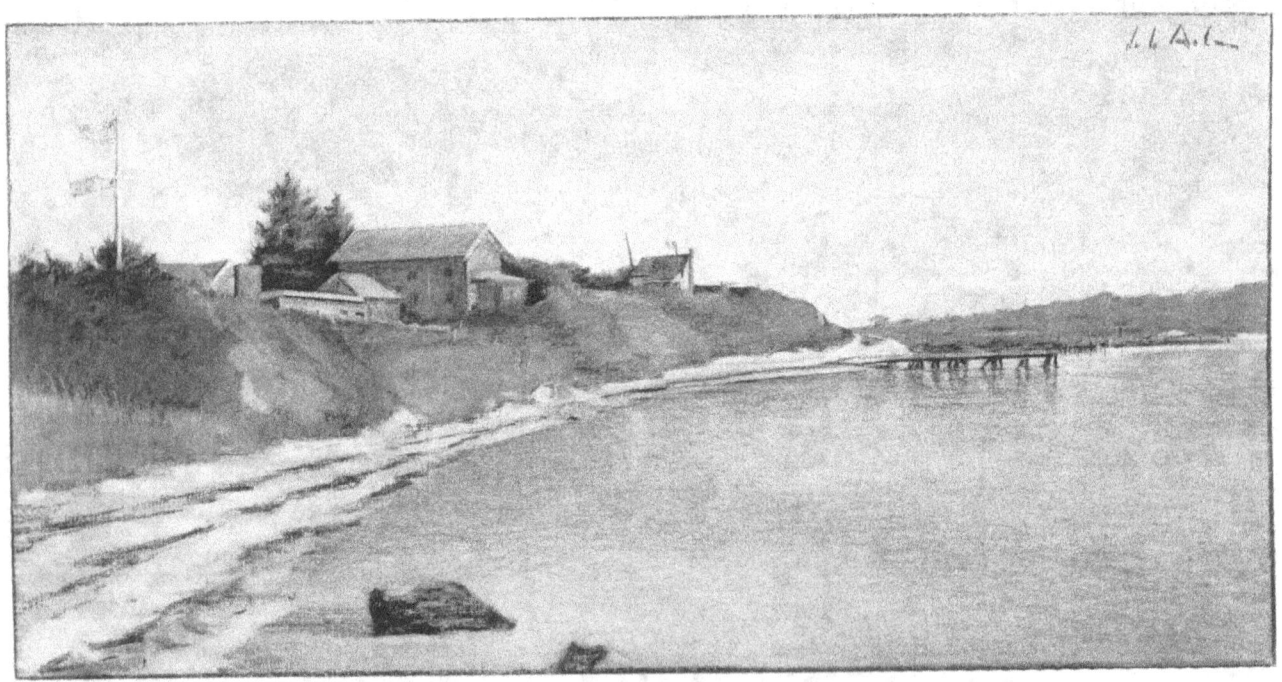

beach for hours that first day—throwing more rocks later on for fun and exercise and not remembrance or ambition or hope, or piling them high into cairns—and scouting other areas for more of the "common" to draw the following day.

By nightfall, I had checked myself into a fifty-dollar-a-night motel and called Teresa, again:

Me: "Hey baby. How are you?"

Teresa: "How are you? I miss you, Gregory."

"I miss you, too."

"Did you have a good day?"

"Yes, I did. I think things will work themselves out, out here. I forgot how beautiful it is up by the lighthouse."

"I wish I were with you."

It is not what you do but how you do it. The first drawing of Montauk was completed at the crack of dawn. My internal alarm clock woke me in complete darkness. The LED display read 4:30AM. Too early to head to the Point? Where could I grab some coffee? In the room, only a Bible: no coffee maker. Outside, I had no idea what was open. I got up and exited the second-floor room, coming out on a balcony that faced Route 27. No cars. Beyond the highway, a flicker of light bouncing on Fort Pond, reflected from a home on the bank. It was colder than I had prepared for, but I was anxious to get going. I put my pants on, picked up my keys and wallet from the nightstand, threw on a sweater, opened and locked the door, and ran down to the car. Frost coated the windshield. For five minutes, I sat tentatively, hands tucked beneath my legs, shivering. Then I made my way east. I passed Mr. John's Pancake House in town; nobody was there. Being the off-season, I wondered if that would change in a few hour's time. Everything was silent, and I would learn later that the only place open that early is down by the docks, a mile or two north from where I was headed.

EXPERIENCE

Perfection, of a kind, was what he was after.
—W. H. Auden

I was glad I left the motel when I did. Taking the same path as the day before, I stepped into the clearing to find the day cracking open behind night. For a moment, the sky mirrored the slate gray/dark blue color of the sea. Then, a perfect horizontal of light split heaven and earth in two, straight across the horizon. The light was more white than I thought possible. Shouldn't it be orange or yellow?

I hurriedly set up the easel as best I could. There was a slight fog, and the water gently rolled in. I placed the small sketch pad on the easel's holding arm, locked it in place by tightening the top latch, and, using diagonal strokes, began to coat the entire sheet of Arches paper with a soft vine charcoal. This was my middle tone to work from. Think: a new mark atop this middle tone will be the darkest dark in the drawing and erasing the middle tone will reveal the paper's original color, creating the lightest part of the picture. Three tones: the paper, the middle grey rubbed into the surface with a shammy, and then the actual color of the charcoal, black, for the darks. Again, quickly! The sun waits for no one. There was not a single cloud in the sky, only traces of fog lingering over the water. The lighthouse read most clearly, so I defined it first, using the soft charcoal stick. Having no coffee in me, and no wind to interfere, my hand executed straight lines effortlessly. I worked fast, marking shapes and outlines as the sun shot through the fog; with the kneaded eraser, I extracted all the lights: the brightest parts of the sun itself, and the great slanting shapes that blazed on the side of the lighthouse, and the small whitecap of a rolling wave. Light bled into middle tones and middle tones created form. Drawing is all about illusion: artists are mere magicians. Within forty minutes, this first sketch of the famous lighthouse was complete. It felt good. I felt good. The drawing wasn't half bad either.

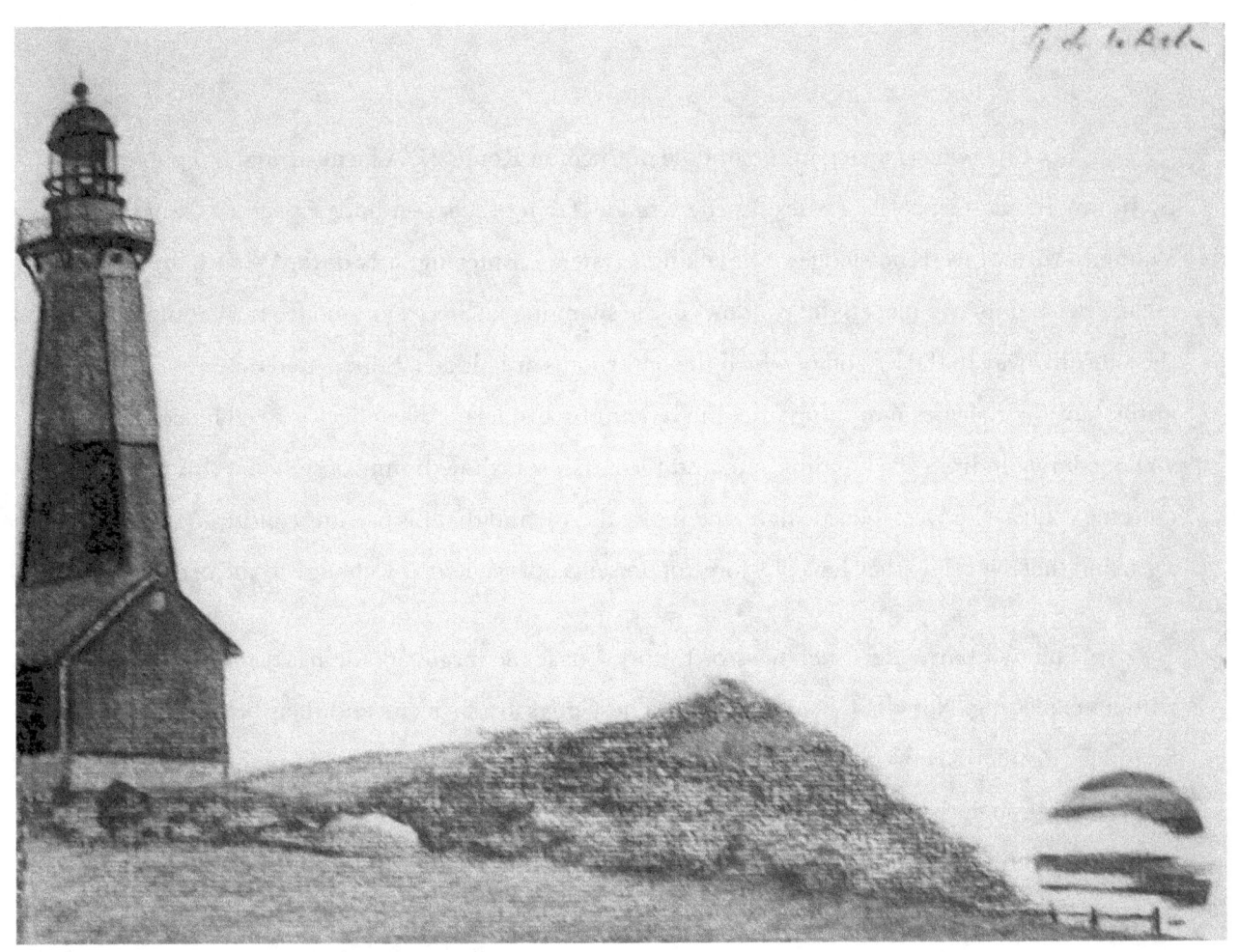

An aged man is but a paltry thing,
A tattered coat upon a stick, unless
Soul clap its hands and sing, and louder sing
For every tatter in its mortal dress,
Nor is there singing school but studying
Monuments of its own magnificence;
And therefore I have sailed the seas and come
To the holy city of Byzantium. Go.

    —W. B. Yeats, "Sailing to Byzantium"

The Shagwong, smack in the middle of town on Route 27. A local stronghold pub owned by Jimmy Hewlett since the sixties. In the window facing the street hangs a sign: "Piano Player Wanted, Must Have Knowledge of Shucking Oysters." Entering, it is dark. What light there is escapes from only two places: the window on the swinging kitchen door and from a ceiling bulb in the short hallway to the left, off of which the bathrooms are hidden. Silhouetted bodies sit or stand at the bar, their shapes morphing into one larger obscure form. The effect is heightened because you're coming in from the blinding sun, and I feel that somehow Jimmy designed it this way—the extreme contrast between outside light and inside dark—and that his patrons conspired in such design, and that over time they have, by force of presence, prevented any change to the original plan.

The two bartenders, nephews of Jimmy, boast the largest potbellies a man can possess without exploding. Not obese men, not slobs. These guys are drinkers and their bellies trophies of first-place distinction—worked on year-round through shots and pitchers and pints. My attention, however, is brought back to my error: I've walked in on a drinking session that isn't mine; they're running it, and they're doing it for their regulars, and now they have to do it in spite of me. It's gonna take a long time and much proving to get a crack out of either one of them, no matter how much tip I leave. In fact, the more I leave, the more they'll growl.

Behind them, the liquor bottles are organized by three stained-glass panels, which lend the Shagwong its air of classic pub. The middle panel depicts the lighthouse. In the first panel, the one closest to the entrance, a small craft and her captain battle the high seas: molded lead engulfed by panes of blue and green. A large taxidermic bird—a black hawk, is it?—sits perched above the bar, and despite its dust and age, it dutifully watches over all drinkers and captains and fishermen, all bartenders and artists, and I think of Circe, the minor Greek goddess of major importance. I look around and take a seat. "Johnny Red and soda with lemon, please." I keep staring at that fucking bird up there, a reminder not to move forward blindly, not to simply go through the grind but to soar and stay focused. That's why I'm here. Or so I believe. Sitting in a bar like the Shagwong, amongst such men, working men, men who labor with their hands and fuss not over their dress attire, and who drink regardless of the day of the week or the hour of the day challenges my theory gifted by the stuffed bird, and alerts the mind that there are other paths in life one can take, other options to contemplate. This much, as this very moment, is certain: The Shagwong is the embodiment of pure abandon and freedom. And it's soothingly enticing. "Another Johnny Red, please."

The adjacent room is the dining area. The red leather booths are well worn and the old wood paneling, faded in color, displays a motley but not haphazard collection of photos. It could be any American's basement built out during the 1950s or 60s. I've seen it before. It was my basement in Flushing, Queens and my wife's in Whitestone, wood paneling and all, but instead of red leather booths we both had red velvet couches, and our framed photos were of relatives and friends and vacations in the family car. The Shagwong's photos are of Montauk and its long and storied past: big fish landed and homes built on bluffs by famous architects; the hunting of rabbits and ducks in the days when cattle outnumbered homes; Teddy Roosevelt's Rough Riders landing at Gardiner's Bay after the Cuban war and enduring months of quarantine up by Deep Hallow Ranch, America's oldest cattle operation and where I had drawn all that day. Drawing in fact, while thinking, too, about home and family. Being here brought back a flood of memories, one of which was why, as a child, I first came here: to fish with dad and the family. And seeing all the black and white photos on the walls, of fishing boats and fishermen with their catch sprawled out with pride on wooden docks, of this place visited often in youth, reminded me of the bond we, as a family of five, had growing up. A bond formed as brothers swimming and fishing together in sight the Lighthouse, of dining on fresh seafood with mom squirming as dad devoured his bucket of piss clams. And yet even with age, marriages, and job changes to other states, the connection to place and between children and parents all those years ago has managed still to keep its firm grip on me, as if the memory itself was the glue holding me in my seat at the bar, begging me to stay a while longer.

The Shagwong wasn't dead, but the staff and those stuck to the bar stools did seem comatose. I ordered a burger and another Johnny Walker Red with soda and lemon, a drink that John Tunney introduced me to back in 1998, in Atlantic City. We would easily order six or seven of them in one sitting as we discussed the mural project for Temple Bar & Grill or we'd talk about famous artists and great restaurants —or goals. Eitherway, it was an absolutely thrilling opportunity to have been challenged so creatively for such a massive, thirty-foot-long mural that year. I ordered one more cocktail and took another peek at my nine-by-twelve inch sketchpad that held the drawing completed earlier that day. I couldn't help but ask myself: Is this what makes you happy, Gregory?

EXTRACURRICULAR ACTIVITIES

Try everything that can be done.
Be deliberate. Be spontaneous.
Be thoughtful and painstaking.
Be abandoned and impulsive.
Learn your own possibilities.

    –George Bellows, 1920

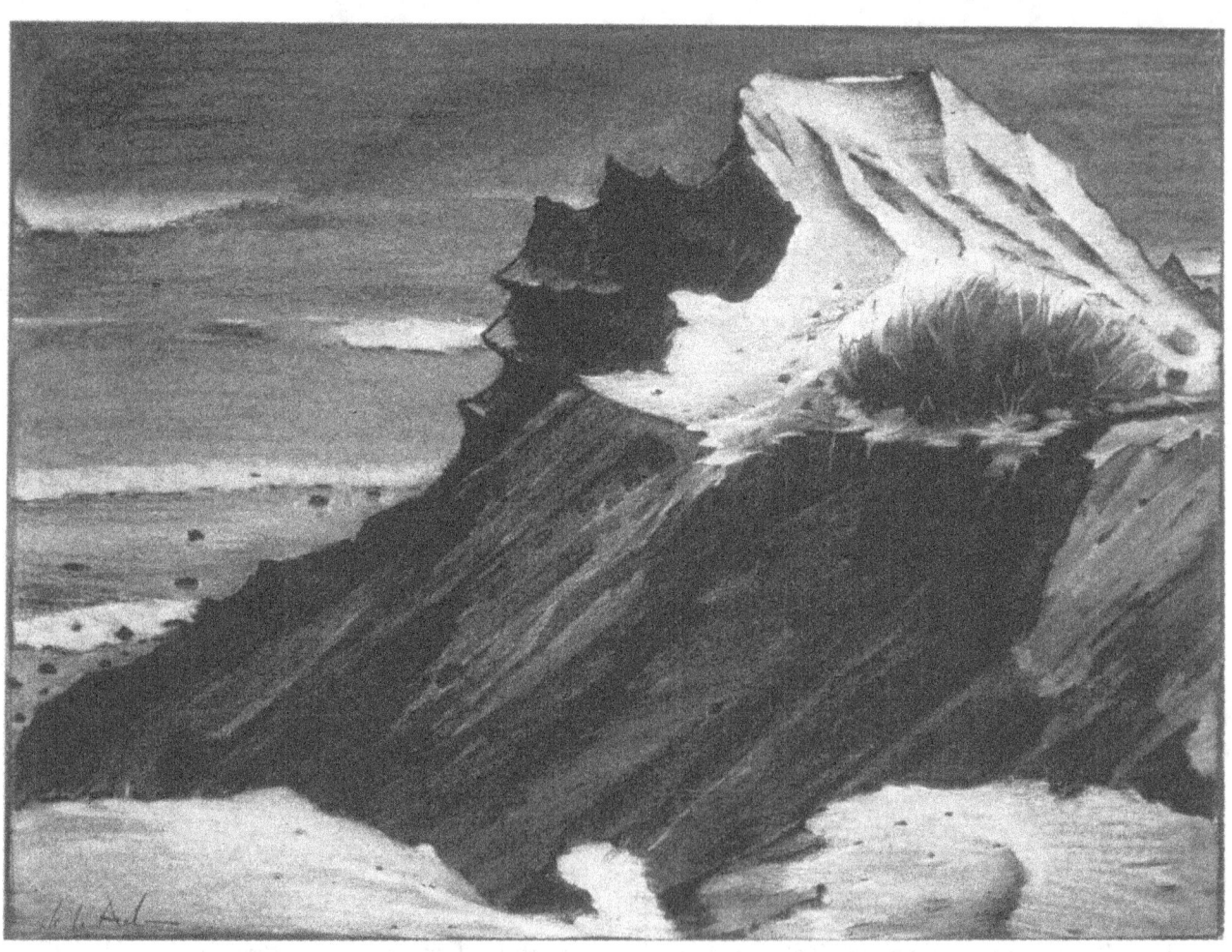

June 5, 2001, Montauk

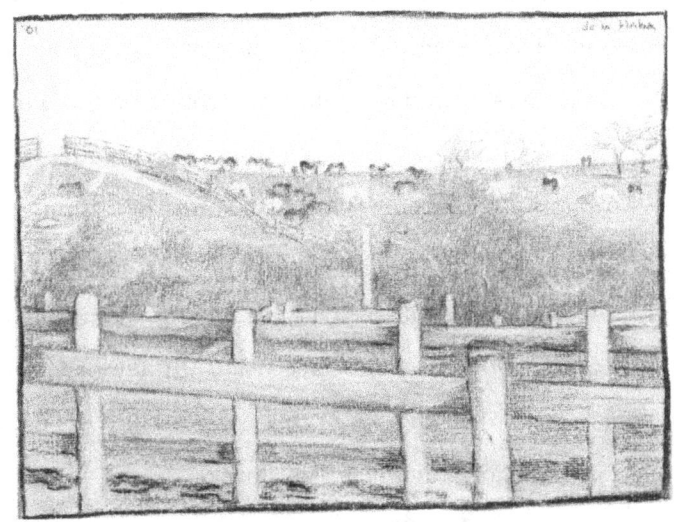

My alarm clock is set for five AM every day. It's one of those digital alarms with the fast-pulsing, techno-beeping sound that causes my heart to miss a beat when it first goes off. But it gets me up fast, albeit a little older and stressed, and the last two weeks have mirrored that theme each day: fog's been rolling in off the Atlantic in large waves, dense and foreboding, making it altogether impossible to see, let alone paint from life. Also, it's been cold and damp, and the dampness makes even a little cold feel colder, and this particular morning the warm blanket I'm wrapped in provides ample reason to relinquish all intention of going anywhere or doing anything.

The window a foot above my head is opened wide, and the screen that keeps the bugs out is wet with condensation, a result of cool northern winds mixing with warm tropical waters that have traveled up from far-away places of the south Atlantic. Nodes of water are held in a pixelated pattern by the screen's array; raising my arm off the bed, I place my index finger on the mesh and drag it in a circular pattern, trying to draw a happy face, but the water won't be pulled along and so the process doesn't work the way it does when writing a name or heart on a fogged-up window. Curiosity pulls me out of bed, having never seen fog this dense. I stroll down to the front parking lot labeled "Town Residents Only," which leads directly onto the beach. On a narrow path that cuts through a small dune, I begin, blindly, walking toward the ocean. It is there, in front, barely audible, a stone's throw away. No wind, and save my footsteps in sand, near stillness pervades the landscape. A slight ripple echoes along an invisible shoreline—broken bits of muscle shells and pebbles turning gently in the tidal flow. It's a sound I trust from childhood, watched over by parents who preferred it this way over big breaking waves.

The water runs up over my feet, over the sand, the last remnants of a wave that formed thousands of miles from here, now exerting its last bit of strength, exhaling its last breath, dispersing itself across Ditch Plains beach. The sand is cool, moist, almost too cold for bare feet, which now begin to sink and force up tiny pools of water. The sand sifts between my toes, removing cuticles and dead skin; maybe this is what the piping plovers feast on along with tasty sand critters? Goose bumps pop from my skin as the sound of a running dog registers, closer and closer, seconds away, toward me. My heart pounds faster: I've been attacked and bitten three times by so-called "friendly" dogs. Dogs that were visible and to whom I offered my hand, palm upwards, for them to smell, to trust. But I must've been cruel to animals in a past life because in this one I'm hopeless with them. I'm certain all dogs know this and get a kick out of jumping on me as this one does, out of nowhere, from the fog. I let out a loud shriek.

Luckily, it was a black lab belonging to a local artist I'd often seen while out walking. I heard Rudy call the dog's name. The lab quickly disappeared back into the fog, and I turned around and headed straight back into bed, eager to get into the story I'd been reading the past few days—In Search Of Captain Zero—penned by another local artist, a writer named Allan Weisbecker. I'd purchased the book from Lily, the Ditch Witch, who parks her eponymous food truck in the other town lot, the one adjoining the East Deck Motel. I normally skateboard over to her around 7AM for coffee and a breadstick or bagel. But she is not there this early, and if she were, she wouldn't want to see me.

I get lost in the book and transported on a journey to Mexico and farther south, on a search for the author's best friend who disappeared without a trace in 1995. Weisbecker begins his trek from Montauk in his "casita," a 4x4 pick-up truck with a camper attached, taking with him his faithful dog and a die-hard commitment to find his lost friend. Along the way, he explores and surfs remote point breaks, the surfing the fuel that nourishes the author and the memoir. It's one of those books that enters your life and then runs parallel to it, because you're on a search of your own and, as it happens, you're also residing at the end of the road from where the author started off. I continue to seek similarities throughout the reading, forming a kindred spirit with the author, in the way college freshman do with Kerouac. I remind myself that this is why I'm out here, to set

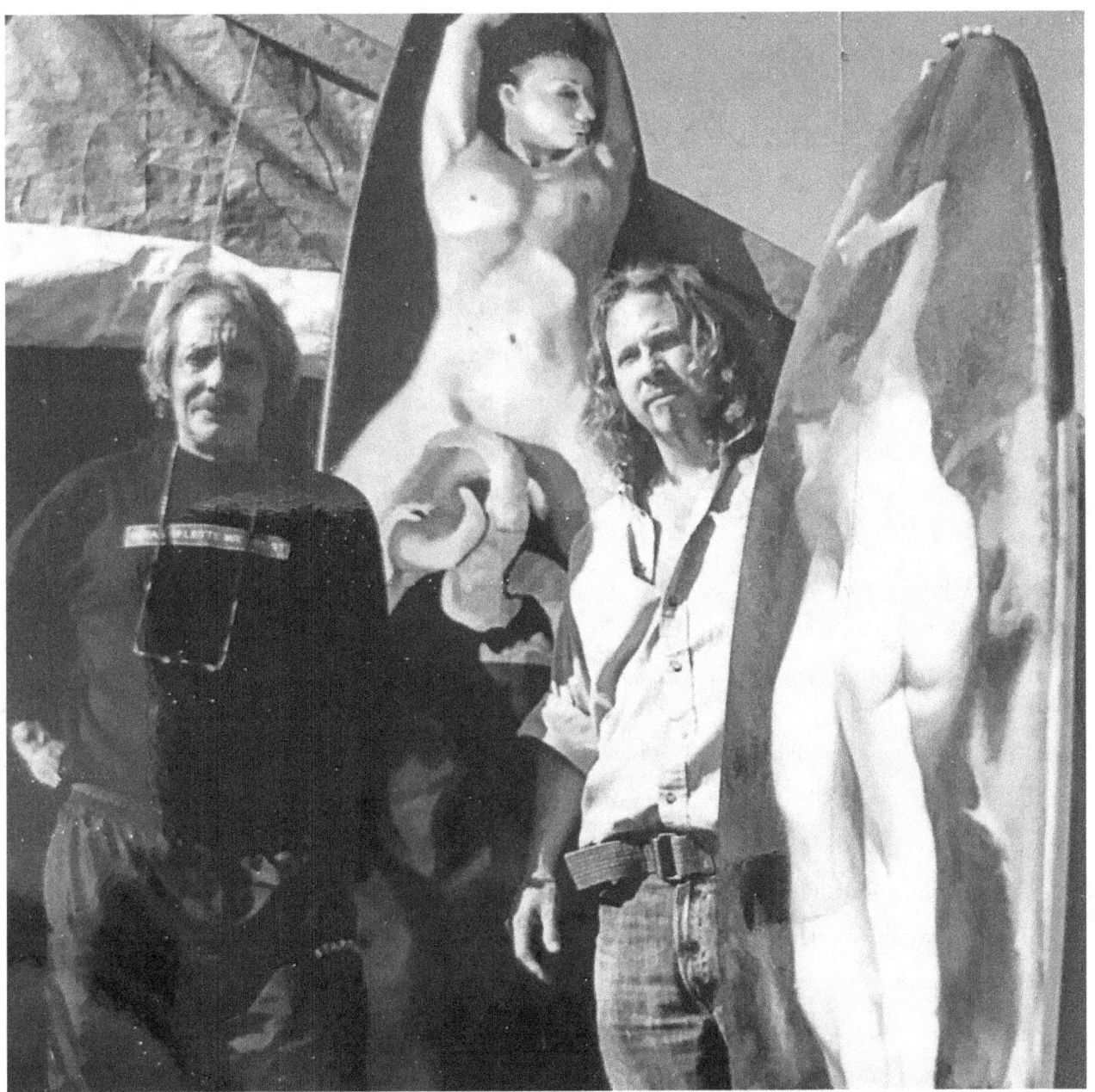

forth on my own search, and to record it in word and image. It's true, I feel, as I turn the pages of Weisbecker's story: the path I've taken is correct, and I'm doing what I should be, moving forward, as an artist. With each new drawing of Montauk, I feel more determined to succeed, to make it as an artist, more confident that I won't fail as one, even though I'm still uncertain of the pictorial vernacular currently being explored.

PERSONAL INFORMATION

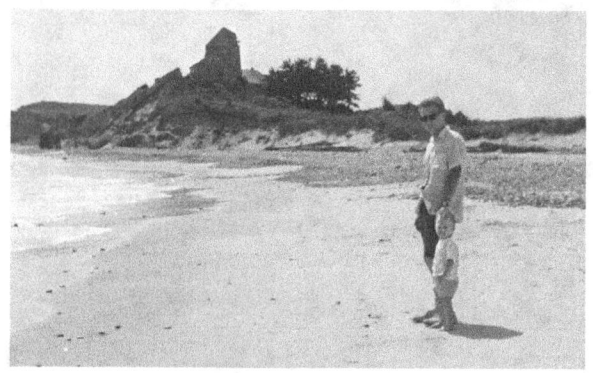

The Ditch Witch doesn't open until eight, but she allows a few regulars to come over to the side of her truck for coffee only. The regulars are all locals, mostly surfers, each a piece of a larger puzzle: individuals who live and breathe the ocean. Their skin is bronzed, hair golden from the sun. Their bodies lean from paddling out to sea and hauling nets of fish up from it. They are salty, and you either like salt or you don't. They are fierce loyalists who live off the sea and have tremendous respect for it and total disregard for those who don't. Fortunately, I'm like them (although more red than bronze); otherwise, I'd be in the wrong place, and we'd all know it.

But this is the right place. It is the place my father took me so many years ago to fish and to swim. The place Allan's father first took him for the same reason years before that. It is a place many fathers take their boys. A place many families come. It's good for that. For growing strong legs, walking and running in the sand; strong hands and arms from swimming, paddling, and fishing; powerful lungs from inhaling fresh, salted, clean air; a free spirit develops in the unfenced space. What grows, too, is a sense of wonderment and awe in the power of it all, of her, mother nature, who can quickly turn on you. The experience of growing up along the shore humbles one's attitude about life. At any given moment, something bigger and stronger than you can take it all away, and all your strength, no matter how much of it you have, is no match. Your existence here on the beach, on Earth, is no greater than a grain of sand. And the best thing in the world to do is kneel down with your father or son and run your hands through it and build something together and murmur in your heart "amen." And then snap a photo. Because, as the saying goes, "time and tide wait for no man." The sandcastle's destiny eventually becomes our own.

There once stood a magnificent hundred-year-old house planted high above the cliff at Shadmoor State Park. The home, long claimed by the sea, had a historic windmill attached to it that the legendary photographer and local summer resident, Peter Beard, saved before it rolled off the cliff. Mr. Beard had the windmill moved to his 6-acre property further east where it lasted until 1977 when a fire turned it and many of his treasured photos and journals to ash. A treasured photo I keep in an old sketchpad is of my father walking along this very same shore. The beach back then in 1964 was empty. Taken in September when the striped bass and blue fish feed wildly and when fishing was still dad's most fervent pastime. In the photo, he's holding hands with my oldest brother, Lawrence, about three years of age, with the house and windmill safely perched in the background, both fully intact and together as one—as my father was with each of his three sons.

This specific locale would be one of the first spots in Montauk I most wanted to draw. To find. To document. To confirm my connection with. But in 2001, all that was left of this home was a water pipe jutting out from the bluff's face and some remnants of the historic home scattered about the beach: parts of a cast iron tub, blue slate from a patio, and a cast iron heater. The drawing would eventually wind up in the collection of Allan Weisbecker because he, too, had a connection to this particular beachfront: It was one of his favorite spots to surf.

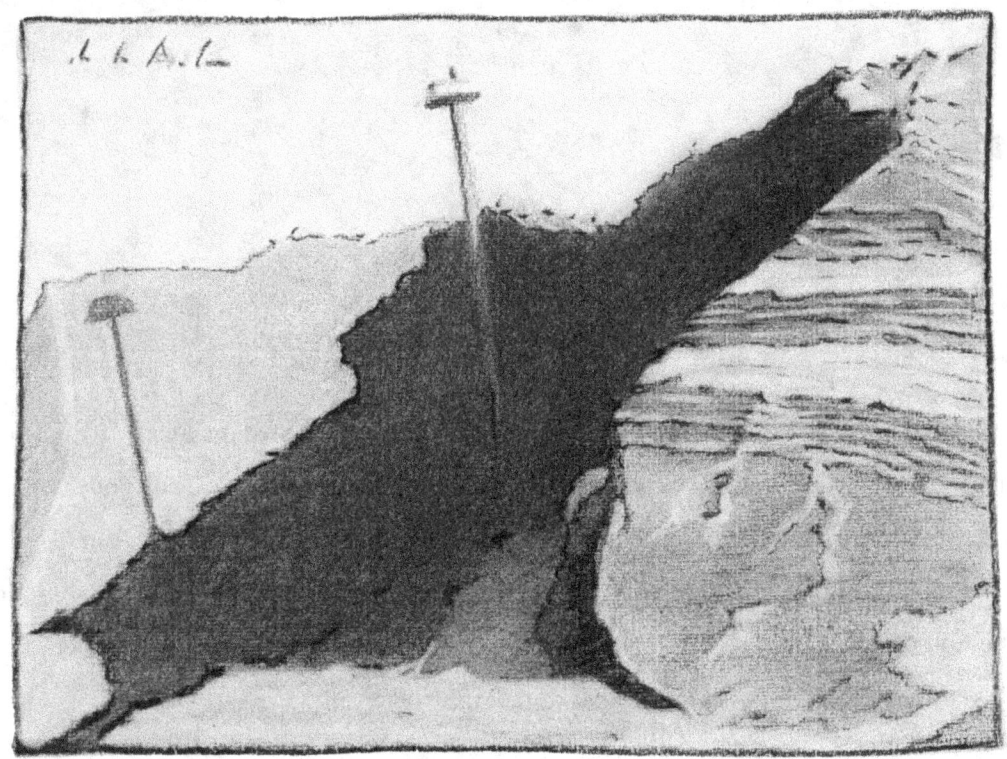

SATISFACTIONS

"Those who cannot begin do not finish."
—Robert Henri

Montauk, late June, 2001

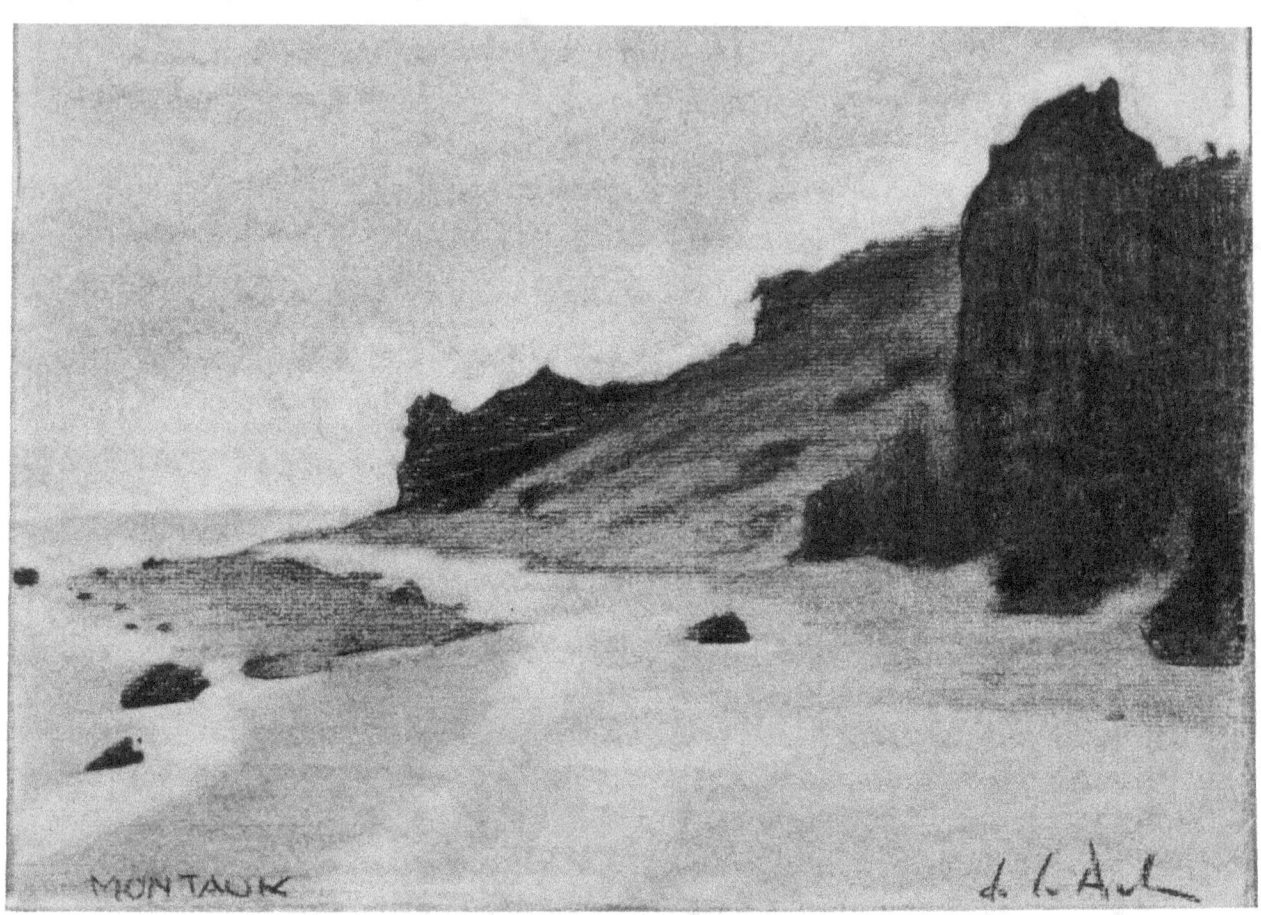

MONTAUK

I like to order a toasted salt stick with my coffee. Having granted me local status, Lili passes the coffee and breadstick out the side door of her truck. I eat and drink as if the coffee and baked flour and salt contain something that my body desperately requires. I ask a local, Jim Goldberg—surfer, shaper, and fisherman—"What's up with the fog?" Without turning in my direction, he smiles behind his dark sunglasses and replies, "You know what they say; fog before seven, clears by eleven," and then proceeds, without looking at me, to stroll away.

Another day of rain and fog. It's not worth getting out of bed, but once awake, falling back to sleep is impossible. So I read while savoring the blankets brought from home and their smell of Teresa. I pulled them off our bed last trip back while she was still in the bed and sound asleep, unable to catch me and scold, "Oh, no you don't!" Teresa will sleep through anything; perhaps that is why she is so beautiful; she gets her rest no matter what. I was no longer in a cheap motel for fifty bucks a night; instead, I had found an inexpensive room in a house and rented it outright for six months. The only problem was that the lady who owned the house was crazy and stuck her nose in my room every day. She smelled horribly, too, the absolute worst body odor ever. And yet, after I take a crap in the shitter and return to my room, she runs over and starts spraying the hallway with Lysol, and with my head on the pillow, I can see the top of the can as she bends down and points it underneath the door, releasing into my tiny space a huge plume of perfumed aerosol. "Mary! What the fuck are you doing? I can't breathe with that shit in here." She scurries back down the hall with her finger hard on the nozzle. Once, when Teresa spent the night, she wanted to charge me double. And it was only one time, because my wife couldn't stand the smell of the old lady either, or tolerate her condescending attitude towards our "lovemaking in her house," which, she informed us, "there'll be none of." Having the stolen blanket from home with my wife's scent attached was a luxurious comfort.

I love the sound of the foghorn. Its life-affirming resonance reverberates as if originating from a far away and sacred place, perhaps from the deep, unplumbed waters off Montauk. It gets directly to the core of a man's being, as any Montauk man can imagine being lost at sea. The sound carries me off the beach and over waters in search of lost ships; I drift farther and farther away before the loud smack of a wave brings me back to the beach to get lost once again, this time on land and within the confines of a four-sided panel. The French easel takes four to five minutes to set up, and with all three legs unlatched and firmly planted in rocks and sand, and with the paint box set parallel to the beach, I am ready to begin. I zero-in on tiny, dark-shelled snails, hundreds of thousands of them, millions, crawling over the large rocks and boulders hunkered below the high-water mark. They are, of course, too small to paint. But the majestic boulders, millions of years old, are not. Nor the crashing waves. And so, I begin to paint them.

Who's Here

(handwritten notes) HEY BABY — MISS YOU! Lili, bought one of my drawings THATS ME

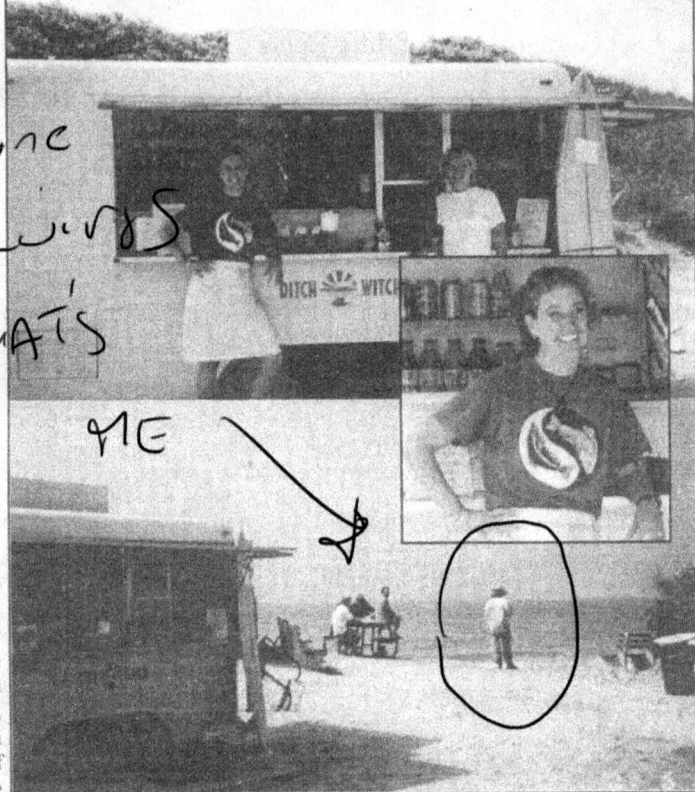

photo by Jesse Moses

LILI ADAMS
Ditch Witch

The 'Witch' knew the name of almost every person who came up to the stand, what they wanted

By Jesse Scaccia

The last way you'd picture a woman known as the Ditch Witch from here to Costa Rica is as, "A momma to the younger ones and a sister to the older guys," or that, "Everyone truly likes (her)," by the people who know her. No, this witch doesn't scare children or ride a broom. She cooks.

Elizabeth Anne Adams, a.k.a. the Ditch Witch has been a chef in the Montauk area since she left White Plains, New York, right after high school (since, like Glenda, Lili is a good witch, we withhold her age). After stints at Eastern Seafood, Laundry Restaurant, and The Dock, Lili has settled in as the owner and chef of the Ditch Witch (this is the name of the woman and the stand), in Montauk, and as the matriarch of Ditch Plains Beach.

The Ditch Witch, which is "the smallest trailer they make," according to Lili, sits at the foot of Ditch Plains Beach. For seven years, she has been "a great source of comfort and coffee for surfers at Ditch," says local author and surfer Allan Weisbecker. While interviewing her, the 'Witch' knew the name of almost every person who came up to the stand, what they wanted to order, and how they liked it. Gregory de la Haba, a local artist who enjoys Lili's cooking on a twice-daily basis, remembers what happened the first time he visited the Ditch Witch, "I just said home," he said. "It's the best deal in town breakfast and lunch."

Lili co-owns the establishment with her husband, Tom, a surfer. Seven

I really didn't... she says.

The Ditch... Not only is... enough to... customers,... describes he... stingy with... originally d... written abo... say that w... Who's Here... "I just try... a sincerity... you see of... attention to... and Abigail... is in the mi... at Elon Uni... calls home.

"The beach has a ce... asked why people love... Witch. "There's a com... surf beaches, people he... There isn't a lot of a...

"I meet so many neat... new people showing u... like for people to dis...

Most of Montauk h... Ditch Witch, known fo... em... eat... ask... use... "Al... eve... del...

COMPETENCIES AND INTERESTS

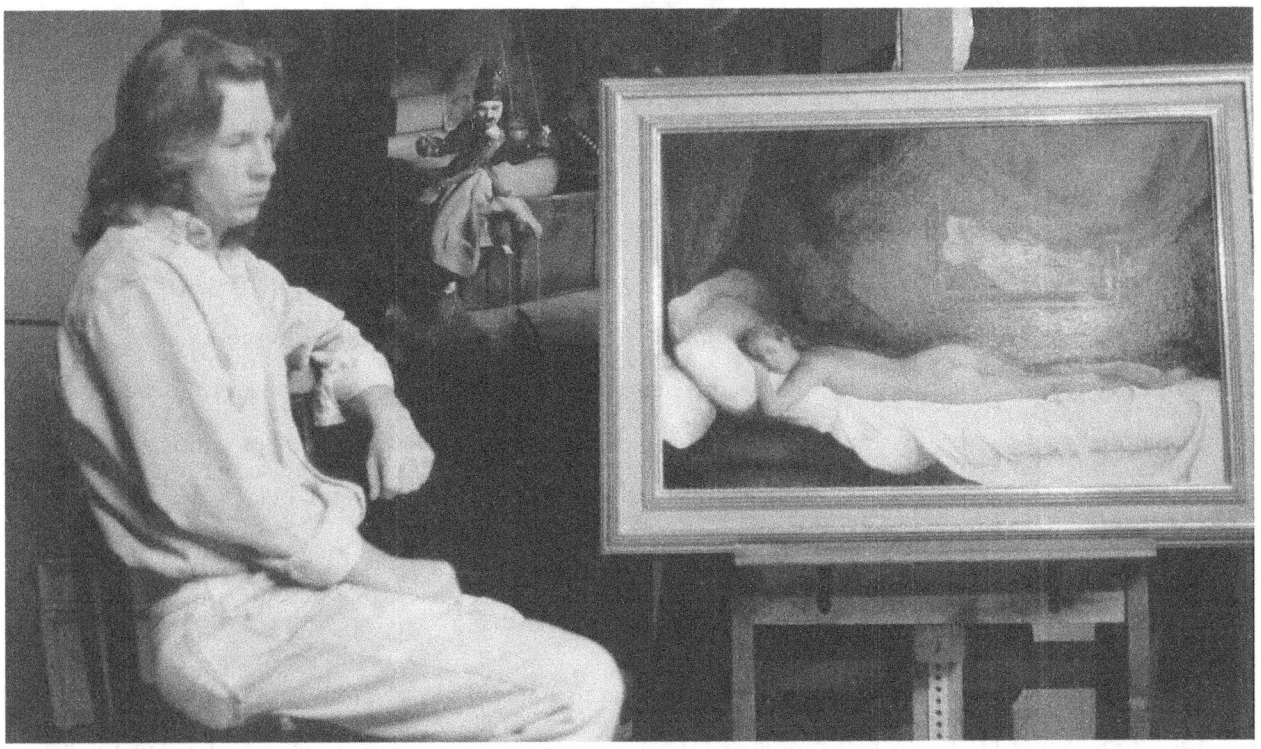

I've never been in search of subject matter or inspiration. Both are all around me and on reserve within. My quest is to do something significant with that subject matter and with that inspiration.
   —November 2, 1994 (Napkin)

Studio, Astoria, Queens, 1996

The blank canvas is primed with lead-white paint and traditional rabbit skin glue sizing underneath that, so that the oil in the paints won't, over time, rot the linen that made its way into the studio all the way from Belgium. The linen is pulled taught over wooden stretcher bars much the same way hides from animals are stretched over bongos and, like the bongo, when the bar is tapped gently at the center, a lovely, perfectly pitched sound emanates. Like the proverbial white elephant in the room, the canvas waits to be acknowledged, paid attention to, heeded, or butchered, even. At times, the blank canvas can be like the forebodingly immense wall in an army's training course, the climbing and conquering of which requires focus and discipline at the get go. Indeed, the canvas can be just as challenging and daunting, especially to a young artist on a budget.

Artist's materials cost a small fortune, and when coupled with self-doubt or fear of failure, the thought of "ruining" expensive supplies—of wasting paints and canvases on poorly executed work—weighs heavy. Managing this challenge means keeping an eye open for paintable surfaces: old wooden doors and plywood, either shoved into trash bins or pushed aside at construction sites. I once salvaged a bunch of six-foot-round table tops outside The Cooper Union, where the kids who pay no tuition throw out tons of valuable art supplies at the end of each school year, when they're required to clean out their cluttered, rent-free studios. Barely used canvases that can easily be painted over and heavy-duty stretcher bars piled high and up for grabs. May is dumpster diving month for smart artists in New York. Painting is hard enough, and any financial advantage that frees up the mind must be gained. This way, a failed work can easily be tossed back into the trash heap, with no reprimand from the conscience.

Some days, however, the blank canvas gets the better of me on a purely psychological front. Like, today: after Heidi, my new model, left, I was wondering why I didn't make a move. Any move. I just stood there for three hours, like an idiot, in front of the blank canvas, hiding behind it, in fact, sapped of the bravado I'd displayed in front of it when she first walked into the studio. The only action was that which took place in my pants as she disrobed. That was the only movement, the only proof that an artist's model was in the studio. Her nudity was all mine, and I did absolutely nothing to keep it, to hold it, to claim it. I bungled the situation for sure. After three hours, not a single mark. And how rare to have one posing exactly how she was told, on the floor with pillows propped beneath; her back to me (thank God!) exposing her soft curves, because she was not so thin that hip bones and shoulder blades are made angular and edgy. Her dark brunette hair was turned up into a bundle. Most of all, best of all, was the round curvatures of her half moons, folding into that dark crevice of glorious womanhood, exposed each time she leaned forward, adjusted, or stood, and her modeling and moving about the studio so easily, gracefully, and without shame. She was here for me entirely and entirely for the taking.

Heidi was captivated and obedient, devoted to being there; she didn't even ask why the

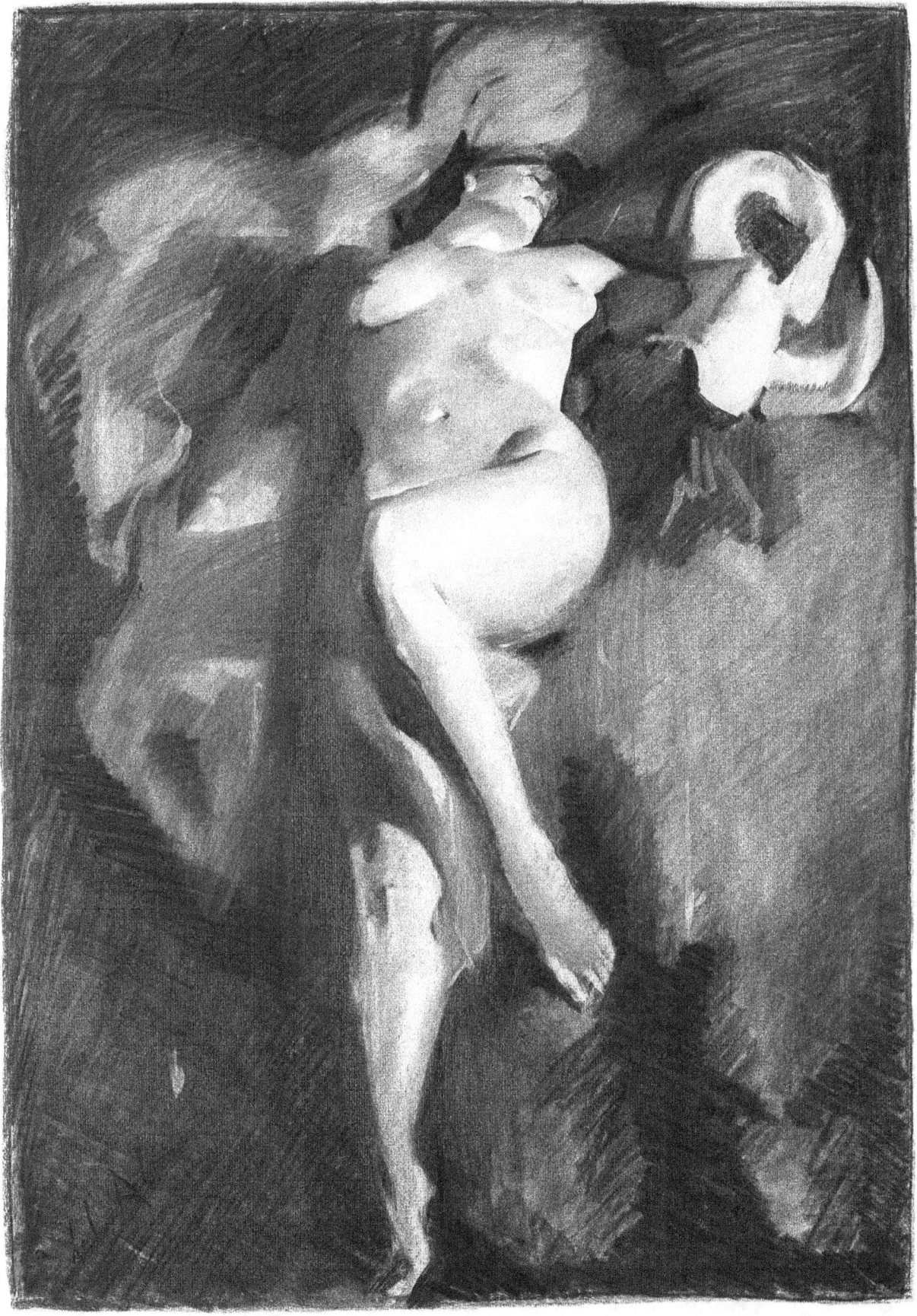

painting was not started after the first hour, nor did she remind me to begin after the second hour. She just laid herself out like the odalisque she was, the one I wished for and was going after. Time was not present, no stop-clock to remind us to break from being still and alone together in a room. Little was spoken, except "turn your body to the right" or "look to the left." How I wanted to instruct, "Look at me." But that would have been selfish and for reasons not to do with painting. And had she done just that and looked at me at my command all she would have seen was a frustrated artist with no paint on his brush and a confused look on his pathetic face.

Some way into the session, she cleared her throat and asked, "And how do I look, Gregory?"

I replied, "You look so fucking good."

She tilted her head back at me. Did I really just say that? I thought for a second how silly writer's block is. Writers don't have gorgeous stark-naked things spread out before them when they're trying to type, do they? No, they have pictures of Shakespeare and Joyce tacked on walls next to bookshelves stacked with first editions and signed copies, interspersed by photographs of loved ones—to remind them of something other than getting laid. What prevents words from making it onto paper or computer screen? Not ripe beauty within arm's length. All I could do was stare. Gaze. She was that much, that beautiful. And when she finally stood for break, she smiled. Her eyes smiled and her body smiled, and I had to sit down because my entire body was begging to smile back. I did smile, too, just a little. It would've been unkind and rude to do otherwise. She didn't even clutch her breasts this time as she walked around, naked, examining my other work. Completed work. Done long before she ever got there. Created back in the days when the models smelled of anarchist's stink, Patchouli oil, when their fifteen-dollars-an-hour cash fee was more important to them than the modeling. And now here she is, nude, when most anyone else would be covered in a robe intended for such intermissions. It made matters worse. These are the moments Teresa is always worrying about. Because she, too, once stood here. And whether it's clothed or nude, the modeling session itself creates that beautifully rare and vulnerable intimacy between two beings, lays bare identity and intention.

After three hours, I have nothing to show for the intensity of our time together. There will be no proof that I went to work. Instead of a Friday paycheck or finished piece to sell, all I have is a disappointed cock. At that, the fun is gone.

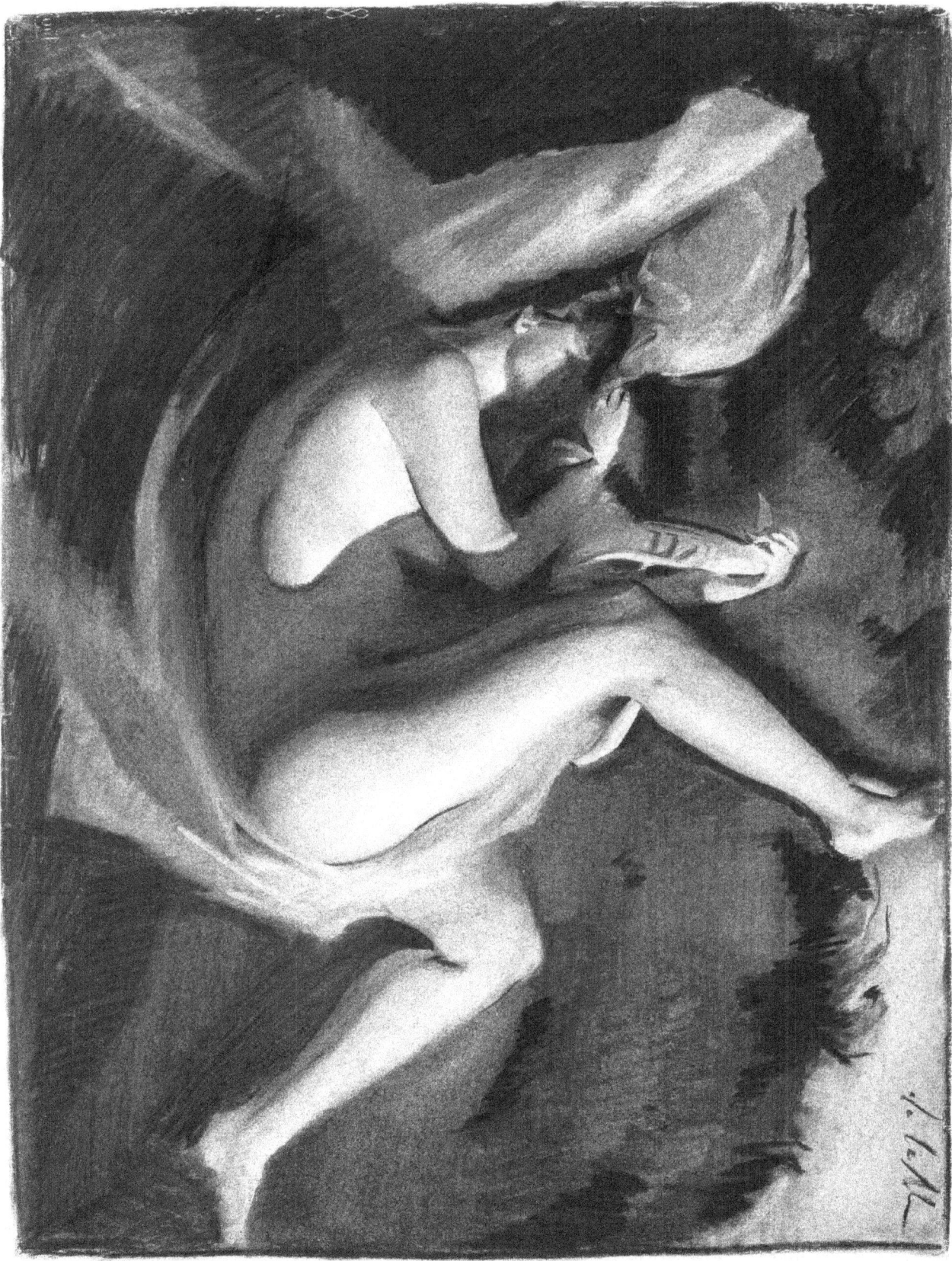

I say goodbye to her and job well done and watch as she walks out. Before stepping on the elevator, she turns "I really enjoyed posing for you today, Gregory." I watched the elevator door close in front of her and imagined the steel box slowly lowering her to the ground, innocence and sincerity descending, and I wondered what other circumstances might happen to her during the remainder of the day. I sank into my favorite chair, feeling like a court jester who's exhausted his supply of jokes. In place of the earlier smile, a flaccid smirk. On the canvas, not even a charcoal outline. In the studio, only her lingering scent, taunting me for not having made a move. I want to run the fuck out of there, leave immediately, go after and follow her, down the elevator and out the building's front door, catch her on the street as she turns the corner. But I don't. I glance over to my palette, cry at the globs of fresh paint squeezed out in preparation for her arrival, untouched and put to no good. Waiting in vain, much like the model was, I am sure of it. By Monday, when she returns—if she does—they'll be dried out. Useless.

Teresa: "I don't like this part, Gregory!"

"I didn't think you would."

"It bothers me."

"But, Teresa, the girl I'm writing about is you."

"Bullshit!"

"Baby, it's true."

"I never posed nude for you."

"Yes, you did. The painting is unfinished, upstairs in the closet."

"But that was after I married you."

"I know, but it's my curriculum vitae, and each time you visited I wanted you like no other and you always looked at me with such a tender, inviting smile, that it stopped me in my tracks each and every time you visited. I so wanted to go up to you each day as you posed…"

"With my clothes on!"

"Yes, with your clothes on, and grab you in my arms and claim you as mine, hold you tight because you were the best model to ever walk into my studio and the most beautiful model I ever had, and you drove me crazy. And I did run after you each time you left my studio, wanting always to get one more look at you as you drove off, to have one more coffee or ice cream with you. I hated waiting till Mondays or whatever day you came to the studio next. You know this is true, yes?"

"Yes, I do. It just makes me nervous you'll find someone else to love. Why did you call her Heidi?"

"Because Hansel didn't give me permission to use Gretel. I don't know...what difference does it make?"

"Well, let's leave Heidi out of it and change the name to Mary, it will be our secret—you using my middle name as me—and then maybe I'll like it."

"OK, Mary, mother of God."

"Be nice! You're so bold! It makes me nervous."

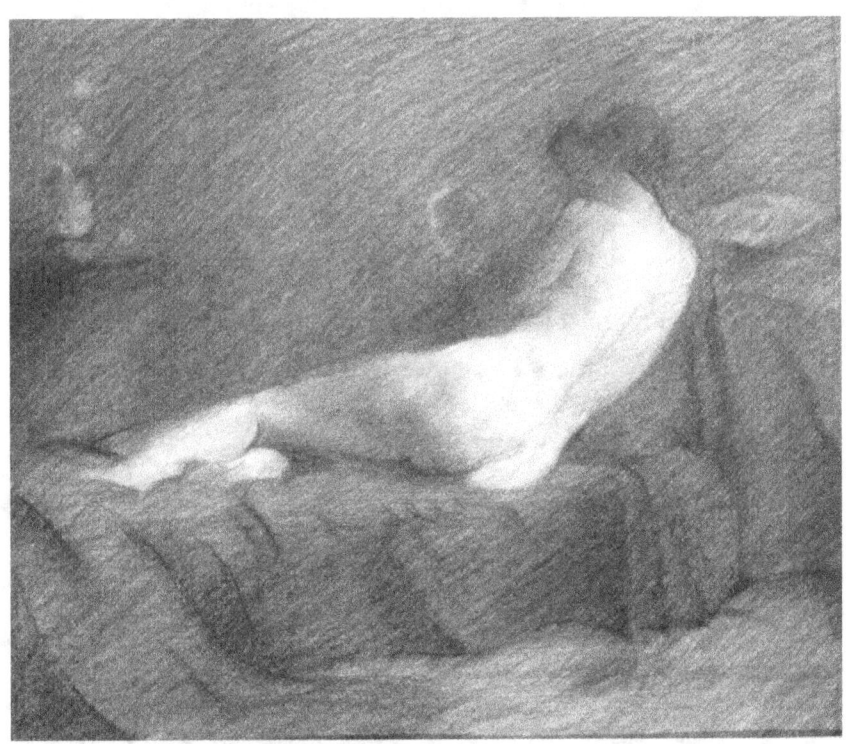

EDUCATION (CONTINUES)

Back during student days, I'd place the palette with its still-good globs of paint into a freezer. But there is no freezer here. No way to store the unused paint for safekeeping. I am slumped in a favorite chair, a nineteenth-century treasure found in the trash, with talons grasping a ball at the bottom of each leg. I reupholstered it myself with a fancy fabric purchased on the Lower East Side. Gold threads weave a fleur-de-lis pattern into the fabric's dark, warm olive green. My hands rest on cherry wood arms, oiled and smoothed by sweating palms. The chair echoes a time when men and chivalry were one, when artists were part of a King's court and when jousting got the girl and jesters had funny tales to tell or died. This chair has traveled with me for the last 20 years, and many a nude model has reclined or curled up in its comfortable embrace while on break. Some even posed in it, dangling a fine, muscular leg or two over the well-worn arms.

While waiting for 'Mary' to open the studio door, I turn my head and put my nose into the back of the chair, longing for her return. Her long, black hair's been pressed against the high back each day as she's sat patiently, waiting for me to announce that I was ready. On this day, I was ready, just not ready to paint. I was ready for her. She returned, as she'd promised, and looked excited as ever to be back. I grabbed her in my arms and have yet to let go.

Teresa: "That's better, baby."

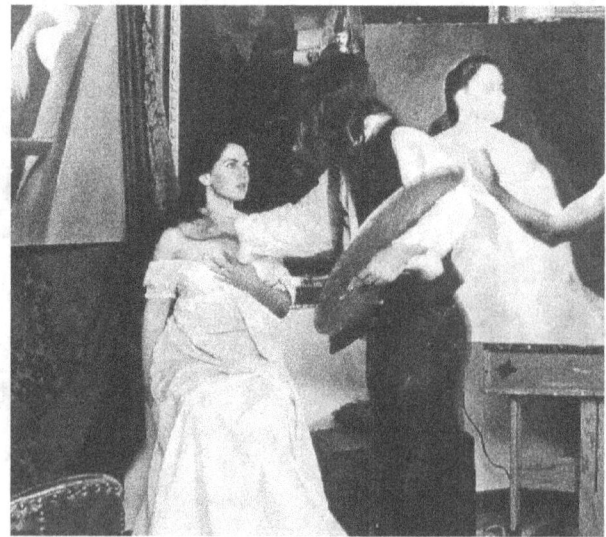

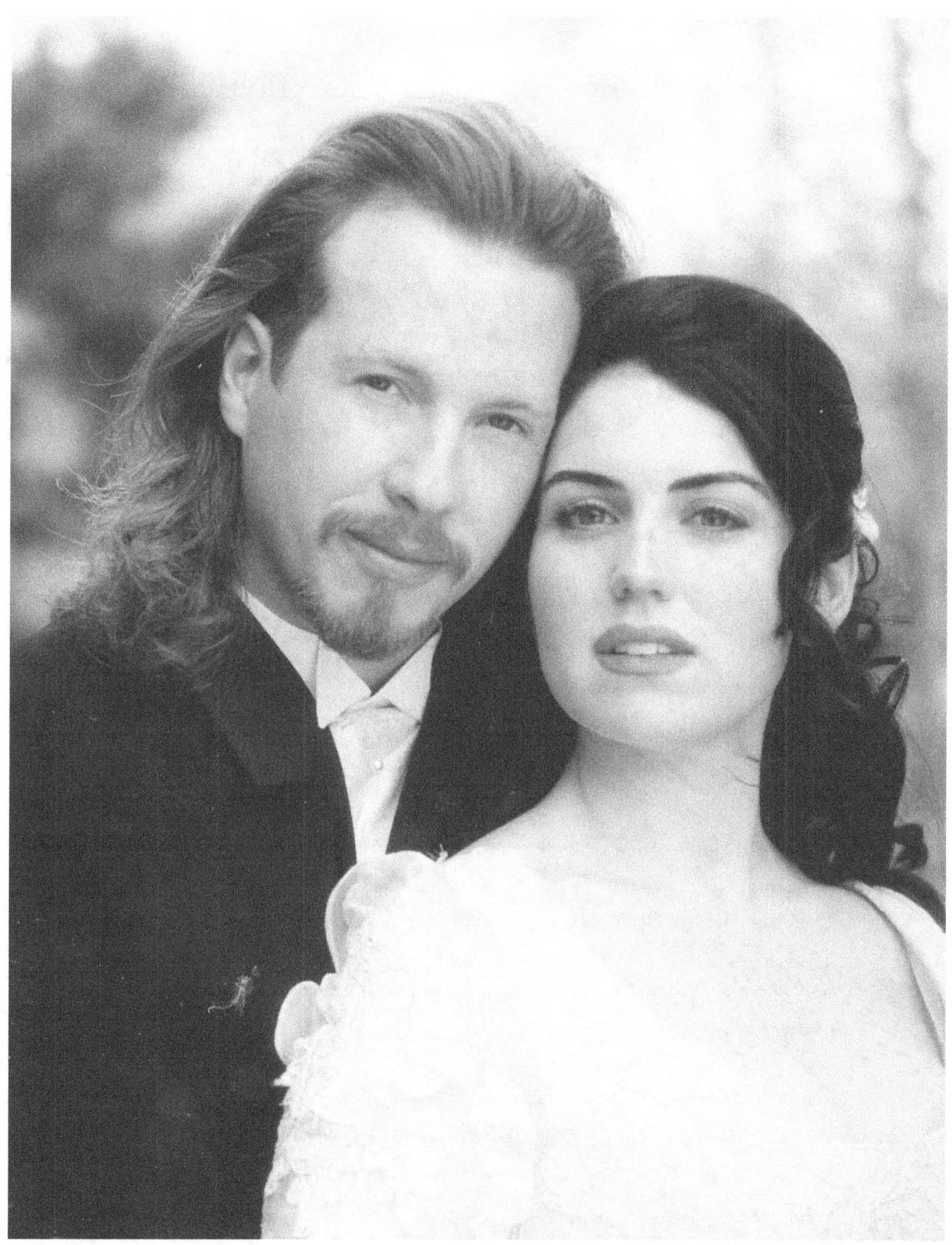

EXTRACURRICULAR ACTIVITIES (CONTINUES)

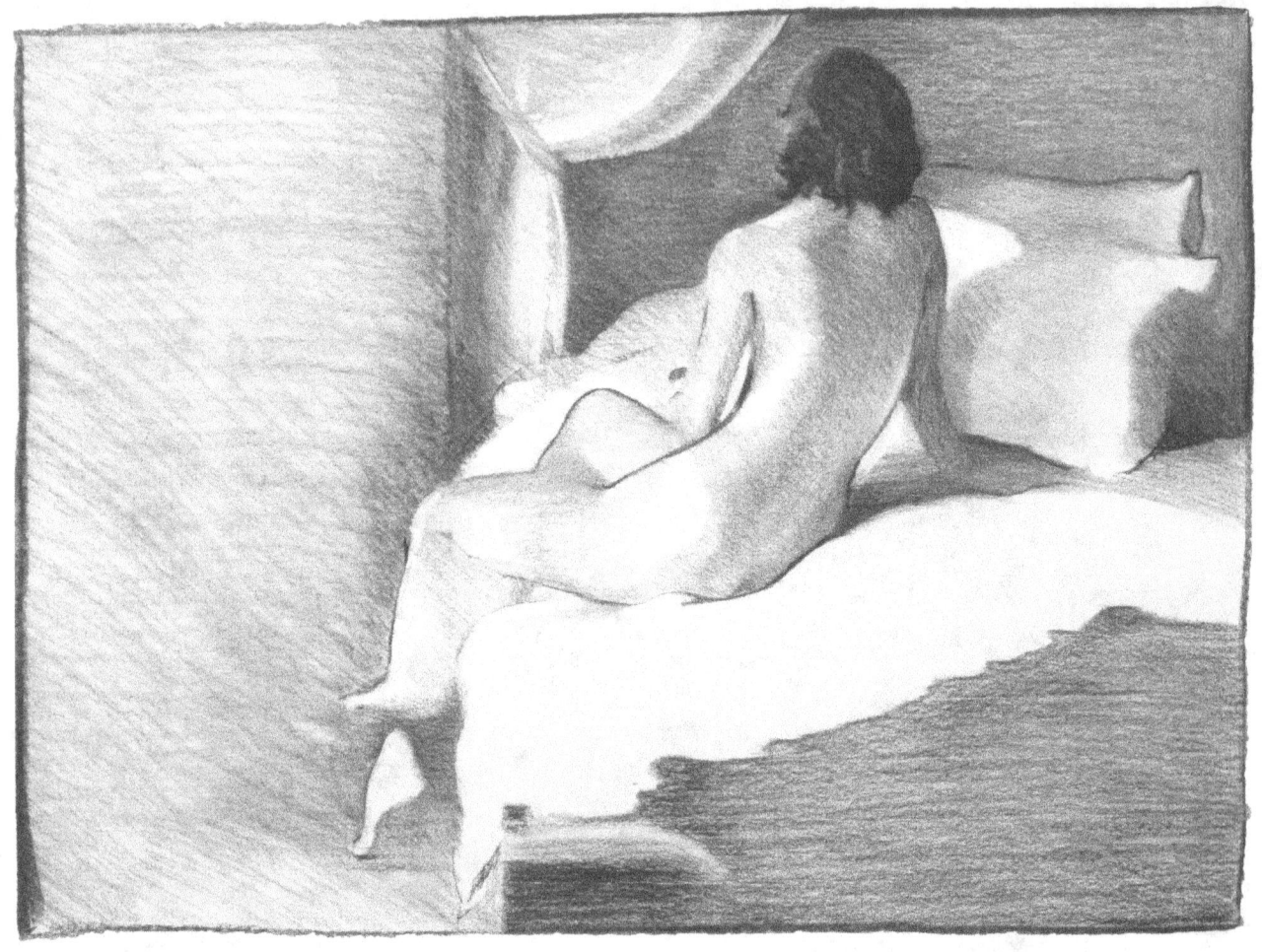

There are patterns. Cycles. Repetitions. Always.

"There is always some madness in love. But there is always some reason in madness."
—Friedrich Nietzsche

It is vital to stay focused. You must! Because you're already out a couple hundred bucks in supplies and materials, model fees for the afternoon or week, plus $50 a day, you've figured, for studio rental, and you know that if you end-up empty handed (without a painting or drawing), your wife will grow suspicious. She wonders—already weeks of wondering—how a man, any man, can stand in front of a beautiful, naked woman, alone, in his separate artist's studio, and "just paint" her. But you try explaining that it's not like that, that your dreams and goals of immortality via picture-making are bigger than that, that it takes so much hard work to achieve, to even approach success. And now you're off again, telling her about the models, the ones you find in your two favorite nightspots, the first on Lafayette Street and the other tucked away on Little West 12th—that's where you first noticed "that look" of this particular model and where she first noticed you—telling your wife through detailed explanation, reassurance, defensive tone, telling her something, but you soon lose grasp of what that something is because it's all running tangential to your recollected fantasies.

And like that, my mind is back at Pravda on Lafayette. I turned a blank sheet of paper into a magnificent rendering of the place in a matter of minutes! And best of all—in terms of your chances of getting her to pose, that is—she loves that you featured her. Poised at the hostess stand, demure smile and distant gaze; black leather boots up to the knees, tight dress; long arms, one hand brushing the hip bone, the other holding drink menus, both drawing attention to her

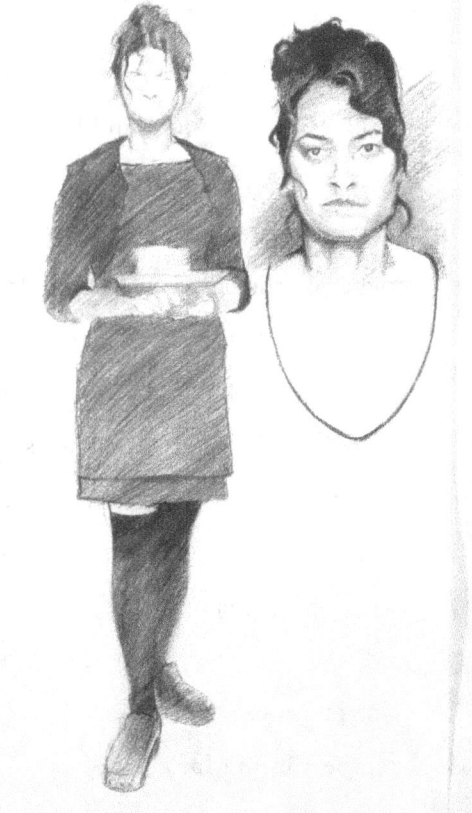

ass, which everyone in the place notices, and you, of these others, imagine how it would look painted. Or drawn. A simple drawing. To admire. And admire she does. Each night, between the seating of customers, she passes your table to glance, or to stay and watch and observe the progress of another night. Soon, there is another drawing of her, and she stays longer than before and the two of you talk.

Though she has never done so before, she agrees to pose nude. It is a wonderful idea, to exchange this act for one of your drawings. Of these models, of this one, you assert to your wife, "They have self-respect." "Integrity," you add, anxiously. "It is needless to worry."

You repeat the last phrase the first time she undresses, but the scene is exactly how you wished it from the first moment you saw her in the bar. At the time, you were making up your mind: professional models won't do. The ones who pose for dozens of easels a day, collecting $15 an hour and demanding 10-minute breaks after each 20-minute sitting. They leave behind the cheap smell of their bodies, the smell of oils purchased with crumpled bills on St. Marks. They use the restroom to undress, or bend and unbutton behind a screen, and disrobe only once on the model's stand. You laugh because you no longer have a screen. You do not share this information with your wife, nor with the hostess, the hostess who is now undressing in plain sight, casting shadows across the leopard print of the chaise love seat. She kicks a red lace thong up onto your easel. She never did this before? You smirk, and try not to get an erection.

But it's too late: you have one, and she's taken a pose that excites you further. Her movement alone is seductive. Without direction from you, she is confidently lying down on her belly, allowing one leg to slip languorously to the floor, the other to point upwards, exposing the shape of her calf, ankle, instep. She lifts her eyes, asking, Who are you? Painter? Viewer? Voyeur?

The tableau is that of an Old Master painting that you know but cannot recall for lack of blood to the brain, and because of this same vascular snafu, you suppose, you stupidly tell her that she looks beautiful, knowing full well that you have just crossed the line. She tilts her head and smiles with a single raised brow. At that moment, you think of your wife and try to forget your fantasies, the ones you've shared with her and which she reminds you of, on occasion, when you're on the way to the studio. What your wife offers is advice, stern but understanding instruction: "Just paint them. Don't have coffee with them, don't take them for lunch, and don't go have a drink afterwards." Because she knows. And maybe she's right, so you say not another word for now; you forget your fantasies and try to stay focused on drawing, but then you notice the black soles of her feet. Charcoal dust blankets this side of the studio floor and you remember how, long ago, you used to clean the feet of your model in Boston. She loved it, and brought you brownies in return. Today, here in New York, it does not matter one iota if her feet are dirty; it is a simple charcoal drawing. So you proceed in the presence of a final thought: Caravaggio did catch hell for painting dirty feet on the Virgin Mary.

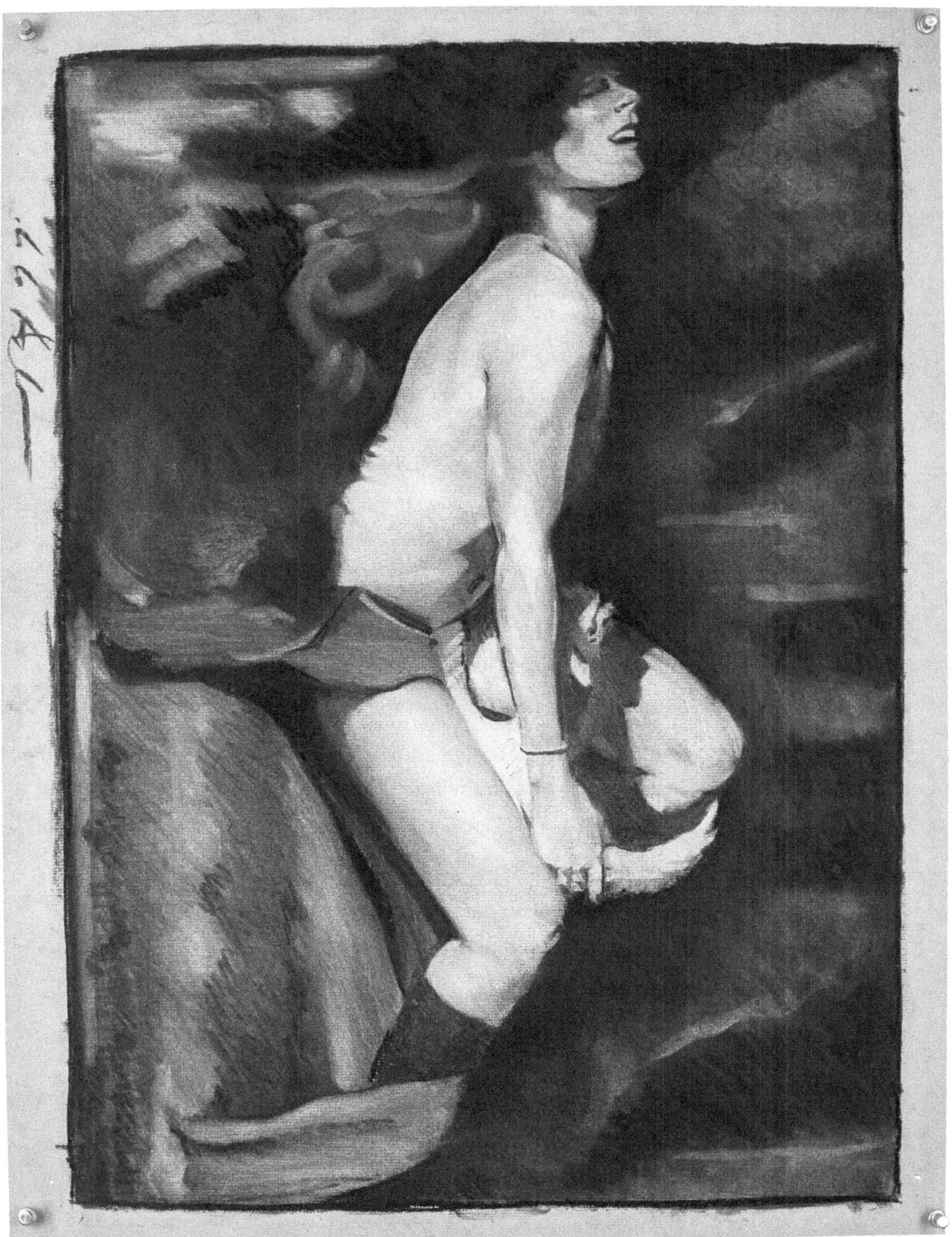

You stay focused: Does the drawing need more sharp lines? How's the composition? Should I smooth out this edge, blend it into the background? What about the pucker in those lips? Get off the lips! The subtlety of form around her small breast? There's that look again that she first proffered you at the bar—look straight ahead, please—(but you say nothing), only now she's missing the black boots and black dress cut above the knees, and you recognize for the first time how beautiful her knees are. She raises herself from the loveseat for her 10-minute break, which you don't mind that she takes because she has no robe and only clutches her small breasts with her wrists as she walks around the studio to examine more of your work. And as she walks, you notice those two small indentations on her lower back at the base of the spine.

She stops at the picture she "loves the most," that of your wife, a pastel. "She's beautiful," she tells you, and you feel pressured, forced to look away from the model's lower back to the picture on the wall that best captures not only your wife but also your ability at rendering from life, beauty. You reply, "Yes, she is," and think of her and why she married you in the first place. "Because you have the most potential," she had explained, and you are saddened at that thought because you still have a long way to go in this business; in fact, at 30 years of age, nobody even knows who you are. You question, momentarily, why you even bothered to become a painter until the model finally makes it over to your drawing and tells you, "It's wonderful, de la Haba." For another brief moment, you forget that she's nude and see instead the lovely girl that she is, and you are thankful that she's here, helping you, allowing you the use of her body. So you go over and over in your head the "rules of engagement" in regards to "painting from life" that you learned as a student so many years ago. After all, this is what excites you the most, this is what you do, this is who you really are, and you forget about your fucking fantasies until later, until after the work is done and her clothes are back on and she is out of your studio and like a good little boy promised dessert if he eats all his "din-din," your erection returns, eagerly awaiting compensation for good behavior.

But all you have is linseed oil because what heterosexual male artist keeps hand cream in his studio? You make a go of it, but the linseed is thick, sun-thickened in fact, and globs form between your fingers and stiffen your stroke. You look immediately to the Turpenoid, instinctively avoiding the strong odor of the regular stuff. You start to wonder, though, what exactly is in Tur-

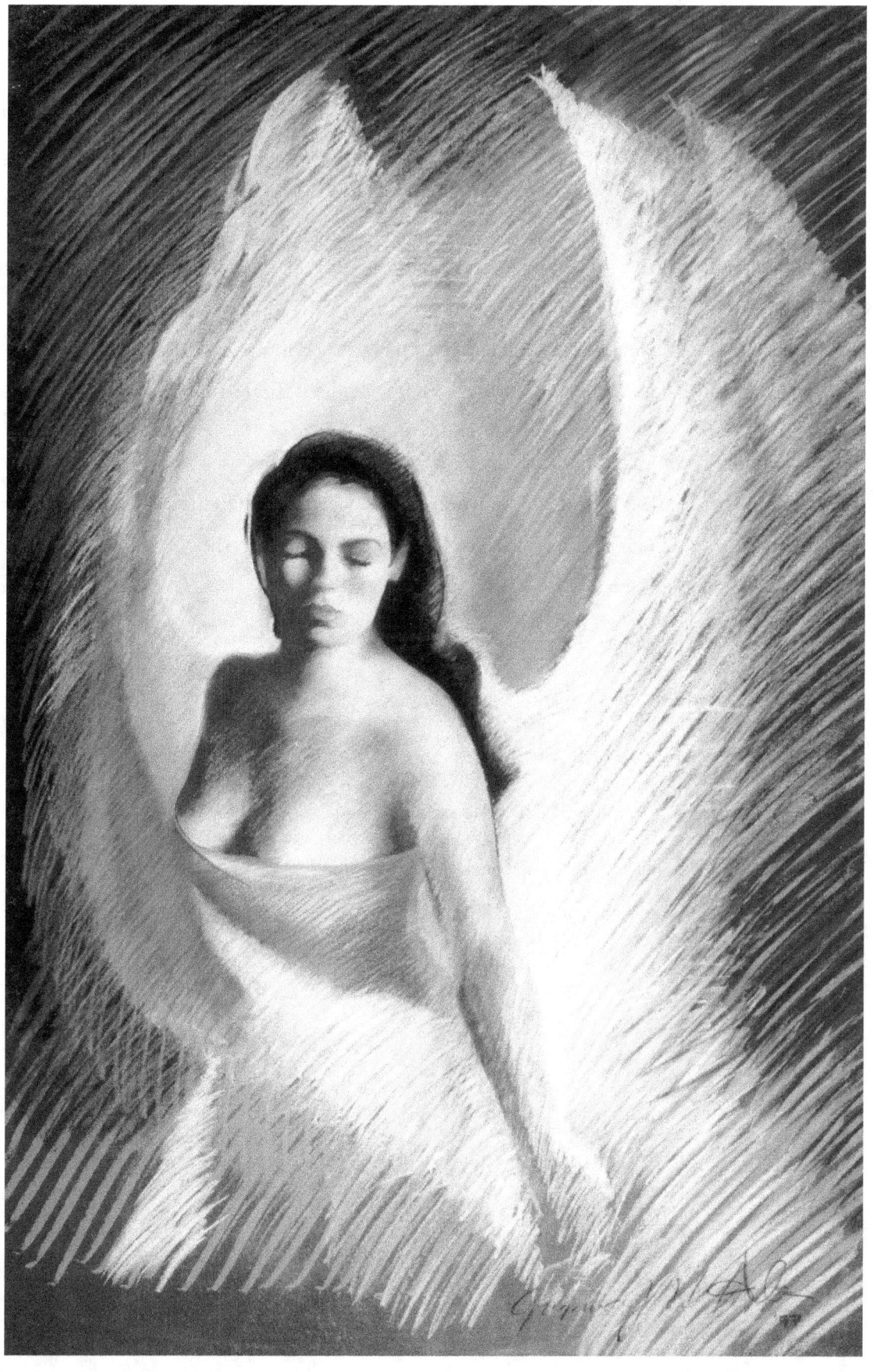

penoid and whether it's particularly hostile to a guy's prick. It's possible because you begin to tingle, and then worry, and worrying isn't good for masturbation either, so you stroke harder and faster just to get the job over and done with.

When you are done, you critique the work of the day, and you are humbled because you see where (and remember when) you went wrong with the drawing, how the tilt of her head is not quite right and how the form in her shoulder needs to be turned more inwards (or outwards?), and you remind yourself that a man feels most like a man when he is successful in his work.

You find a cloth and wipe yourself clean. You place a call to your wife. You say that you love her. You let her know that you will be working late. When nightfall arrives, you tell yourself that it is OK to go to the bar and see the model. You want to confirm the next session. You want to tell her what a great job she did.

Teresa: "Really? You're not putting this on your CV, are you?"

"What? He wants an interesting art life; I'm gonna give him one."

"How is this going to help you? I think it makes you look like a sick creep."

"It makes me a human with flaws and cracks."

"I don't think you're taking it seriously, Gregory."

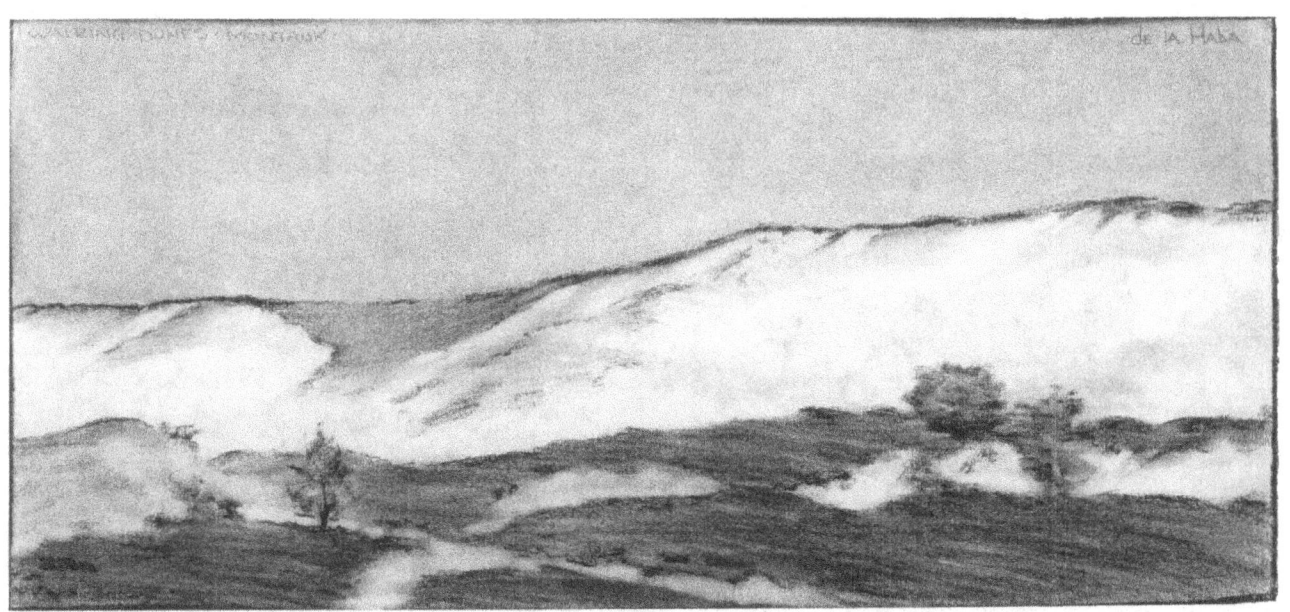

HONORS (AND REWARDS)

"I like things that don't look like you're in control. It's like life itself. You just learn how to benefit from accidents and chances that you take."
—Peter Beard

Montauk, late Summer, 2001

I'd see Peter Beard around town every now and again, in the Shagwong late at night or the Italian restaurant in East Hampton. In the city, I'd see him working his large-scale collages at The Time Is Always Now gallery, usually surrounded by gorgeous models, half clothed, if clothed at all.

The proprietor of the gallery, Peter Tunney, younger brother to John Tunney, my Atlantic City patron and partner at the time in a race horse called Imagineer, was as much a part of the show at the gallery as the work on display inside it. He was always cordial on the many occasions I visited to gawk at the Peter Beard show Carnets Africains: A Retrospective, which remained up years past its original closing. It featured a lifetime of Beard's work: Africa: elephants and giraffes being fed by six-foot-tall nude models. Portraits of friends and colleagues: Jacqueline Onassis, smiling, arms around her fatherless children. Karen Blixen: her majestic profile recalling that of the great Egyptian queen Nefertiti. Francis Bacon (who painted Beard's portrait 26 times). Andy Warhol: at

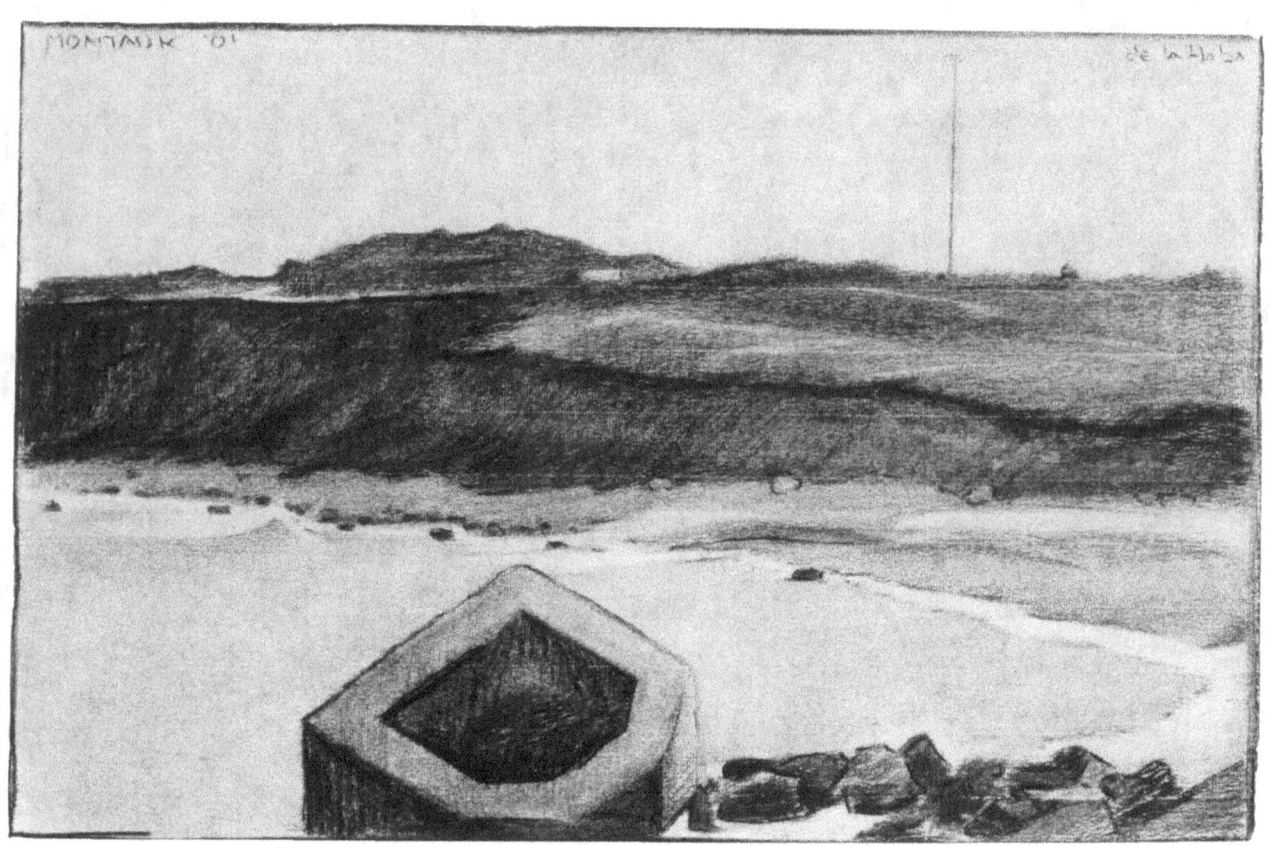

his 'first light' estate Eothen in Montauk. Mick Jagger: licking a giant lollipop after water skiing on Lake Montauk. Photos of them arranged and mixed and glued with feathers and skulls, crumpled Marlboro cigarette packages, and other accoutrements found in the gutter, on the beach, or dug up on one of his properties after he buried it the previous year. Too, there was zebra blood, large bugs, million-year-old rocks, matchbooks, and tattered and torn ephemera collected over the years during his travels: years that criss-crossed his ranch in Kenya, his Montauk home, and the route from Cipriani's on West Broadway to the gallery around the block on Broome Street. Never, for him, was there a moment, locale, or object too precious or too broken to become a fragment in one of his colossal collages. His work was his self-portrait—of a man who did what he wanted, did what he pleased, and did so, judging by the gestures, looks, and sheer number of nude models, with unbounded enthusiasm. His work exemplified that when honest and simple are done right, breathtakingly grandiose becomes par. To see Peter Beard and witness his work first-hand ignited a fire in me.

It was an honor when I finally met him, end of summer 2001. We were enjoying an epic spliff and cocktails of Kettle One and Clamato, sitting on the edge of a 100 foot bluff on a huge log of drift wood, at the end of a sprawling lot that kept his house, the last one in Montauk (or the first one if starting out from the Lighthouse) isolated and in place. I met him through Noel Arikian, who had landed in Montauk years before and had come for the surfing and not the fishing. Noel lives to surf and to enjoy life and, like most surfers, does whatever he must to make that happen. During the cold months, he travels to warmer climates to surf some more, but while still here, he works with his hands, making furniture or, in my case, frames for art—custom frames hewn from old barn wood, driftwood, sun-dried and weathered fence slats; frames that are aged and have character and are made for art where mistakes are embraced and not worked over. My charcoal drawings of Montauk looked a million times better in Noel Arikian's frames than they did in the store-bought rectangles I had ordered earlier in the summer, when I had sucker written all over my face and cared more about having a show than how the work looked.

Noel and I were out drinking at the Shagwong to the wee hours of the morning; that was when the party was about to migrate to Peter's. Everyone was going, but I couldn't even stand. I said goodbye to Peter, Nejma, his wife, Noel and a few others; I said I'd love to stop by another time, and Peter replied, kiddingly, I thought, "Come by tomorrow afternoon." I thanked him and stumbled home, my body used to getting up at 5AM, not going to bed at that time. I woke with a massive pounding in my skull. The remedy simple: jump straight into the cold Atlantic Ocean. It always works. It reboots the body and the electrodes of the brain. Then coffee at Lily's before drawing along some stretch of beach, and finally, by noon, a stop-off back at the Ditch Witch for lunch. I spotted Noel on the beach, in front of the low dune, eyes fastened on the water. When he felt me approach, he smiled and offered, "Peter would love to see you later." I felt honored that he'd even remembered, let alone had Noel request me.

By four that afternoon, I was cleaned up and in the liquor store picking up a bottle of Kettle One—"Peter's favorite" according to the man behind the counter at White's. I followed Noel's car, and we headed to that last house in Montauk at the end of the dirt road off Deep Hallow Ranch. A bunch of people were about. Peter was dashing between cottages. But within five minutes of meeting him again, there at his home, I felt like a total fucking idiot. The first thing I said was that I knew Peter Tunney. Nejma turned and looked as if I had just dragged a dead rat into her home, perhaps one that Peter would've used for his work but one, also, that she didn't want near her.

"Tunney and I are no longer on speaking terms," Peter said baldly, without looking at me, while heading into the kitchen to mix drinks.

Being in my own world since May, without much use for Page Six, I hadn't heard that they'd parted ways. There I was, thinking I'm cool, one of the guys and hanging in the right circle, finally, and as soon as I got in, I blabbed, "I know Peter Tunney; his brother John commissioned me to paint this big project down in Atlantic City." I felt like a heel, a fool, a jackass bragging to make himself feel important.

A braggart's poetic justice was in order, I suppose. But Noel was already stoned, and my adolescent display didn't seem to faze him, and Peter Beard carried on as though nothing uncouth had been uttered. Nejma, meanwhile, just walked away and disappeared, and Mr. Beard remained nothing short of a gracious host.

"Do you like Clamato Juice, Gregory?"

Of course I said yes. It was true, too, I did like Clamato Juice, loved clams, but agreeing felt like I was only trying to make up for having put my foot in my mouth earlier. The three of us proceeded to go outside where Peter was working on a large collage and unburying some things he had "planted" in the soil last year. Noel went home after that first drink. Before long, Peter and I had polished off the first bottle of Kettle One—mixing it with tomato and clam juice, flavored with salt and pepper: absolutely delicious. I had brought with me to Peter's house a black portfolio box of drawings. My precious drawings. The ones that pleased my wife. The ones I had by now sold to many a Montauk local. The ones that were giving me great joy in completing each day. Peter Beard asked to see them.

"Let's move to a quieter spot, Gregory."

We soon moved to another location on the property because of an encroaching Ralph Lauren photo shoot, and Peter wanted some peace. Out on the south bluff, he rolled a huge spliff, and we spoke of bullfighting and surfing and how both are great arts that are dependent upon what transpires in tiny, fleeting pockets of time, and I kept my mouth shut and didn't brag about the de

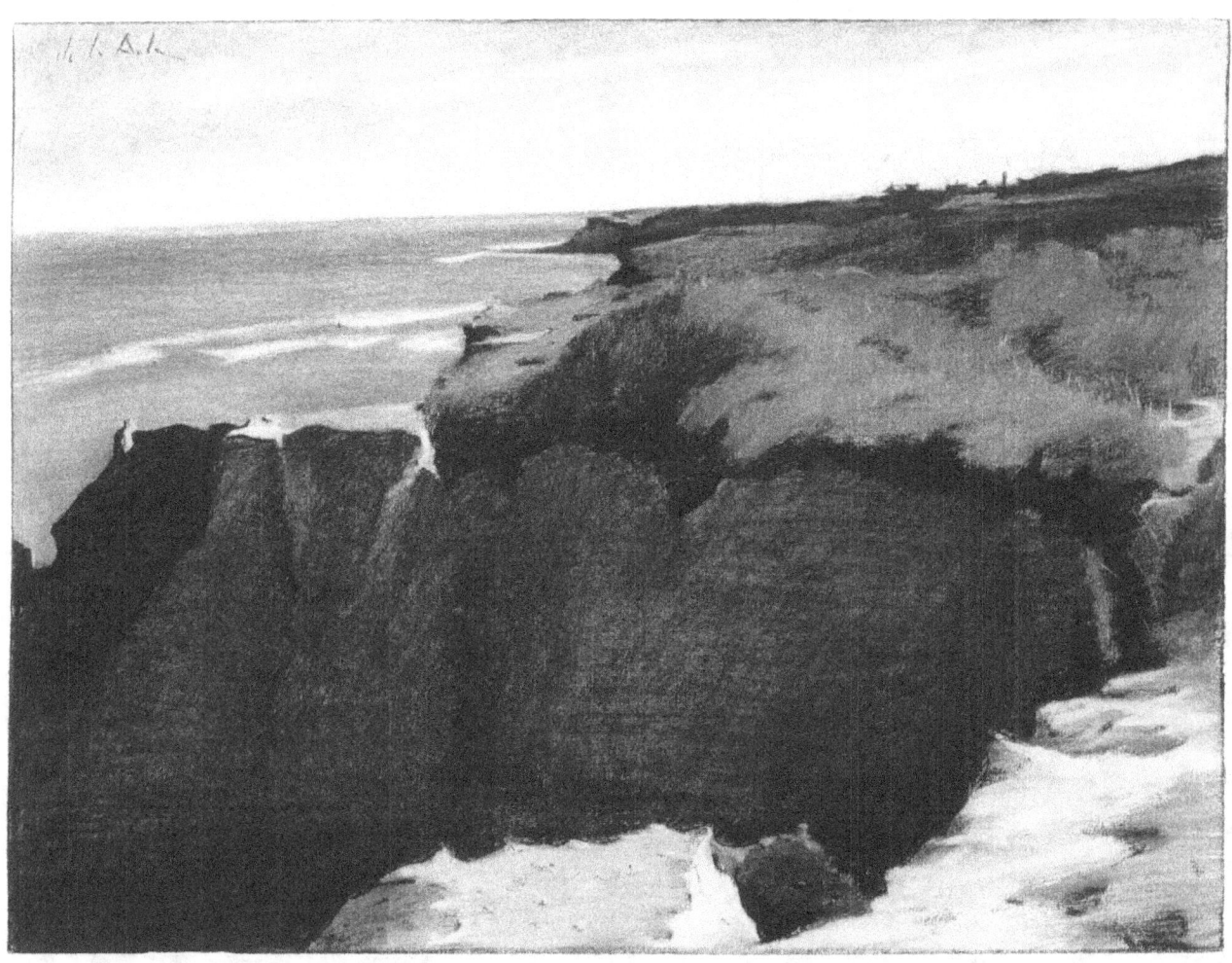

la Haba's of Spain being the bullfighters that Hemingway wrote about in Death In The Afternoon; instead, I stared out to sea and inhaled. I was thankful for the absence of morning dew because as Peter removed the drawings from their protective box, he tossed them on the grass, one next to the other, one atop the other, as if they were washed-up buoys that required only the quickest glance in order to be catalogued. I was too happy to be there and too proud to show him my work to interject "but wait" or "be careful!" Rather, I sat in a drunken stupor and watched as his bare foot came down on one, his uncut, grossly yellow toenails standing out against the charcoal hues.

On another drawing, his fingertips left ink swirls, and dirt from his other hand smudged but more work. He wasn't saying anything, only lighting that monster joint a second, third, and fourth time in between hastily handling yet another one of my delicate drawings. Back and forth it went like this, and after a long while he looked at me and smiled, took another long hit, and without exhaling asked, "Pretty art school stuff, don't ya' think?"

VISUAL ABERRATIONS

I felt like jumping off the cliff. It would've been one of those pathetic attempts at suicide, landing in the brush twenty feet down or on a boulder jutting out from the bluff's face and only

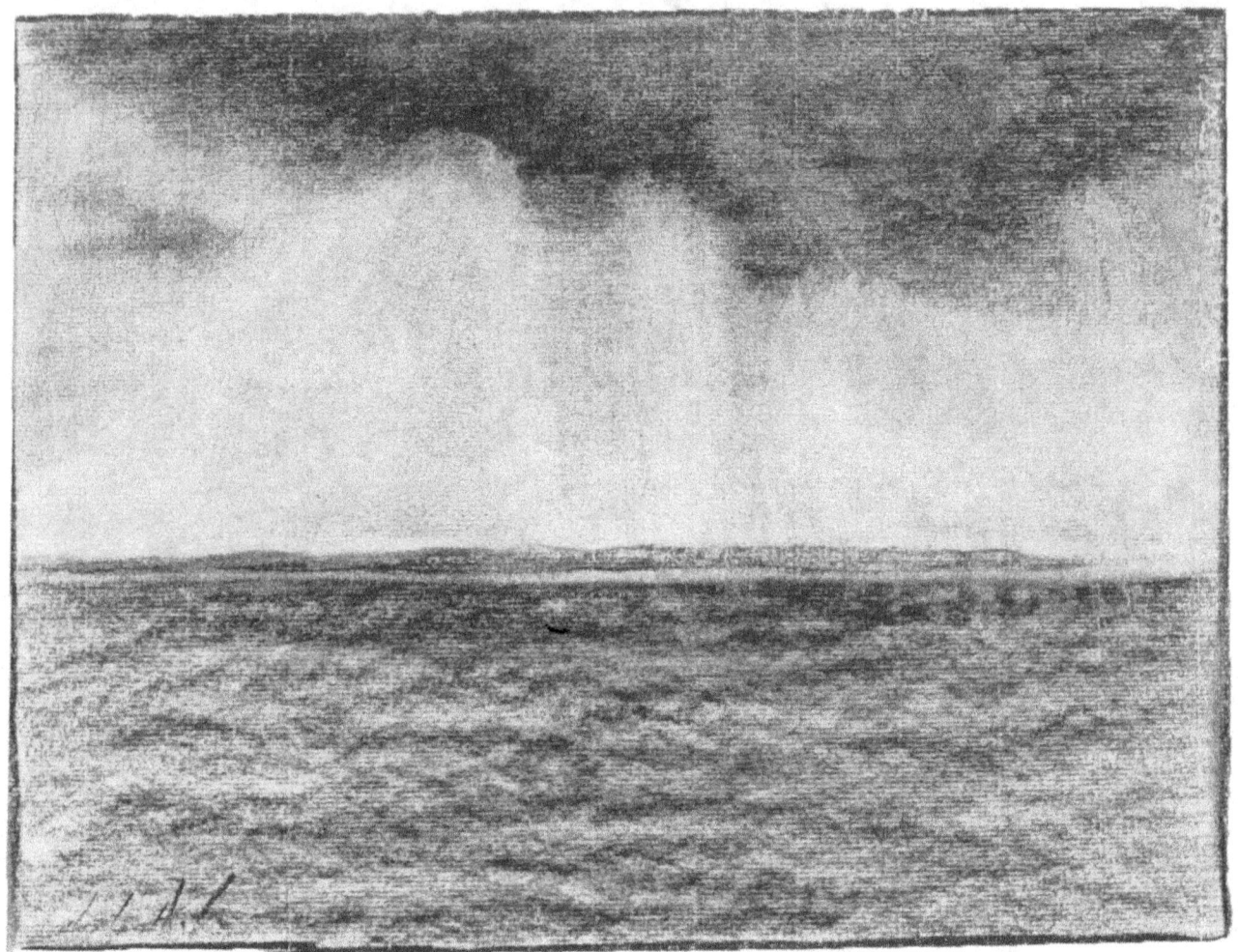

getting hurt really bad. I looked down at the drawings and knew, without having to look down at them, that he was right. Absolutely right. But that was all I had. That was all I had amounted to. A technician who could render form. A master craftsman who could paint from life and here, now, was showcasing pictures and drawings that were entirely devoid of vision. The last hundred years of modern art, the art I avoided, flashed through my head and I realized, and now admitted, how far behind the curve I was operating. Peter spoke the obvious: what I drew in Montauk was nothing different from what those rich fucks painted in watercolor or drew in sketchbooks as they made the grand tours of Europe in the 19th century; what amateur artists with time on their hands could do. These were postcards from Montauk and not high art derived from the depths of someplace important: the place where Basquiat went and the result of which I only mocked because it looked childish. I had failed as an artist and knew it. I was so bent on drawing like one of them (the Old Masters) that I forgot to draw like myself, and worse: I couldn't trust what I did as good enough, ever. And how can anyone say they've succeeded when they can barely make a living?

Here I was with such pride, at 30 years of age, and all I had to show for my artistic legacy was a bunch of charcoal drawings and a few paintings, of cliffs, beaches, lighthouses, dunes—done so in mediums and on surfaces that were insultingly common. I couldn't have become a more traditional artist. I offered nothing new for this gentleman to see, this man who I admired and felt so horribly small next to. I was too stoned to cry. I just sat there looking stupid and feeling numb, staring out to sea and not knowing where I was going next with my art, my life, with this crap that lay idly on the grass. Where's that gust of wind when I need it most to sweep this whole pile of shit from my sight?

The silence lasted an eternity, and Peter refused to exhale from his last hit, as if to punctuate the absurdity of my life up to that point. I looked over and up at him, his older body still erect on the log, his eyes focused on the world, the bigger picture, from up here, high on a cliff—a vantage point where one could almost feel the curvature of the earth—and I watched his face as he spoke these words, still not looking at me:

"Gregory, yours is a slow maturity."

He paused for a moment. He had more to say, he had to have more to say, because he didn't say "Wow, Gregory, these drawings are so fucking cool, I love them." I looked back out to the water and focused on the incoming waves—details—and then on the massive sea and then, farther on, the unseen that exists, somewhere. What out there was for me? I wanted to tell him that I really was, am, a good artist and that I wanted to share with him and the world all the big

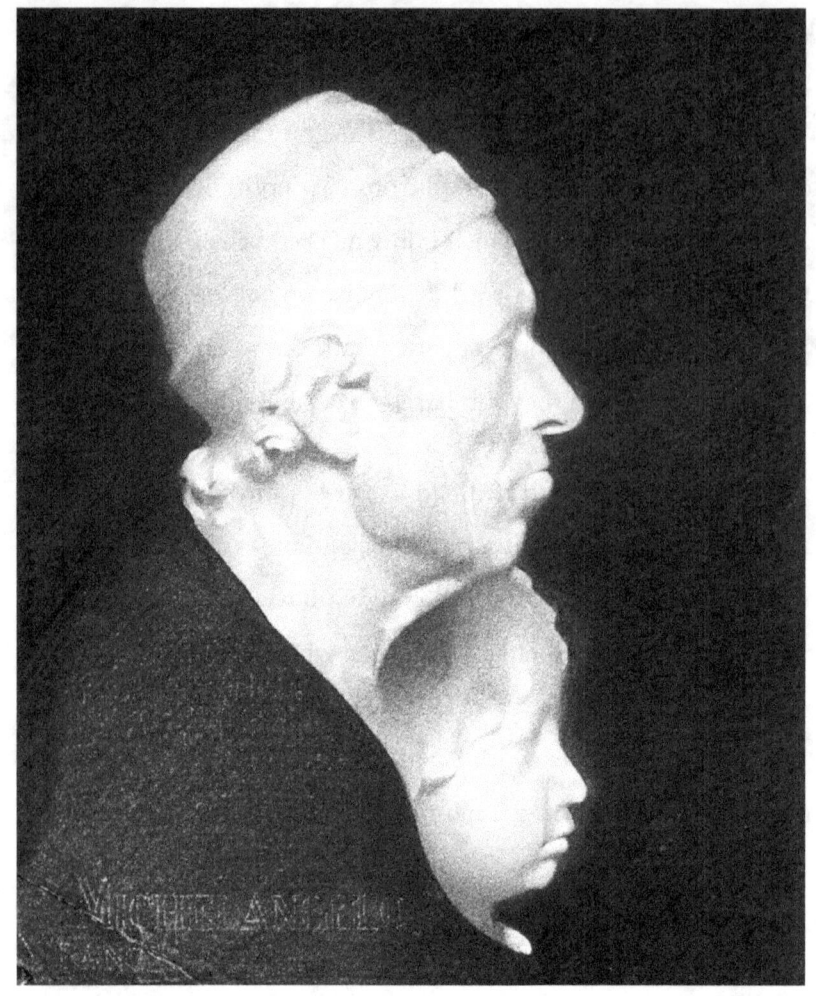

ideas I've always had, of paintings and things I hadn't yet had the opportunity to make. Had I only a patron. Had I only a bigger studio or more money; yes, with more money just imagine all the things I could make, or—and I shut myself up. Again, the cliff looked like a good escape, because it all sounded like fucking excuses, and I lit up that joint one more time and looked back over to Peter, who finally turned to me and explained, "But that's the best kind, Gregory."

He had thrown me a life vest. I was going to be OK. Yes, he must've seen this shit before. I immediately recalled my grandfather's words of wisdom: "Life is beautiful if you don't weaken." He told that to me when I was a boy, while we were walking to the local OTB to place bets on other people's ponies. This from a man whose front teeth had been knocked out in a bar brawl, who survived the Great Depression with eleven kids to feed, constantly moving when the rent couldn't be met. Now, up on Peter Beard's cliff, my grandfather's words unraveled, rearranged themselves, and spoke to me in a different, more relevant language: you must keep the faith.

AWARDS AND HONORS

September, 2001

"I feel ever so strongly that an artist must be nourished by his passions and his despairs."
—Franics Bacon

A few days after Peter Beard simultaneously shattered my world and gave me hope, I was back home in New York, finished with the extended stay out east. Teresa was happy to have me home and glad to see so much completed work. She was also glad to know a few dollars in sales from other drawings would be coming in during the following weeks. Sharing a sense of accomplishment, we were content to be in each other's arms again.

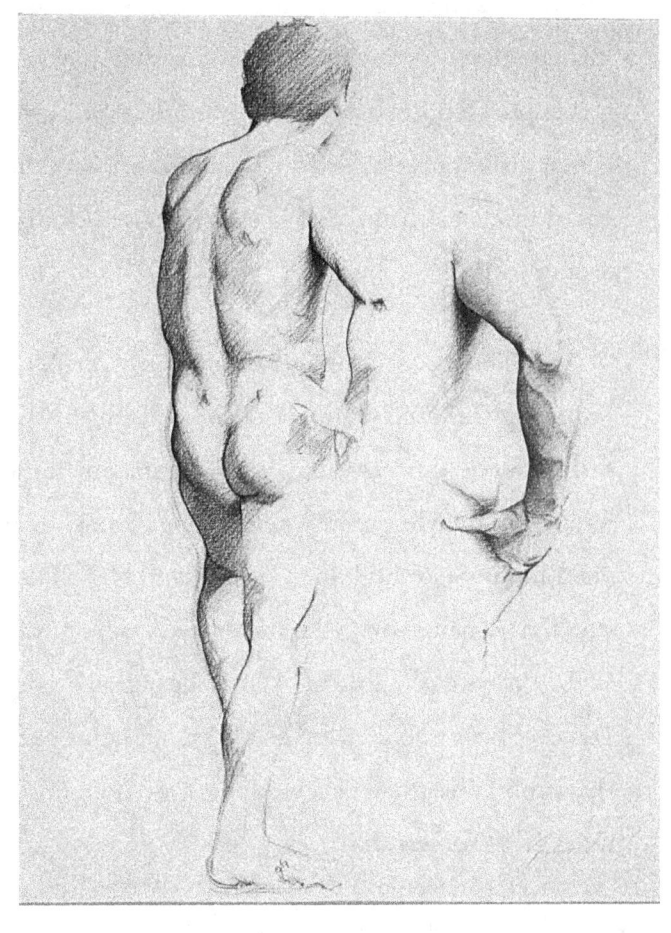

I didn't tell her all that Peter had said, only that four hours passed at his home rather quickly and that we spoke of art and the world and Francis Bacon in the 60s and Studio 54 in the late 70s and the Rolling Stones' Sticky Fingers tour, and how Peter had rolled all those years into one big joint. I told her, too, of how we discussed bullfighting and surfing and other arts that are only alive when you experience them at that very moment and can never be replicated exactly, unlike the second big joint we shared, which was exactly like the first one. I explained to her what a great privilege it all was, while still trying to digest the good kind of maturation compared with the other kinds that weren't so good, and I wondered which kind described the successful artist who, although young and still maturing, sold at auction for high sums:

the likes of Matthew Barney and the Young British Artists, who were plastered all over every art magazine at the time.

Teresa wanted to celebrate my return. She made plans for dinner and had our friends join us—Darcy and John and Adrianne and Mike—and she chose a nice Italian place in the West Village off Hudson Street. It was a beautiful night, and we spoke of Montauk, of work and pending vacations, and we drank red wine and made toasts to all things. And for some reason, somehow, this question was posed: if a plane crashed into one of the Twin Towers, would it stand or would it collapse? John worked on the 83rd floor of Tower One, his wife across the street at the Federal Reserve Bank. He believed it would stand, as it did during the bombing in '93, which he experienced first hand from his office high above. I said it would collapse. It was September 10th, 2001, around 10PM.

The next morning, I resumed my pre-Montauk routine and went for coffee and pastries, returning with Teresa's favorite cheese Danish. We enjoyed hot coffee and each other's company, sitting by the windows at an antique table my father refurbished when he was a young man. The wraparound skyline view was amazing: Brooklyn and Queens, Lower Manhattan, the Twin Towers, Empire State Building, Triboro and Hell Gate bridges. It was clear and beautiful except for a small, dark plume of smoke we noticed from one of the Towers. I asked Teresa to call John, but she said, "I'm sure he's alright." When the plume became larger, she called nonstop. A scream, a sound I'd never before heard from her, filled our home as the first tower collapsed. We cried together when the second tower fell, believing that we'd not only just lost our best friends but tens of thousands of other New Yorkers, too.

Around 10AM, we got a phone call from John, informing us that he was in the basement of the Federal Reserve with his wife. He had managed to convince all ninety of his company's employees, many reluctant, to leave the building, even though they were told via intercom to go back up the stairs, because "everything was fine" and it was "all in the other tower." When his tower did get hit, John persisted still when told to stay inside because of falling debris; he forced his way out with his co-workers. Had they listened to the loudspeaker, they would've ended up dead. The first thing I said to John when he called was, "So much for your theory." Again, I'd said something stupid and terribly timed. He had no idea what I was talking about, that the building he'd worked in for years and the one next to it had fallen, collapsed. When I told him, he replied, "What do you mean they fell?" He was six stories underground, in the bank's vault, and he had no idea that the world as we knew it was ending above.

"What matters? And when does it matter most?" —scrawled on a piece of paper in the days after September 11th, 2001

From Montauk, I brought back a few unfinished paintings and piled them with all the finished charcoals against one of the walls in my studio. Paintings that I had started when the sun, after baking color into the land all day long, began its descent, and early evening's kaleidoscopic cools initiated their daily dance with the final remnants of the day's intense warms. Some paintings were never completed because the rich shades between crimson and violet, which emerged in shadows of shadbush and boulders, were too much. As I stood motionless at the easel, sepia tones, at first revealing themselves from deep within the cliff's creviced and scared face, soon blanketed the rolling landscape, as if a giant cuttlefish had squirted from its anus a load of darkening ink. Night fell too quickly to paint, for my eyes to adjust; my mind, instead, preferred to wander outside the picture frame, to ride the curling waves breaking a hundred feet below on the beach.

Once back home in Queens, there was one picture in particular that I really wanted to finish. It was of the lighthouse, and the composition was already there, primary colors blocked out, a fine start. But I couldn't bring myself to work on it, or on anything else for that matter, any time soon after 9|11. The city, and life in general, was unreal: art seemed inconsequential. But that's the thing about art—it's not inconsequential. It took time, however, to realize this: time to leave things alone and reflect on the bigger picture, which had changed more dramatically outside my window than the entire South Shore's coastline had changed during a generation's upbringing. It was a time to leave desire untended, to put the brushes down and be OK with that, for once.

But paintings cry, too. They scream for what's needed: proper waves to crash the shore, a meandering path to welcome the eye, a seagull to guide you round the lighthouse, a moving cloud to carry one out to sea and back again, occasionally, even, taking the viewer on a quick jaunt out-

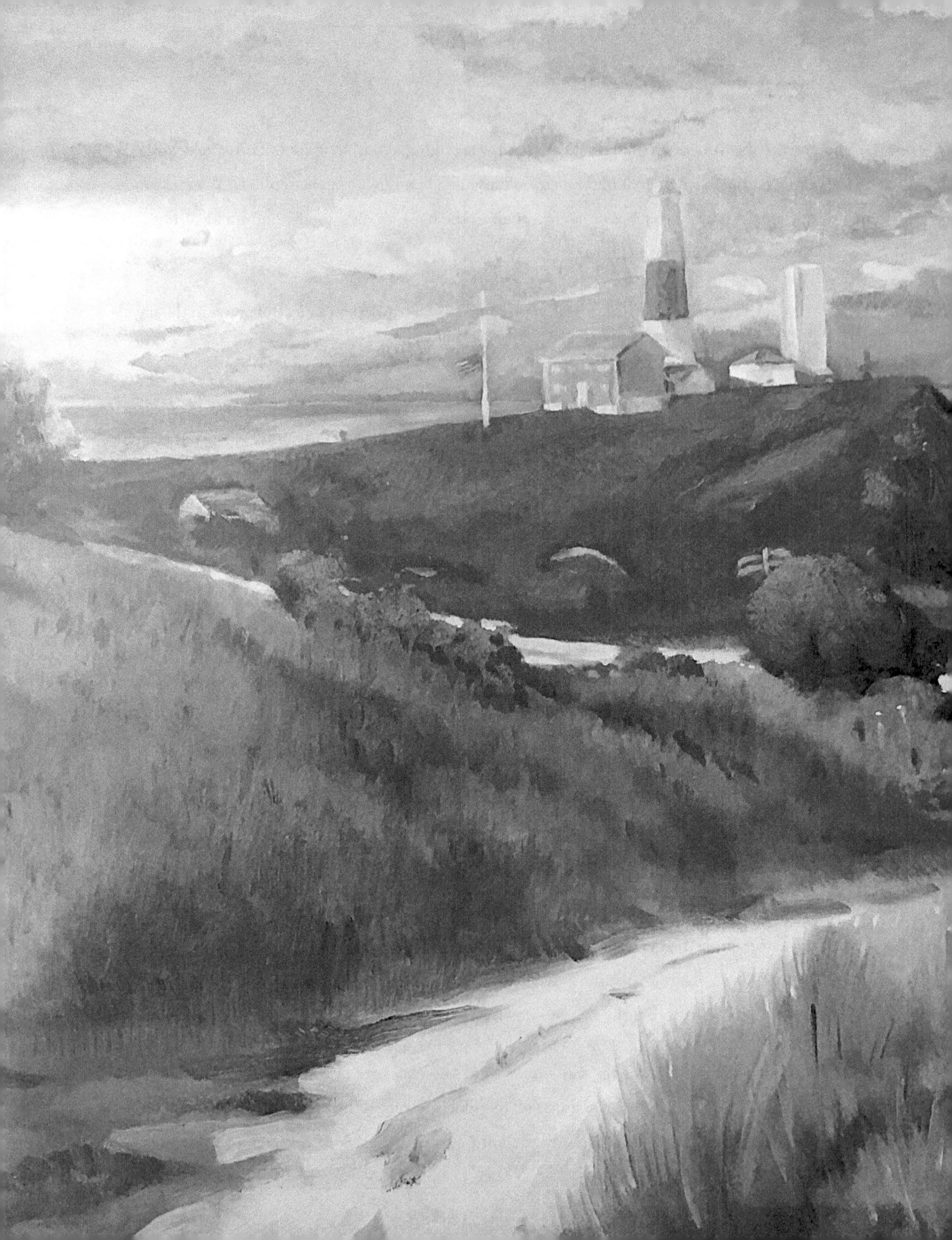

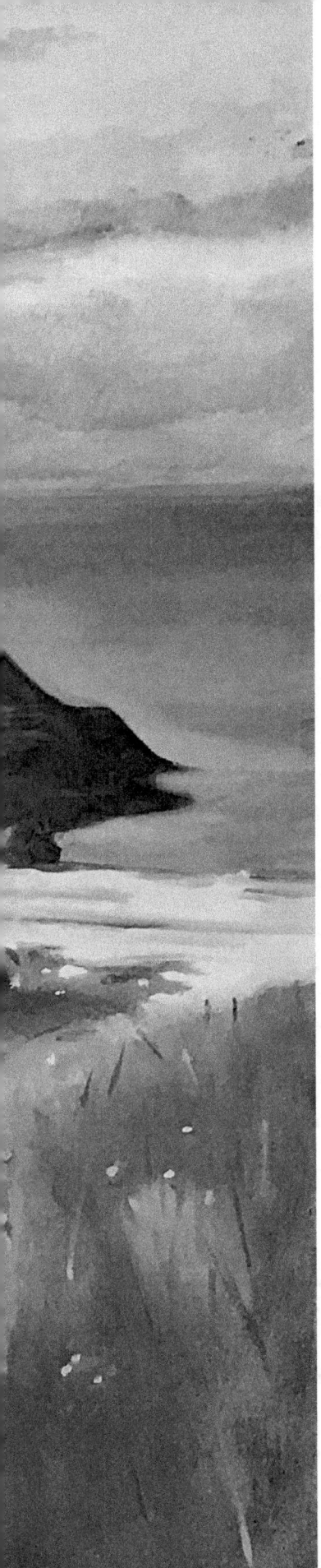

side the painting's four-sided boundary. But the painting would have to wait for these details. The time that elapsed became an exercise in restraint. How long to mourn and not work? How long to leave what you do, undone?

Ultimately, it took weeks to finish in Queens what I started out in Montauk. By Thanksgiving, I told myself, I'd begin. I'd keep the day a sunny one, with the wind going strong, the way I like, but I'd make the lighthouse sit even farther back in the picture by bringing attention to detail in the foreground, vertical flicks of the brush to hint at blades of grass, or a horizontal dab to indicate a pebble on the pathway. Waves would roll and crash onto the jetty, a cloud would whiz by. But it was the flag flying in the wind that'd change the painting most: I'd now bring it down to half-mast in honor of a fireman friend who died on 9|11. He was two years older than me and had attended the same all-boys Catholic High School, Holy Cross. I remember drinking beers with him in a Bayside, Queens, home as a teenager and after a play we both performed in, where I got to know him better. A smile always stretching wide across his face and a story in his pocket, he was friendly. That's what someone would say. But more: he was authentic.

FELLOWSHIPS

Between The Artist And His Muse

Queens, New York

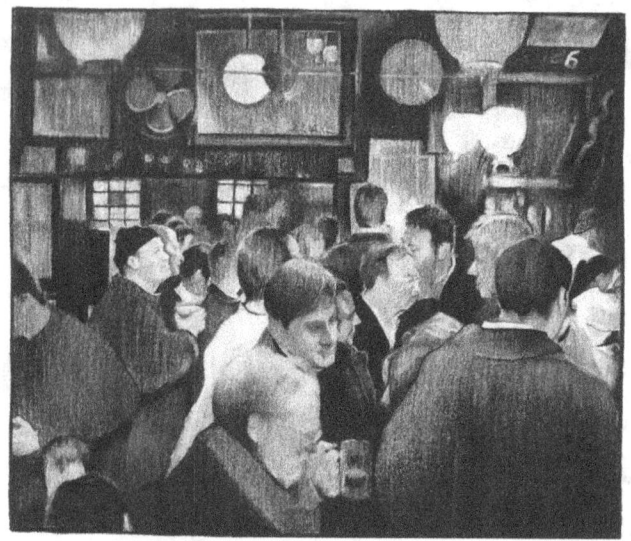

My Irish-Catholic grandfather, Joe McShea, started driving a coal truck around the year 1927 when he was only fourteen years of age and when both his parents had died unexpectedly. He desperately needed to take care of a younger brother and sister, ready or not. A forged birth certificate made him age faster than he was. One of his coal-delivery stops was McSorley's Old Ale House. Family lore would have it that he made this sacred, ancient bar on East 7th street in Manhattan —where Irish freedom fighters like John Devoy, Thomas Francis Maher, and Jeremiah O'Donovan Rossa, members of the Fenian Brotherhood and of the Clan na Gael, met and drank—his regular pit stop before returning home to a growing family of his own doing in Corona, Queens. Prior to the building of La Guardia Airport, Corona was New York City's main dumping ground for the copious amounts of ash from all the coal-burning furnaces on 24 hour overdrive throughout the ever-expanding city. Described by F. Scott Fitzgerald in The Great Gatsby as "the valley of ashes," Corona, Queens, was "where ashes take the form of houses and chimneys and rising smoke... of men who move dimly and already crumbling through the powdery air."

By the mid 1980's, while still a teenager myself and when New York driver ID's were still absent a photo on them, McSorley's was my go-to destination each weekend, where I would get my Irish-up, as they say, courtesy of an older brothers driver's license, and throw back as many mugs of ale as my weekly, very weakly, paycheck from a Queens sporting goods store would allow. It was the only place missed while away at college, and where I visited piously when Teresa was working and especially after we first met in 1995. My excuse to see her back then was always the same: "I was just in the neighborhood" or "I'm here to do a little sketch" for the portrait commission. The other bartenders and staff would always poke fun at her during and after my visits, gossip that "something was going on" between the two of us which she always denied or ignored. She, in her most gracious, smiling way, always made me, and everyone who visited the bar for that matter, feel right at home, unlike the other, rough-around-the-edges, old-time staff. And the bar, like the staff, seemed straight out of an old western movie, swinging doors and all. The surly, burly guys who worked there were legendary, characters of yore, ready to rip your head off at any moment for stepping out of line or for not keeping pace with the place and the fast action of the swinging suds. And there, in the middle of all the memorabilia, between the aged, beer-stained wood, and the pipe-smoke-stained etchings, surrounded by brittle newspapers and fading photographs, amongst all the energy in a bar that bustles like no other in a city like no other, stood Teresa, the most beautiful and recent bar acquisition—minus the dust. She was truly "about her father's business" and her presence ever so purposeful. Her youthful vigor and bright blue eyes, her porcelin skin and joyous demeanor all a complete and total contrast to everything inside. She stood out like a sore thumb yet filled the space with such dignity and gravitas it was clear she was standing and being where she was meant to stand and be.

McSorley's Old Ale House was always more than a place to drink for me. It was a portal to the past, a connection to my Irish roots—to my grandfather. But since meeting and marrying Teresa, McSorley's became more sacred still, where love brewed and spilled over the hundred and fifty year old mahogany bar top as generously as the Light and Dark ales they're famous for serving. McSorley's became our second home, our place of work, our pride and joy. It's where our fates met and forged solidly together and as permanent as the momentos forever embraced on the walls of the greatest bar on earth.

In February 2004, the week before the bar's 150th Anniversary celebrations, an exhibition at NYU's Glucksman Ireland House of drawings and paintings of McSorleys that I created since meeting Teresa was slated to open, festivities of which my father-in-law had planned as homage to the bar's longevity milestone. I wrote a letter to my wife:

Dear Teresa,

Nine years ago, on January 5th, to be exact, you walked into my studio for the first time, to pose for a portrait at your father's request. Having met him in the bar a few months prior, I recall how he wanted something special to commemorate you being the first female bartender in McSorley's history. To him, a portrait sounded like a great idea. You thought he was crazy to send you off to a stranger's studio, and I remember how awkward you felt. How nervous you were standing there for me, in the middle of a 2,000-square-foot room with no furnishings, atop a huge old factory building nearly vacant. A single easel, some newly stretched canvases, a piece-of-shit radio, and a nightstand filled with materials were all that occupied the space, except, of course, for me. And my own anxiousness did little to help ease the tension, which was heightened and framed by the dark gray walls and the yards of opaque, black fabric that covered the 16-foot-high windows. And of all the things I could have said on the way up in the elevator, I went with the first stupid thing that came to mind: I told you that they killed cats on the third floor and used their guts to make strings for musical instruments. I was fully aware of how difficult the task at hand was for you. My eyes studied every detail, and for you, it felt like I was looking you up and down.

I searched for that perfect pose, telling you to position your body this way and that. Ten unobstructed feet between us, and you continued to make the adjustments I asked, but never looking right at me and clearly still shocked by your father's request. A chair to rest your hand upon, a prop to lean against, that would have made things easier for both of us, but I wanted to see you. I wanted to see you with nothing else around, nothing to distract. The way you looked, however, was also making things way too damn difficult. If the subject is ugly, how can anyone complain of a poorly executed portrait? If the artist fucks up, the sitter can be blamed. But I was obliged to get beauty right. That the proprietor of my favorite bar granted me this first big commission exactly one week after my return to New York from my formal training in Boston was unbelievable to me. Up until then, no one had paid me as much for a portrait (and not too many since). The thought of failing followed my every move. I want to apologize (just a little) at the pleasure I took in watching you not know what to do with yourself. Your naïveté was my amusement, the only distraction from my own uncertainty.

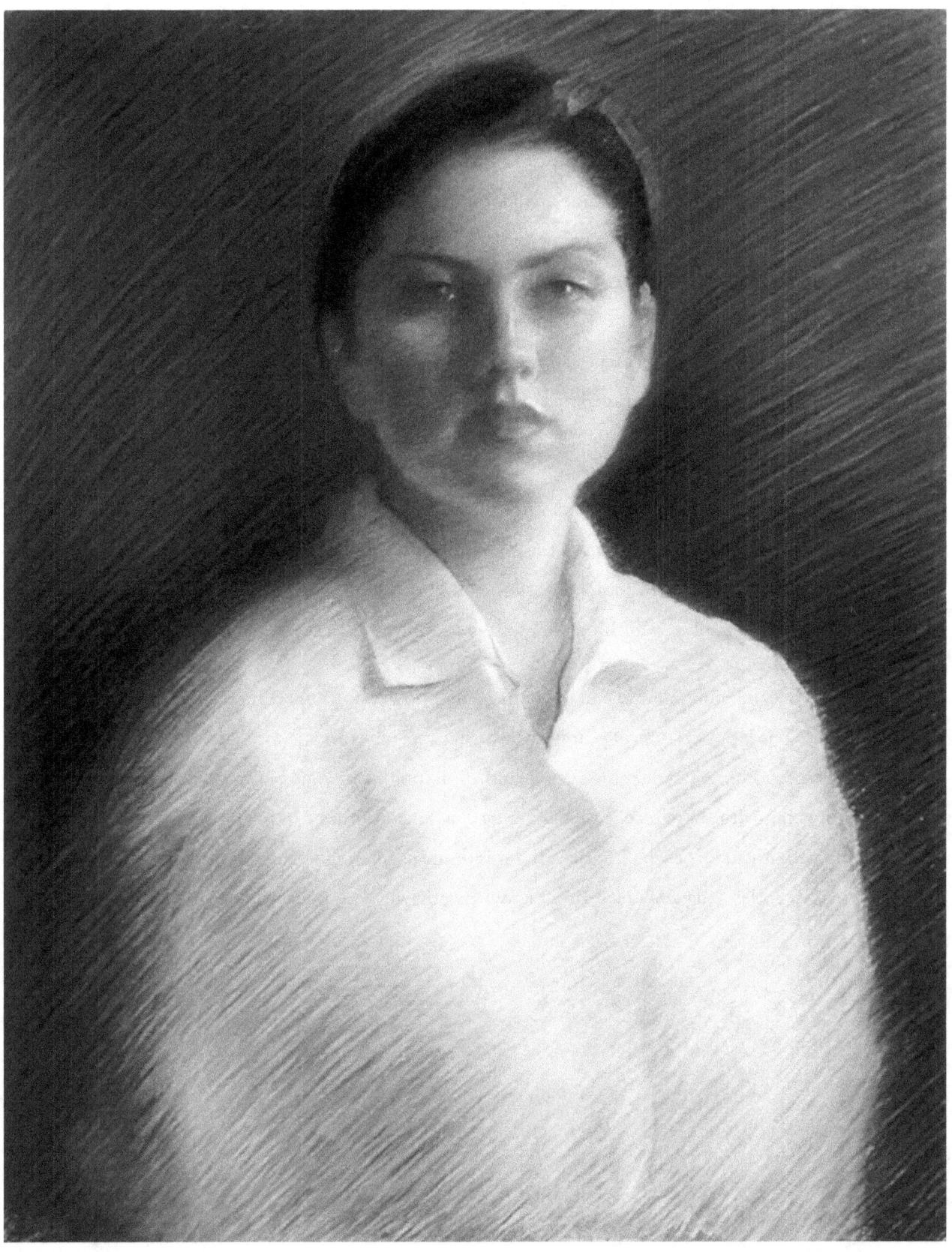

I remember asking, "What kind of music do you like?" and before you could reply, I suggested Van Morrison, thinking to myself that it was the only vaguely "Irish" music that I had. I would learn soon enough that my "McSorley's girl" was as Irish as a fortune cookie is Chinese. In the course of our sittings, it took no time at all for me to completely lose hold of the artist-in-charge-of-his-subject role. The size of the commission. The work it would take. You, Teresa. My anxiousness took the form of questions: "Are you OK? You sure? Is it cold? Hot? Change the music? Need a break? Coffee?" Still-lifes, landscapes, hired sitters, no, this was a world entirely different. It's no wonder it took three sittings to start the damn thing. Finally, we recognized that we were both in a similar boat. At that, you encouraged me: "Gregory, I'm fine. If there's one thing my father taught me, it is never to bother a man while he's working." I've been working alongside you ever since.

The loft became our home soon after the portrait was finished. Right now, I am looking through the French doors that separate the studio from our living space, that first portrait of you hanging on the far side of the room, beneath the latest one, finished three days before the birth of our son Matthew. Thank you for him. And for Sebastian who'll arrive when he's ready.

It is freezing out today, like many of those first times you came here, bringing with you the gift of coffee. The light this time of year is my favorite, cool blues and neutral grays, like slate but not as cold; crisp, soothing, heightening the warmth radiating from your blushing face. I don't know where I'm going with these recollections, Teresa, just like at times I haven't always known where I'm going with my art—or why I bother. But it is a much different feeling on the occasion of these works, my McSorley's Sketchbook series. I know exactly why—and for whom—they were created.

Love,

Gregory

Glucksman Ireland House at NYU is pleased to present

the McSorley's
Sketchbook

by Gregory Jos. de la Haba

POTBELLIES

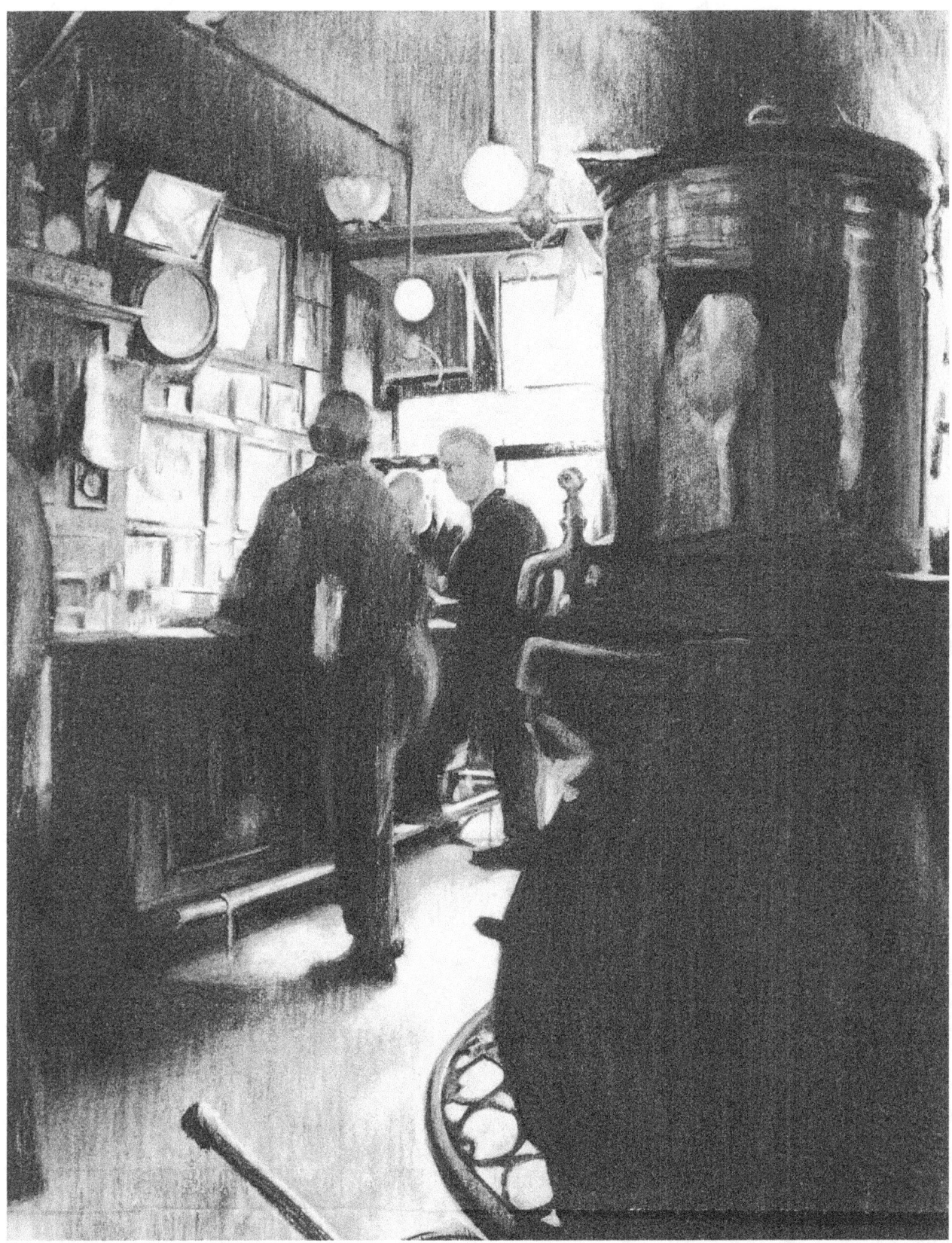

LOST IN THOUGHT

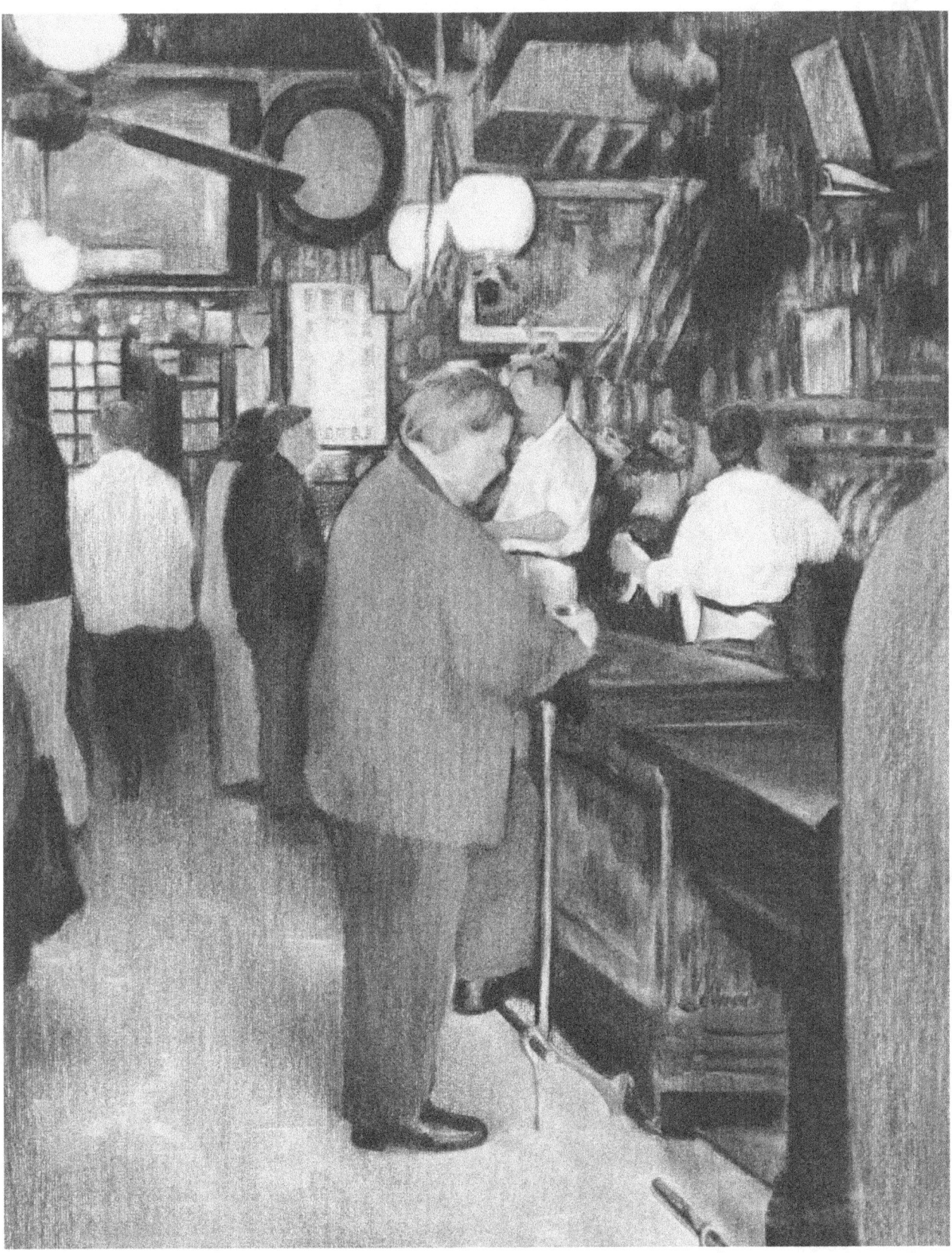

SWINGING DOORS #2

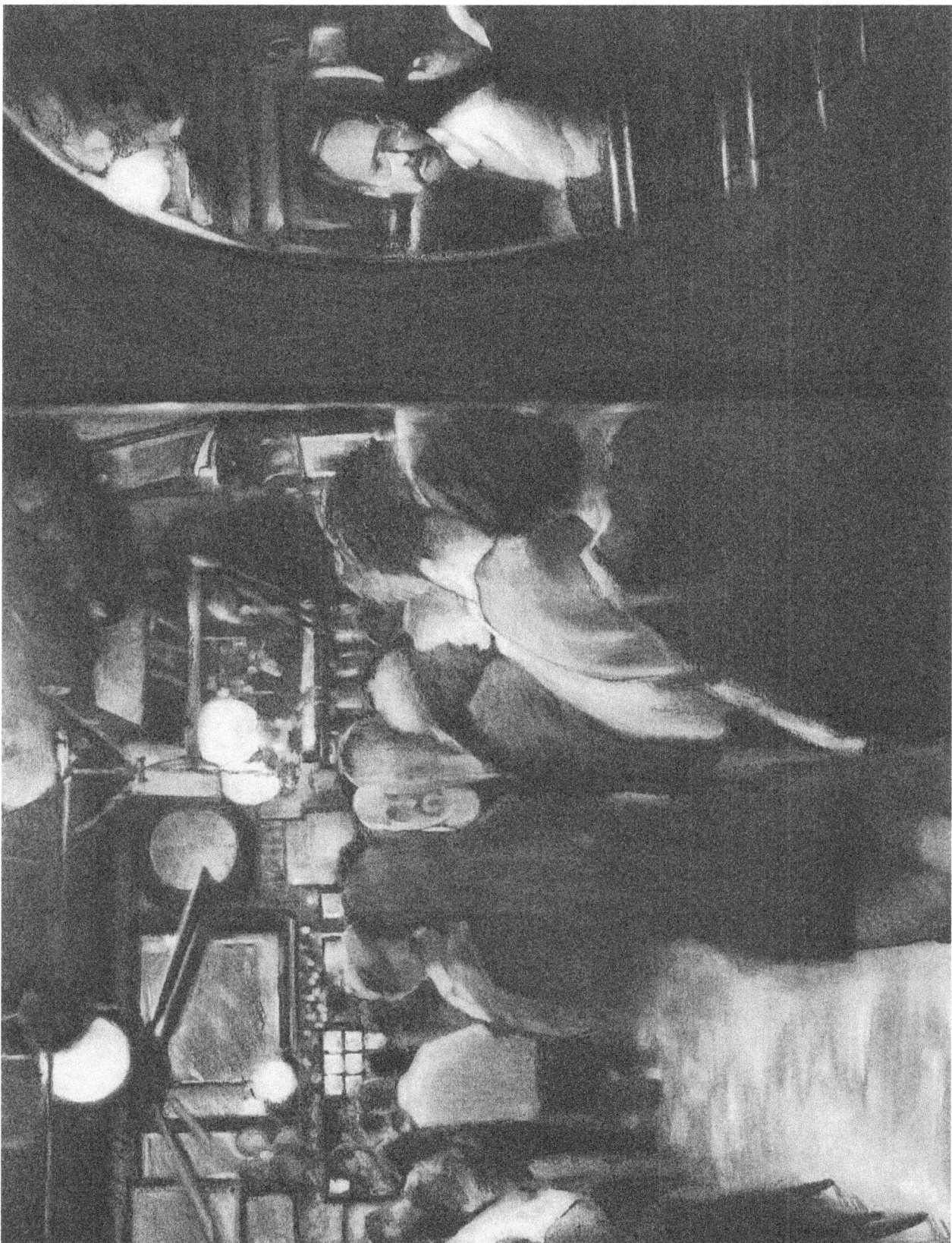

TOM'S FANS

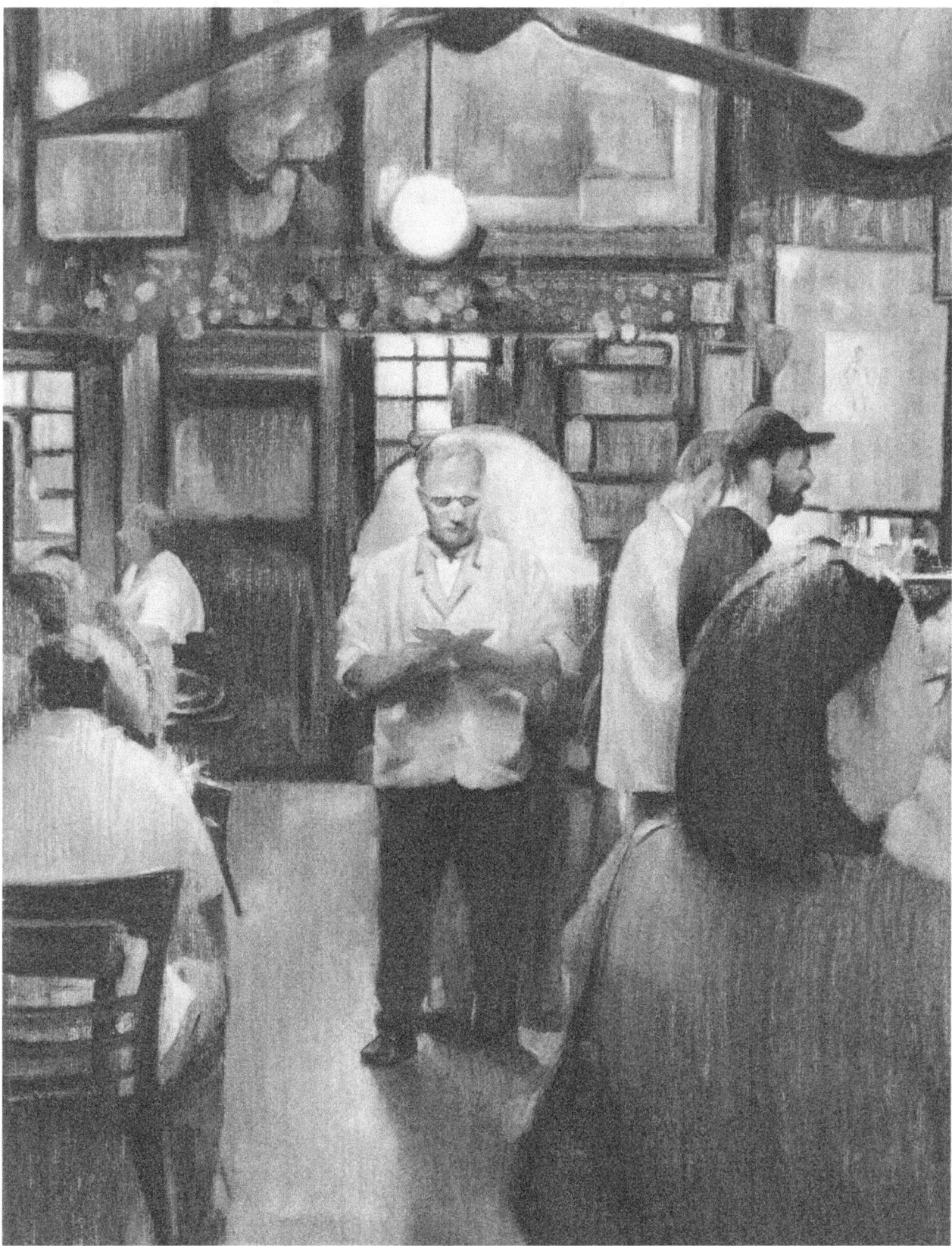

FRIDAY NIGHT

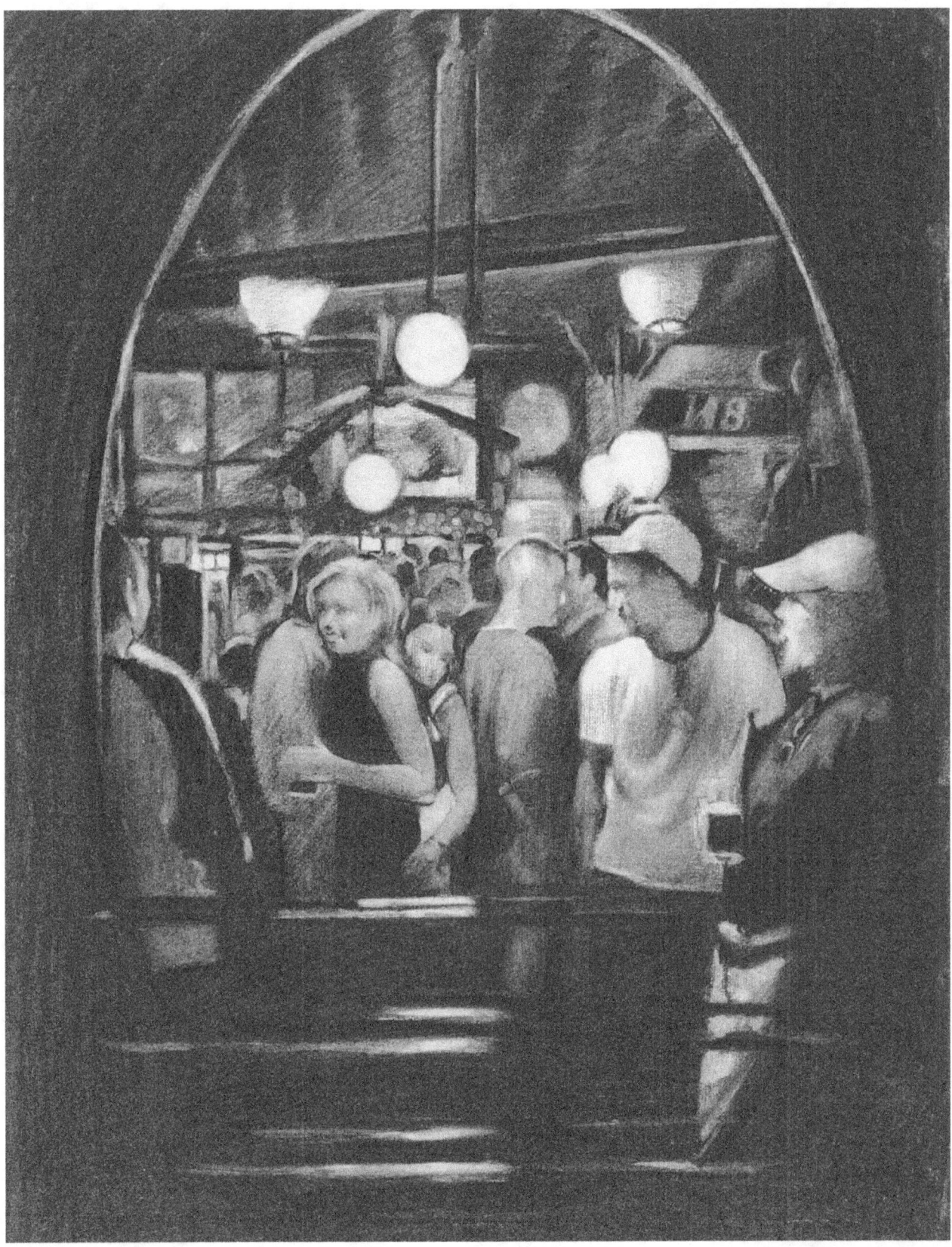

NIGHT WATCHMAN

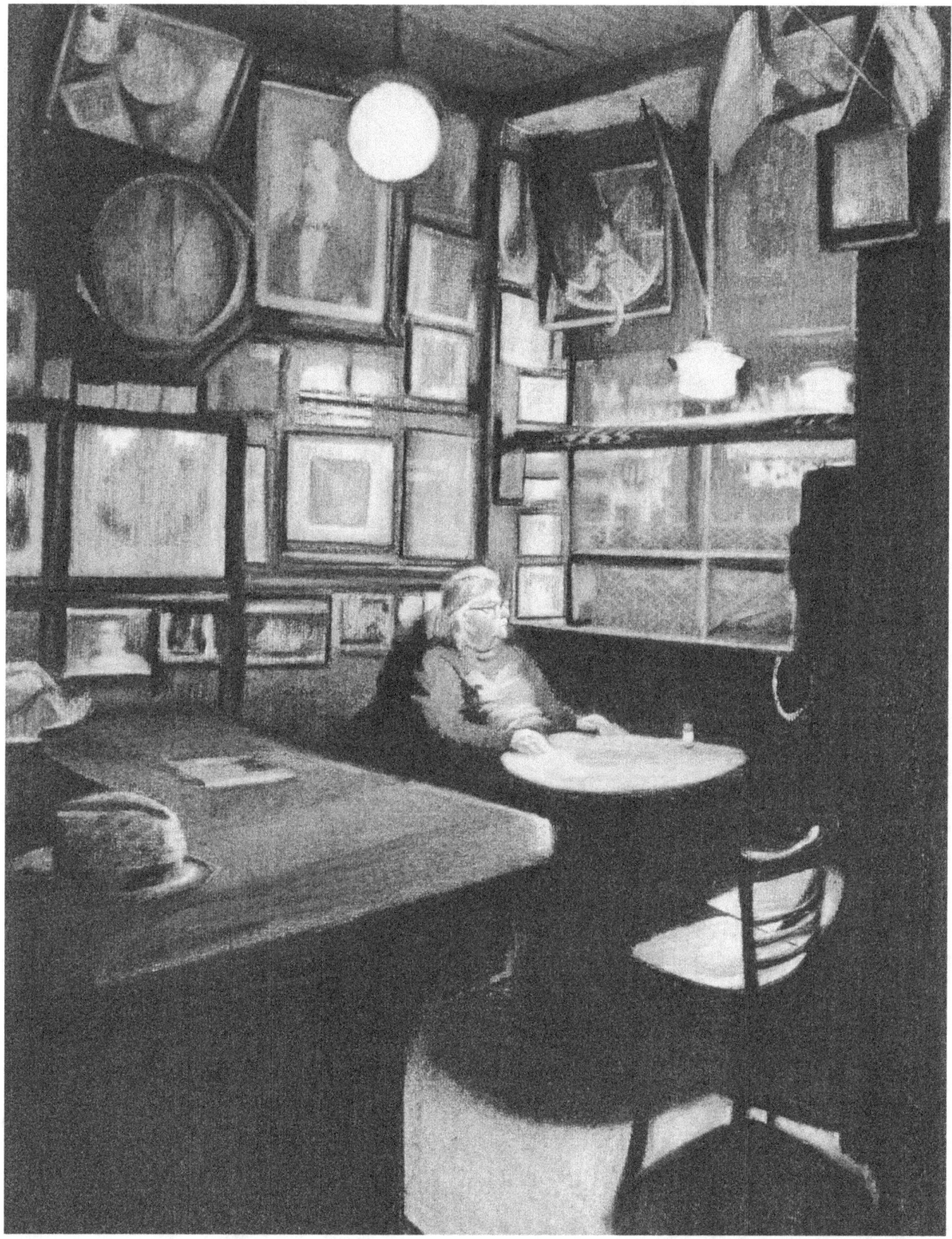

ALE'S WELL

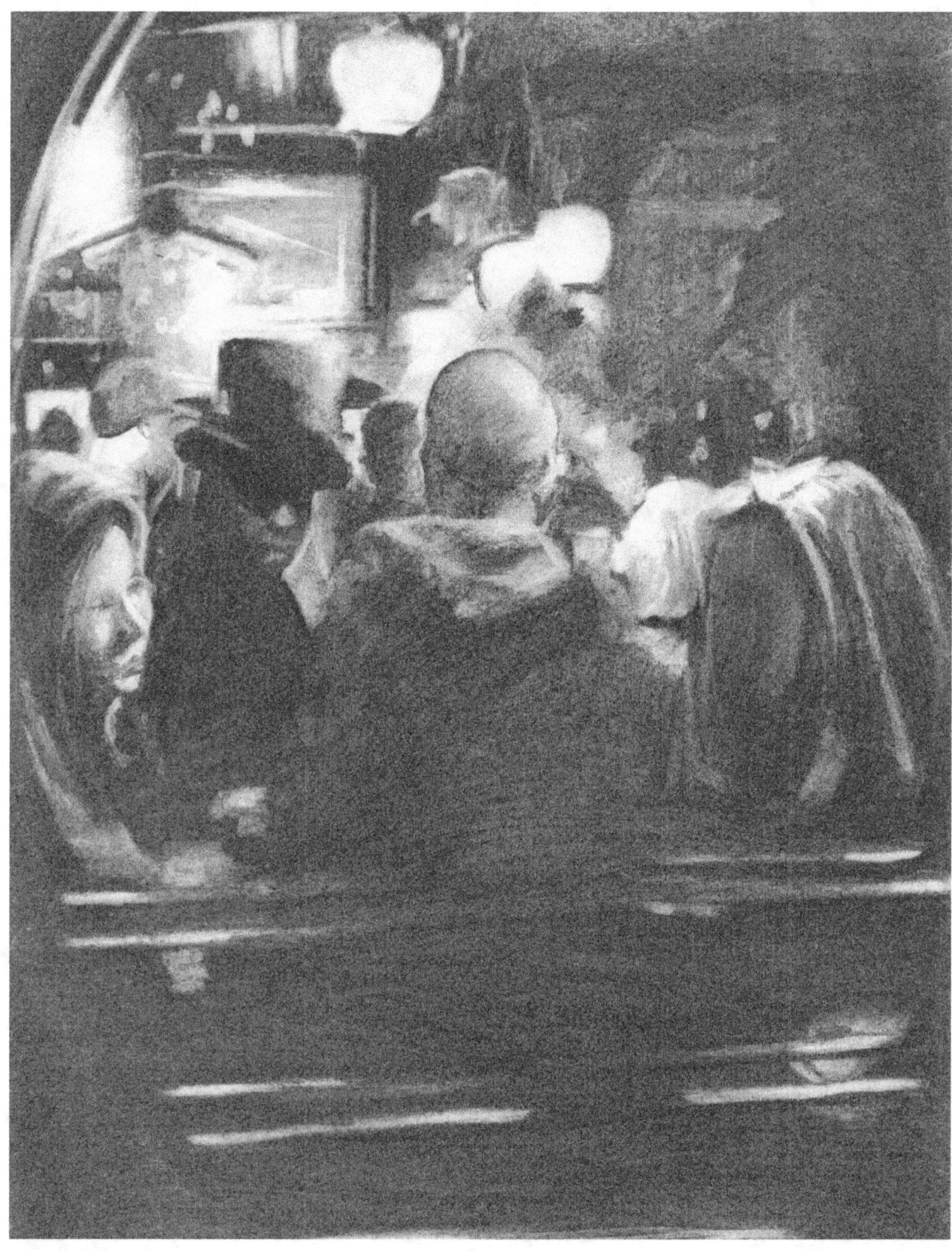

LOST WISHES #2

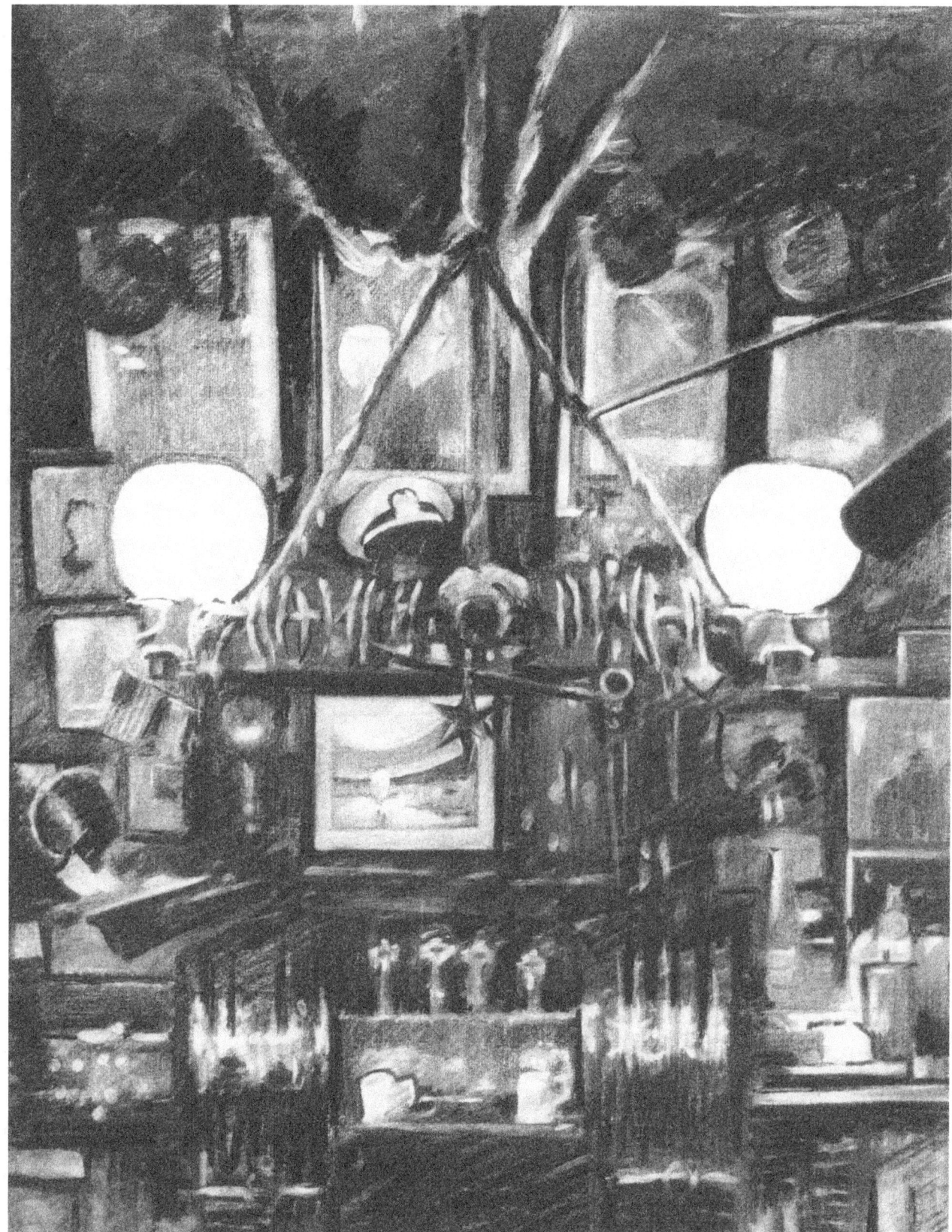

WHEN ARE THEY GONNA LEAVE

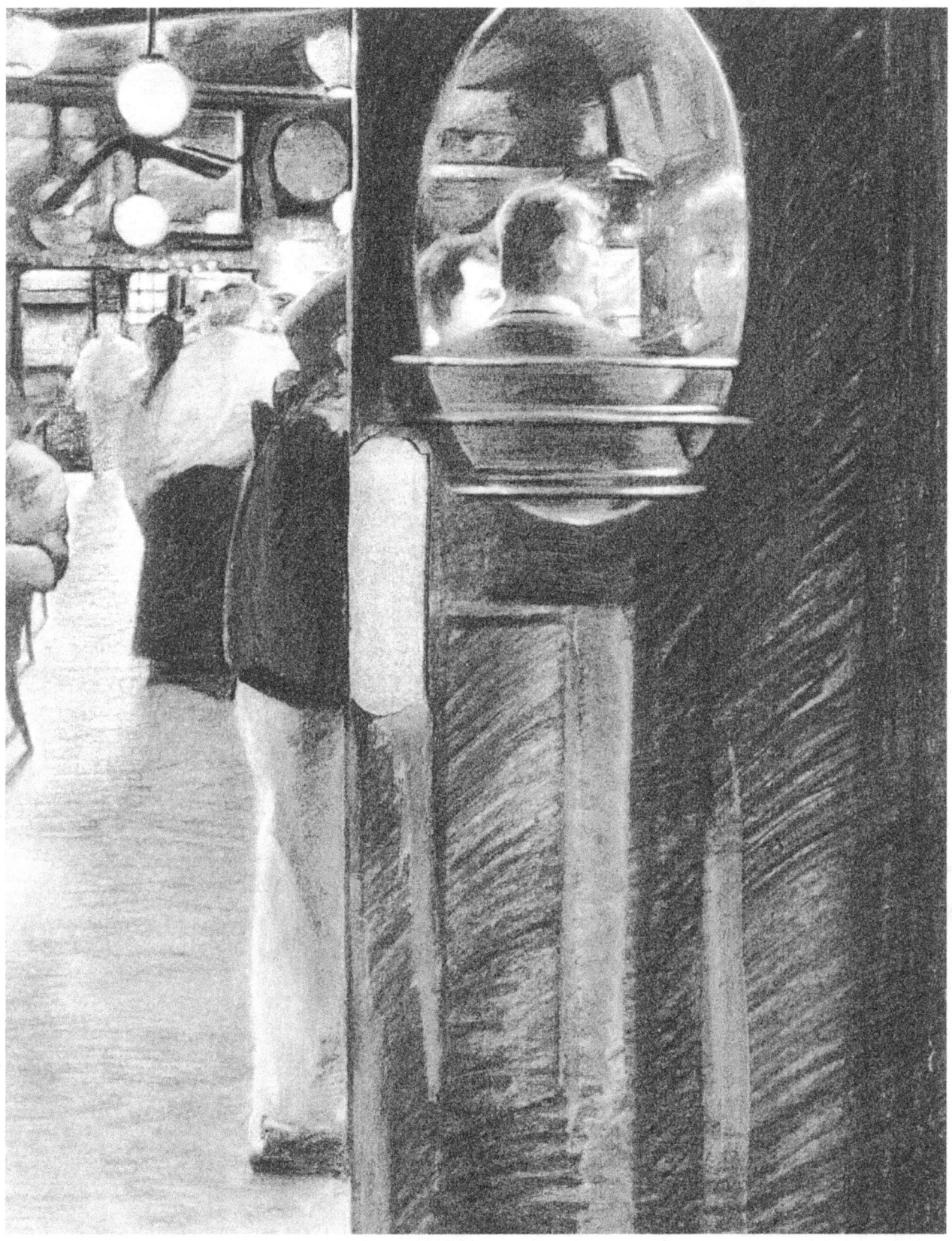

LOOKING IN

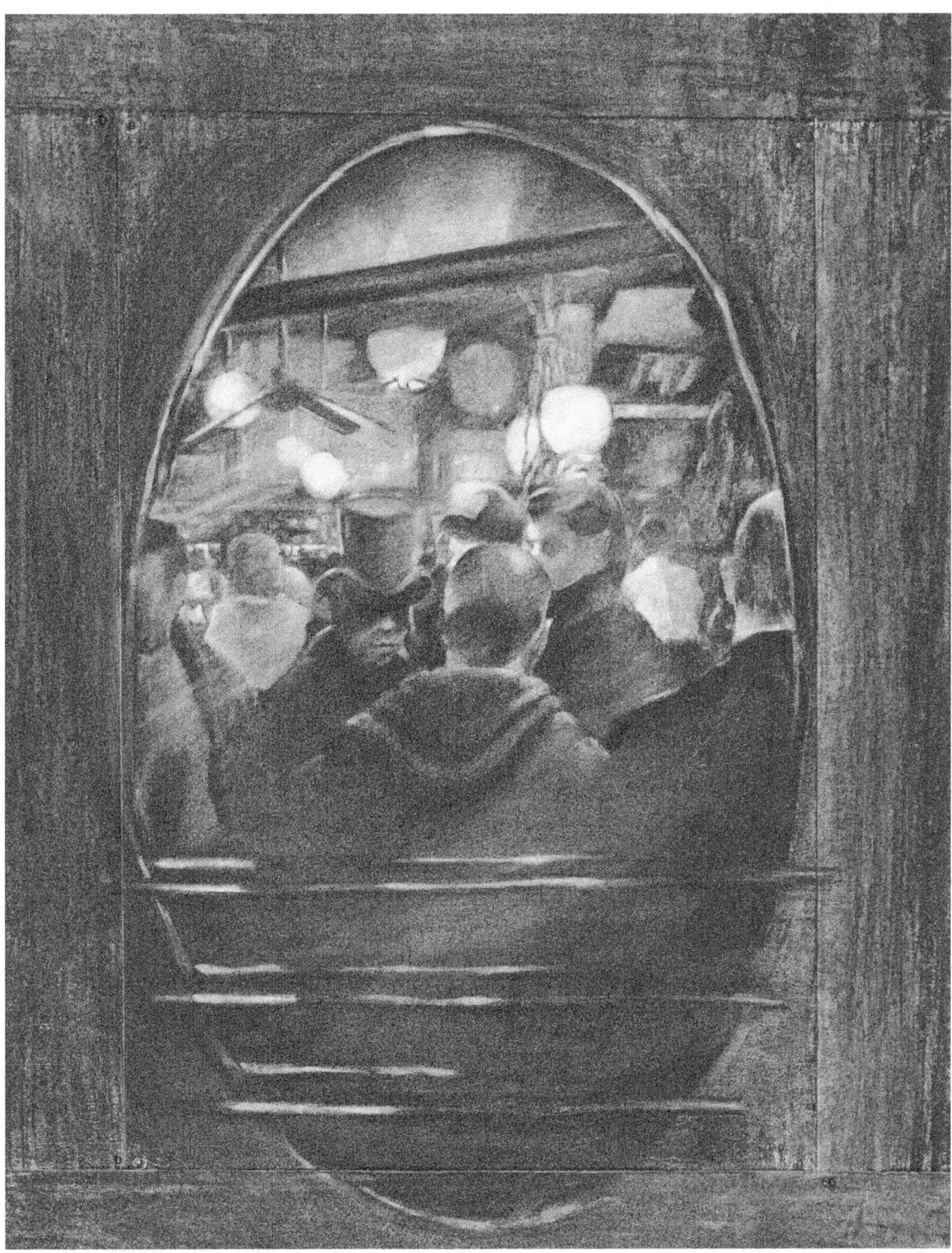

FAT CATS

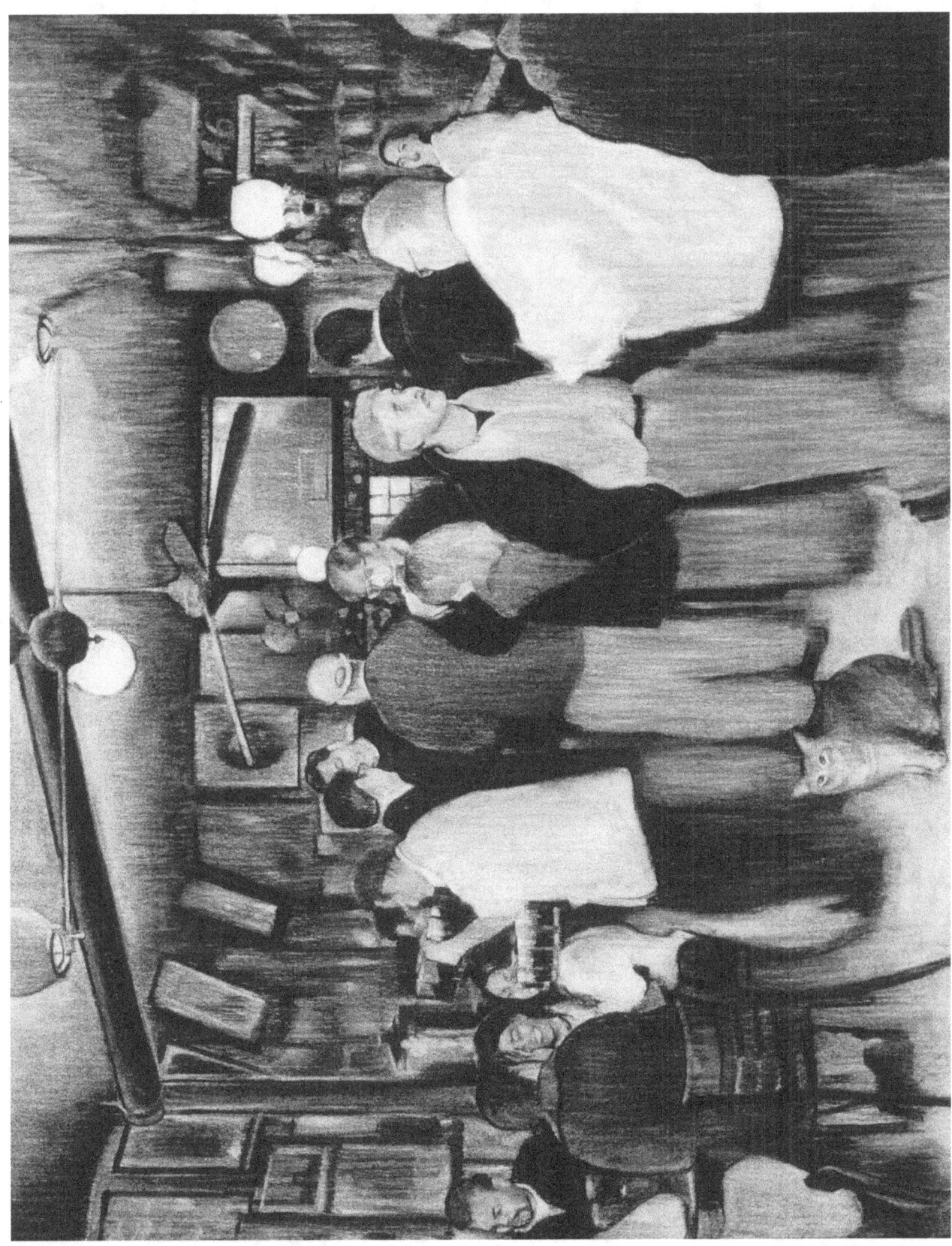

CHEESE PLATE

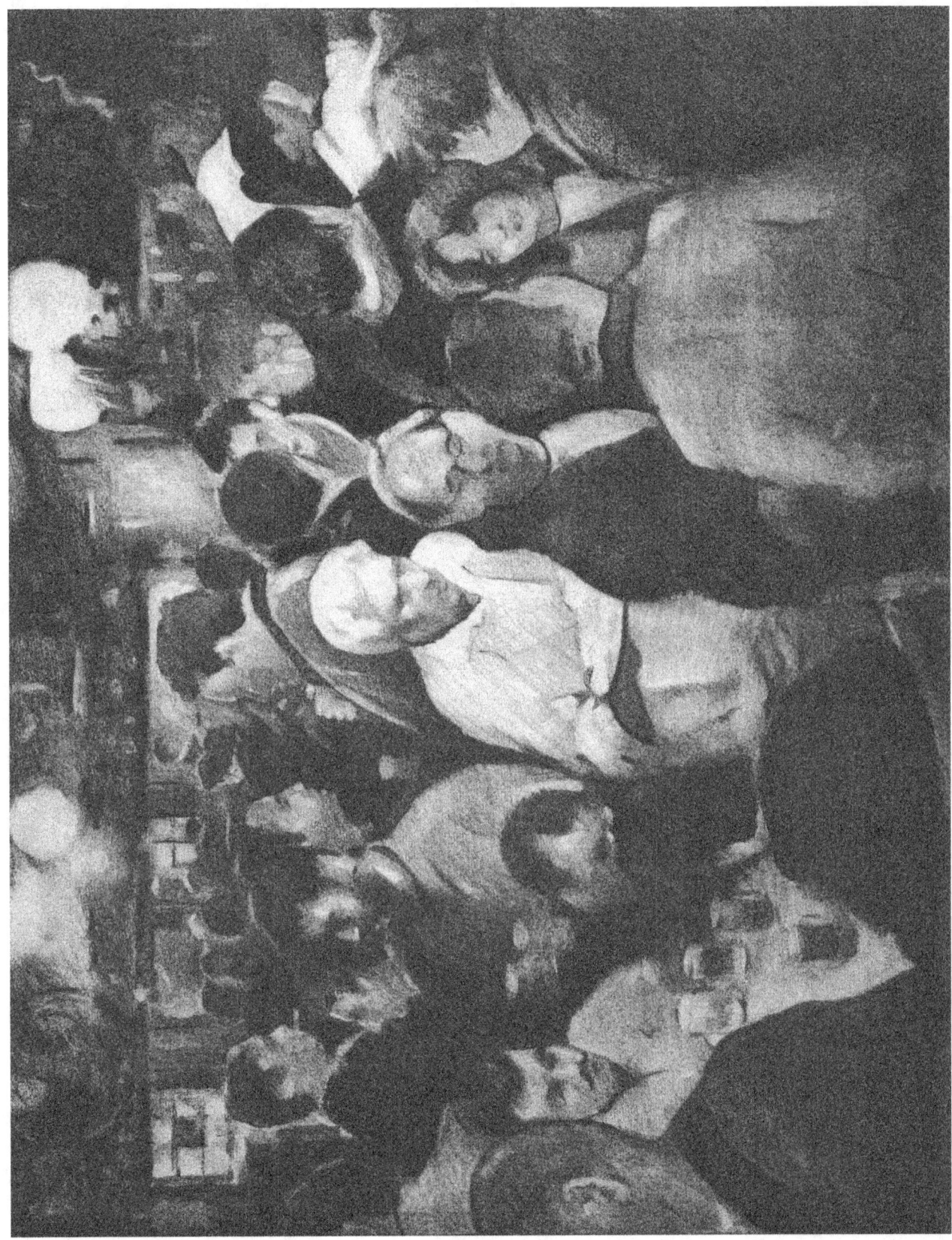

THE BARD OF MCSORLEY'S

Geoffery Bartholomew

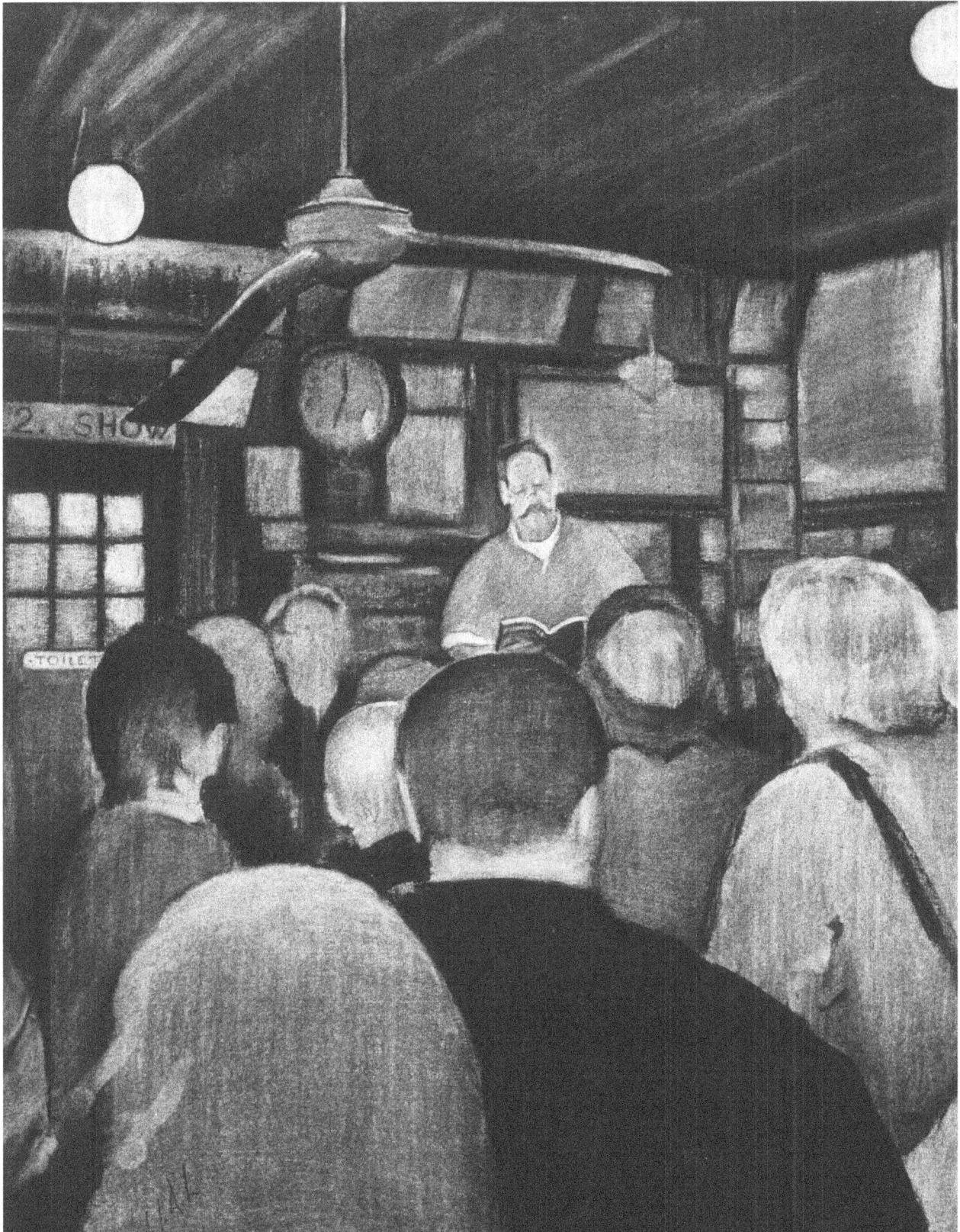

LET ME JUST FINISH THIS

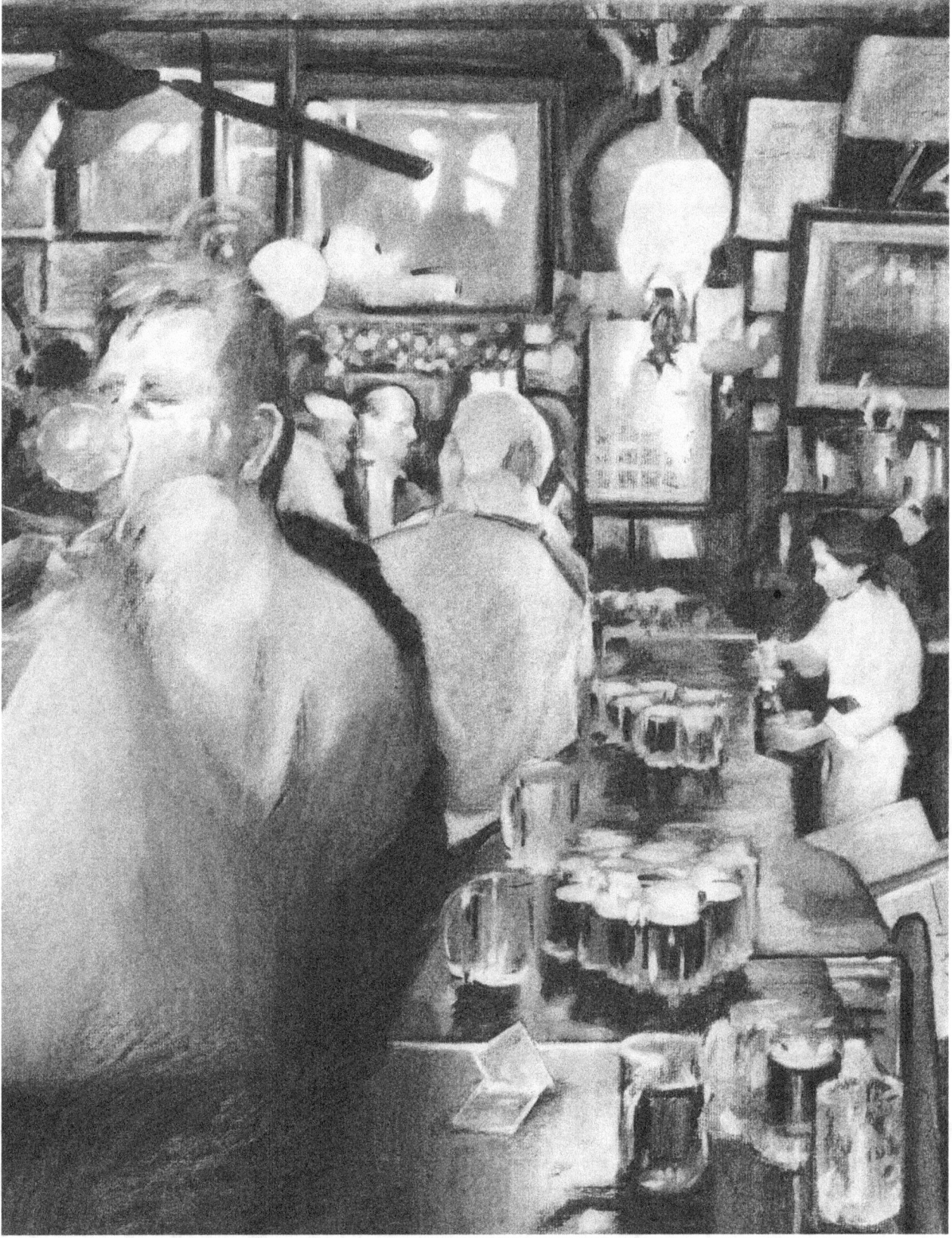

SWING DOORS #1

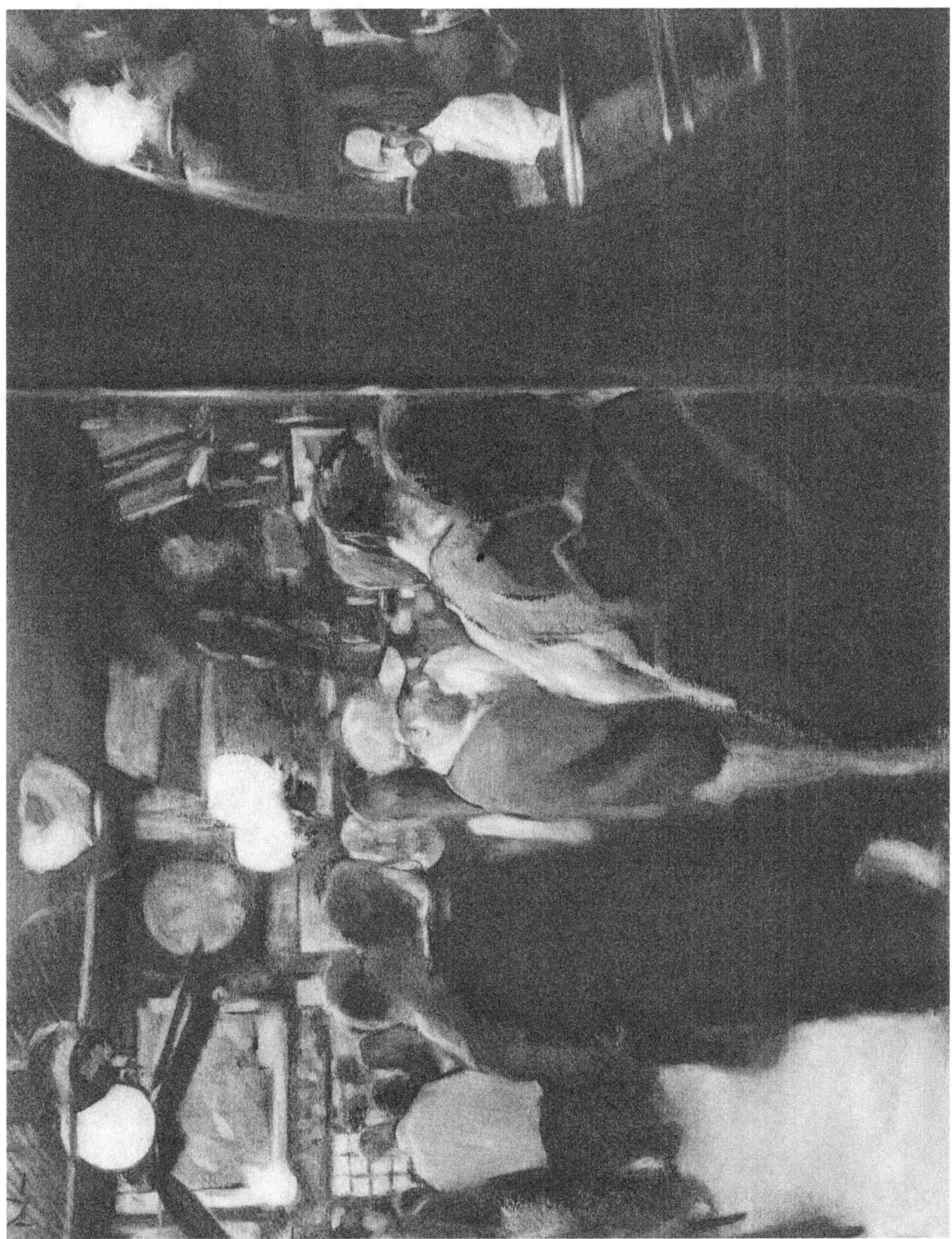

MARCH 17TH

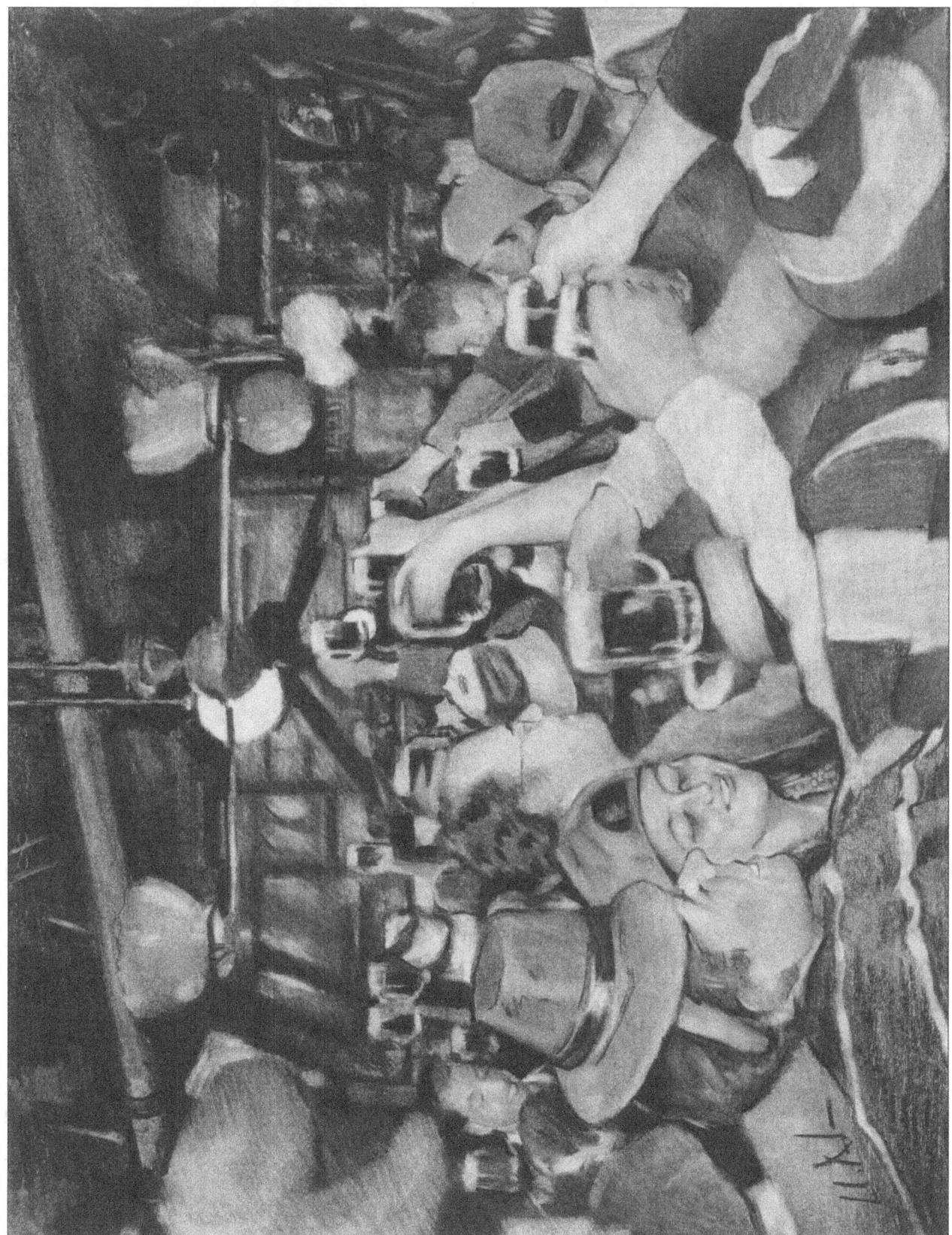

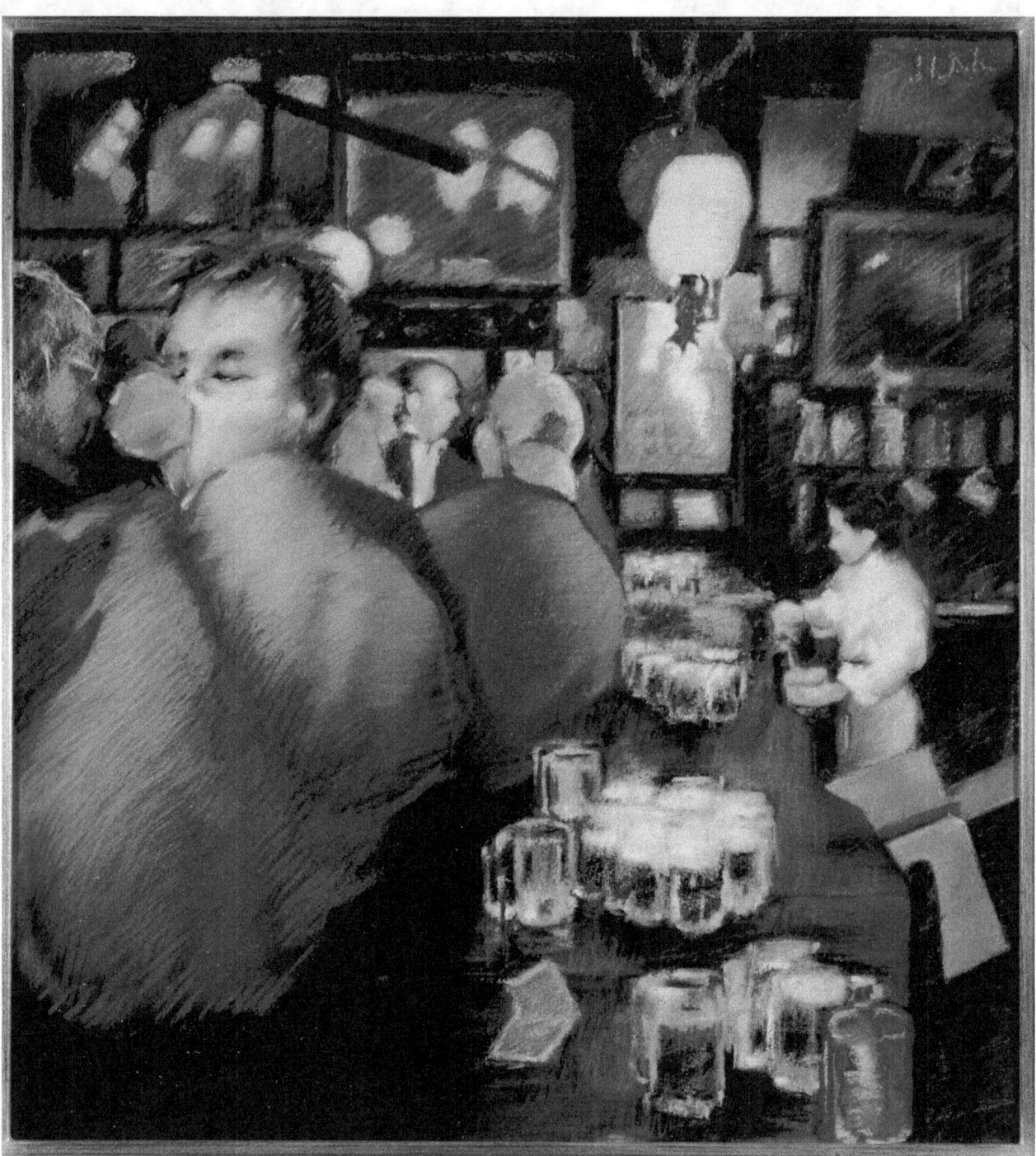

Teresa: "But, Gregory, this is supposed to be about you. It's your CV."

"Teresa, remember the story I told you about the artist Whistler, how he'd walk around London with a white chrysanthemum in his buttonhole because he wanted other people to know who he was and believing full well that if anyone acknowledged his flower, that if they were sensitive to its charms, that they, too, must hail from a similar place as his soul abides. And that those were the types of people he wished very much to meet in life. To surround himself with. Do you remember?

'Yes, I remember. What does it have to do with your CV?"

"Teresa. You're my white chrysanthemum."

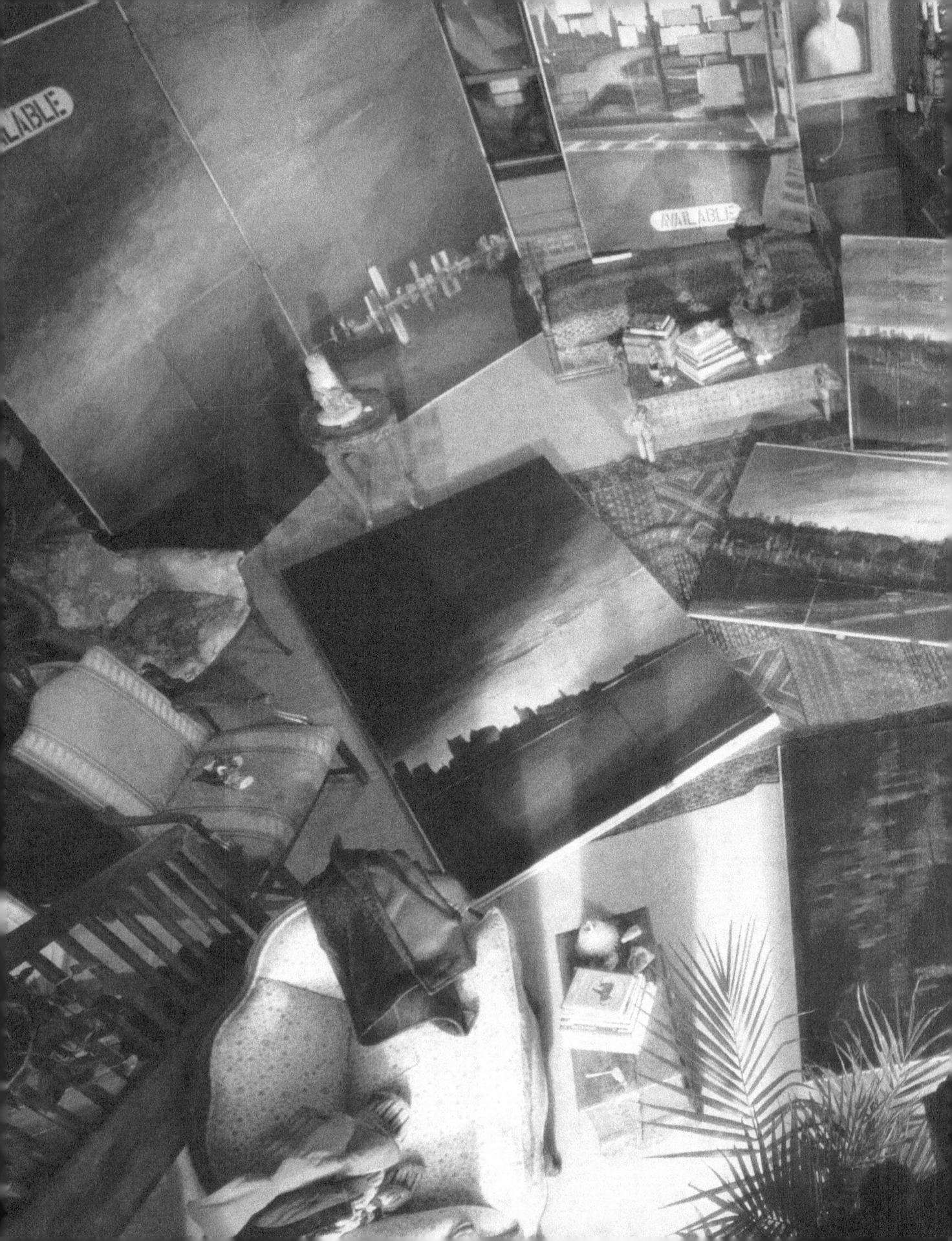

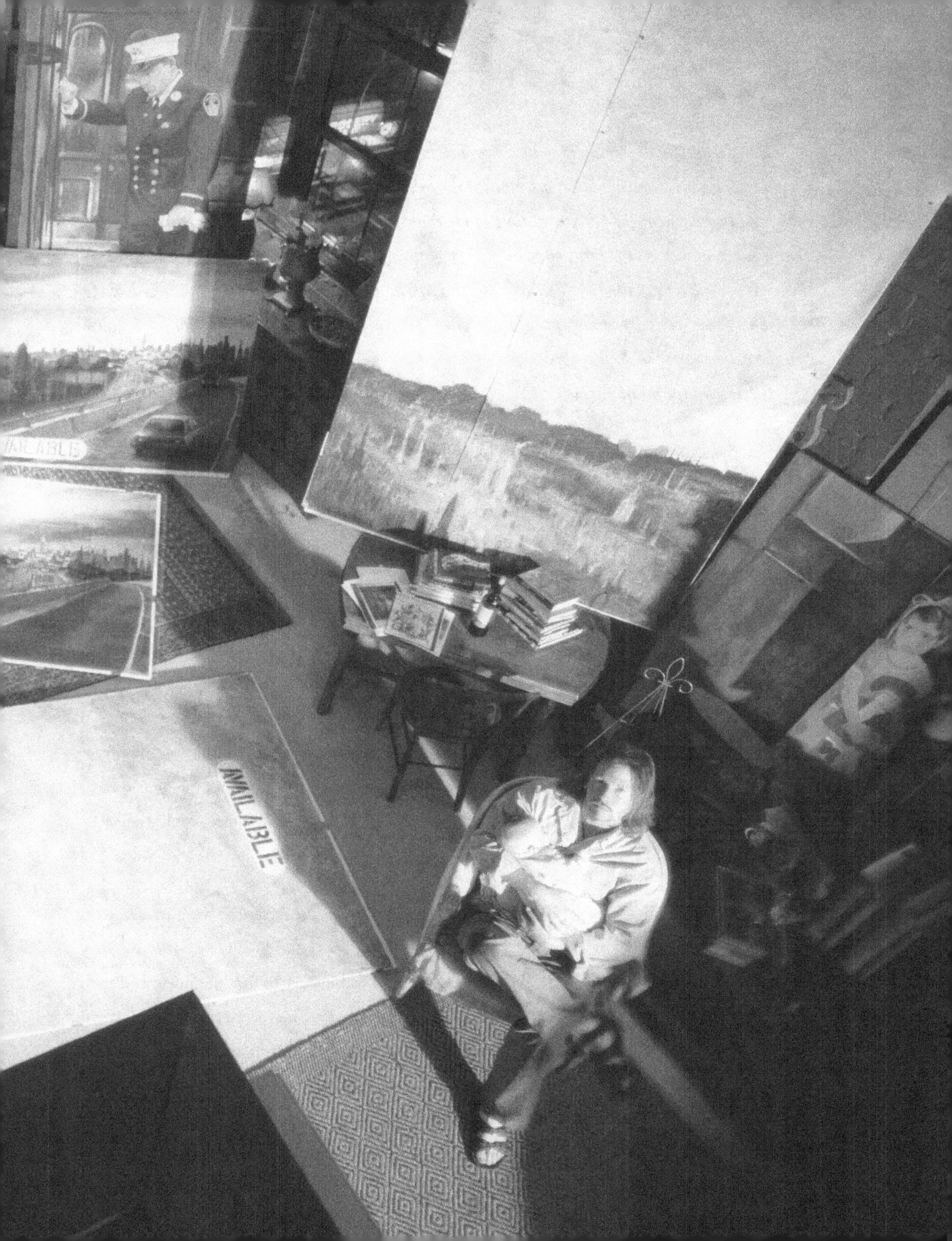

Life flows as a ripple, unseemingly so at times, but always steadfast, unmasking and unraveling itself slowly, in continuous undulations, until it doesn't. Each rippling can be seen as a fraction of something larger unseen, the passing of time made evident in a family's photo album, each page an older memory: smiling at the birth of a child; crying during the burial of a loved one; a ball caught at six years of age with dad or the catching of fish with him later in life and the reflections looking back act as gentle reminder to keep pushing forward, purposefully, during the course of life because when the action stops, so do the ripples.

—GdlH, Sketchbook entry

Studio, Astoria, Queens, 2003

English dramatic soprano Florence Easton was singing Puccini's "O mio babbino caro." The album is only one in an immense collection of classical and opera given to me by my grand-mother's girlfriend Trudy when I graduated college, right before she graduated into a nursing home. I sat in my talon-footed chair, my favorite one, listening to this gem of a song while holding tight a gem of another sort, my first born son Matthew, named after Teresa's father, barely a year old and tucked into soft little pajamas. We were waiting on the arrival of photographer Becket Logan, who was going to document my current work. Peering out a south-facing window, I wondered where these works—created because of and after 9|11, and now laid out across the studio floor— would take me. Where would they wind up in fifty or a hundred years, how'd they be received at the upcoming opening and, for the little guy looking straight up at his babbino, would they sell? Uncertainty is the artist's true course and companion.

Beyond the windowpane, it was perfectly clear. The fog, the clouds, were in my head only. I recalled the horrible moment two years earlier when Teresa and I watched from this very spot and our hearts trembled. I considered the texture and framework of that memory, and then thought of the chair in which Matthew and I sat: a hand-carved replica of a French neoclassical model, solid and sturdy, upholstered with a white, cheese-cloth-like fabric and stained here and there by paints and oils, much the same way that envelopes and books become stained with coffee and red wine when left lying around a dining room table. Aged wood and pull-out flap extensions—I thought of the table that Dad purchased from an antique shop off Route 25 out on

Long Island, long before Antiques Roadshow, when a hand-made oak table with ten oak chairs could be had for under a hundred bucks. This was back before everyone believed that what they owned carried more value than it really did, before people needed to care about getting every last nickel and dime for their possessions because their homes were still worth more than their mortgages. But the table's real value was this: Dad bargaining with the aged flower-print-dress lady who smelled of rotting flesh. With stale breath and through gaps in her mouth, she told us that her dentures were in one of the wooden dressers that lined the wall. Dust and cat hair coating everything inside the low-lit shop, including her soiled sundress, we couldn't wait to bolt out with our new purchase. I helped Dad quickly tie it atop the car so we could drive it back to our little summer home on the Island's north shore.

Over the coming weeks, I watched him restore its lost luster; and in the sun room that fronted the house, we immediately began to enjoy what would be many happy times gathered around its ovalesque shape: eating snappers caught by the dozen right down the block, at the water's edge; we used short fresh water poles in order to feel all of the fish's fight. After burying their scales and innards by the rose bushes, Esther, my Puerto Rican grandmother, who stayed while my parents worked, would pan fry the whole fish, adding flour, butter, and Adobo seasoning. Almost every day that the snappers ran, we'd sit and enjoy the day's catch. Then there was the arroz con pollo that my mother cooked at least once a week; I can still see the tomato sauce and fried green peppers against the swirling browns of the tabletop. Once, when the table was set up to hold its maximum, I told a Jewish joke to a gathering of my older brother's friends. I was thirteen or fourteen at the time and, being polite, asked beforehand if anyone was Jewish; they all smiled and said "no" collectively, except for Big Bruce, who just smiled. After the telling, they all laughed, not because the joke was funny but because Danny, my older brother, cracked an egg over my head and proclaimed loudly, "The yolks on you!" Big Bruce was Jewish. Danny and his friends took their time prizing my mortified expression and first lesson in table manners.

Moments to recognize and claim what really matters in one's life are always there: like the first Christmas Eve spent with Teresa, decorating a little artificial, silver-tinseled tree taken from the apartment Esther lived in for 65 years; the tree I'd decorate as a kid every year during sleepovers,

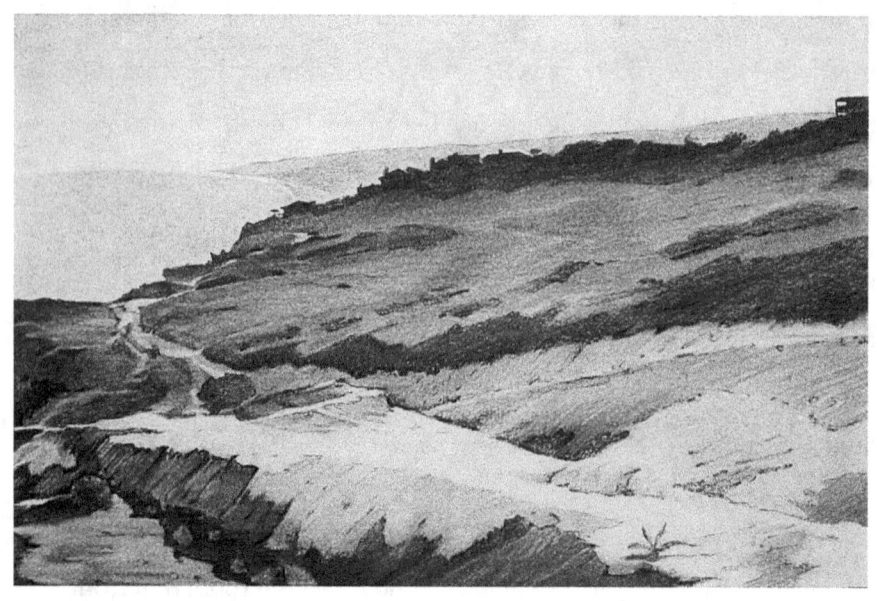

which was purchased at Sak's Fifth Avenue when Dad was still a boy. Esther had hand-blown German ornaments, original ones from the 1930s and 40s—doves, musical instruments, fruits and the like—carefully wrapped and packaged away each year in shoe and hat boxes from Wannamaker's and Depina's department stores, where Esther worked long before she ran the Children's Department at Sak's Fifth Avenue. Each boyhood Christmas provided an opportunity to retrieve these things from the top shelf of a packed closet that also stored crayons, Cutty Sark, and Listerine. The warmth of the tree's lights glowed and spread across the small living quarter, casting shadows of yellow, red and green onto aged white walls. The lights would sparkle in the cherished hanging ornaments, twinkling like the star that guided the Three Wise Men to Bethlehem.

On our first Christmas together, Teresa placed the tree atop the bar in our loft. As she unpacked boxes, I started to tell her to handle the ornaments carefully: "These are family heirlooms, my dear, especially that first one." It was in the shape of a bell, pulled from the top, wrapped in tissue paper older than the two of us combined; she held it up to ring it, but it fell out of her hand, smashing to pieces on the cement floor; a bittersweet demise and the bell's last toll. I can still see her saddened, heartbroken look and hear her "I'm so sorry" apology. How could I mind or be upset when the most beautiful woman was sitting opposite, sorrowful, and apologetic? Lessons on learning to put what matters most front and center, though, aren't always so obvious.

LIFE LESSONS: PART 1

The artist's charcoal—the charred remains of a tree, a once-living entity—has been an easily accessible tool for creative expression since the dawn of mankind and was selected for use in the "Billboard Series". With what better medium would an artist comment upon 9|11 than with ashes?

—GdlH (catalog entry for The Billboard Series)

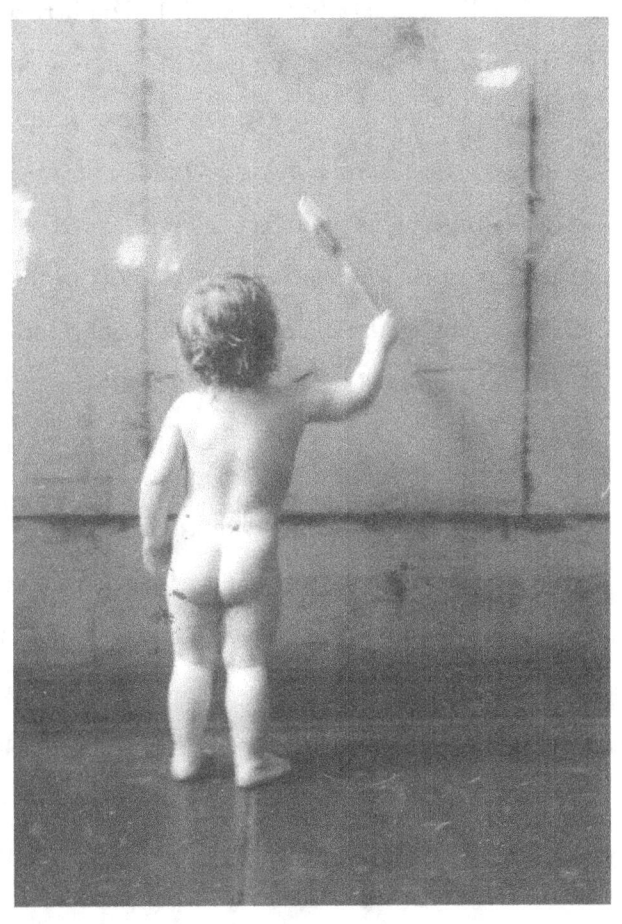

He grabs hold of the French easel to pull himself up, wobbles over to a chair, then to a table loaded with brushes and charcoal sticks and looks to see which will be his toy for the day. The studio has become his own little playhouse. So long as he's not chewing on aluminum tubes filled with cadmiums or lead, it's fine. I watch him carefully, he giggling always, as he watches me, seeking approval on the brush chosen or to see if I'm laughing also. Matthew's tiny body, his milky white flesh and loose baby diaper hanging precariously from his chubby, cherubic bottom, draw a sharp contrast to the art work I've created during the first year of his life: dark swirls of compound charcoal, extra black. Like an alien mold, they gradually invaded the studio, multiplying every week and month. At night, it was an apocalyptic landscape—multiple large billboard replicas, all empty of advertising. The process of drawing starts up again. The clean white of new paper is wiped with charcoal dust, the middle tone thus formed. Darker darks can be added with charcoals of specific density, or light can emerge by subtracting the middle tone with an eraser. But what to draw, exactly?

However, this first: the black smoke spewing from the North Tower, the phone calls to friends in the South Tower and the Federal Reserve Bank, the collapse, Teresa's scream, the shattered glass refracting bright sunlight, the static on the television, news on a radio, incessant phone calls to friends and family, the disbelief, traffic into and out of the city stopped, arrival of the military at all bridge and tunnel crossings, jets overhead, a resolute mayor, a president and country standing tall, American flags, outpourings of love and kindness. But there's more, as the titles of the work capture: the "Exodus" began almost immediately. As soon as traffic could flow again, it seemed to move only outbound. U-Haul trucks everywhere, packed and heading east. Bagpipes from funerals arriving daily at McSorley's. All the "Stoic and Vacant" billboards because who's paying attention to advertisers? Cranes standing idle in their Maspeth home yard, construction halted everywhere, stirring a "Post Perspective: The Sky Was The Limit Then." Will it continue to be limitless, as politicians and developers debate the need for ever-higher buildings? And what to do with an "Available: 16 Acre Plot" in the center of the universe? Lower Manhattan seemed doomed as death's shadow descended long and ominous over Brooklyn, seemingly forever. Was this the city's post 9|11 "Inheritance"?

The Billboard Series grew into my most ambitious body of work accomplished until then, both in scale and scope. A first-hand account of events witnessed and observations made on the days and months after the attacks; pictorial commentaries on what was and what was to come, apart from the obvious: uncertainty. Goya commemorated Spanish resistance to Napoleon's armies during the 1808 Peninsular War in his "Third Of May" masterpiece. The Billboard Series, I hoped, would be just as epic, providing a glimpse into the city's metamorphosis and marking the beginning of the war on terrorism. But it also took the form of plea to keep commerce and philanthropy alive during New York's darkest hour; to capture and rally for resilience.

And how could I use anything but charcoal to work, and how could I not work large? Drawings measuring from five feet wide and eight feet high to twenty feet long and ten feet high. The show would be installed at 48 Wall Street—the site where Alexander Hamilton founded America's oldest bank. To underscore this new, unwarranted skyline and the surrounding times, drawings would be mounted atop sixteen-foot-tall Erector-Set-like scaffoldings, mimicking actual bill-

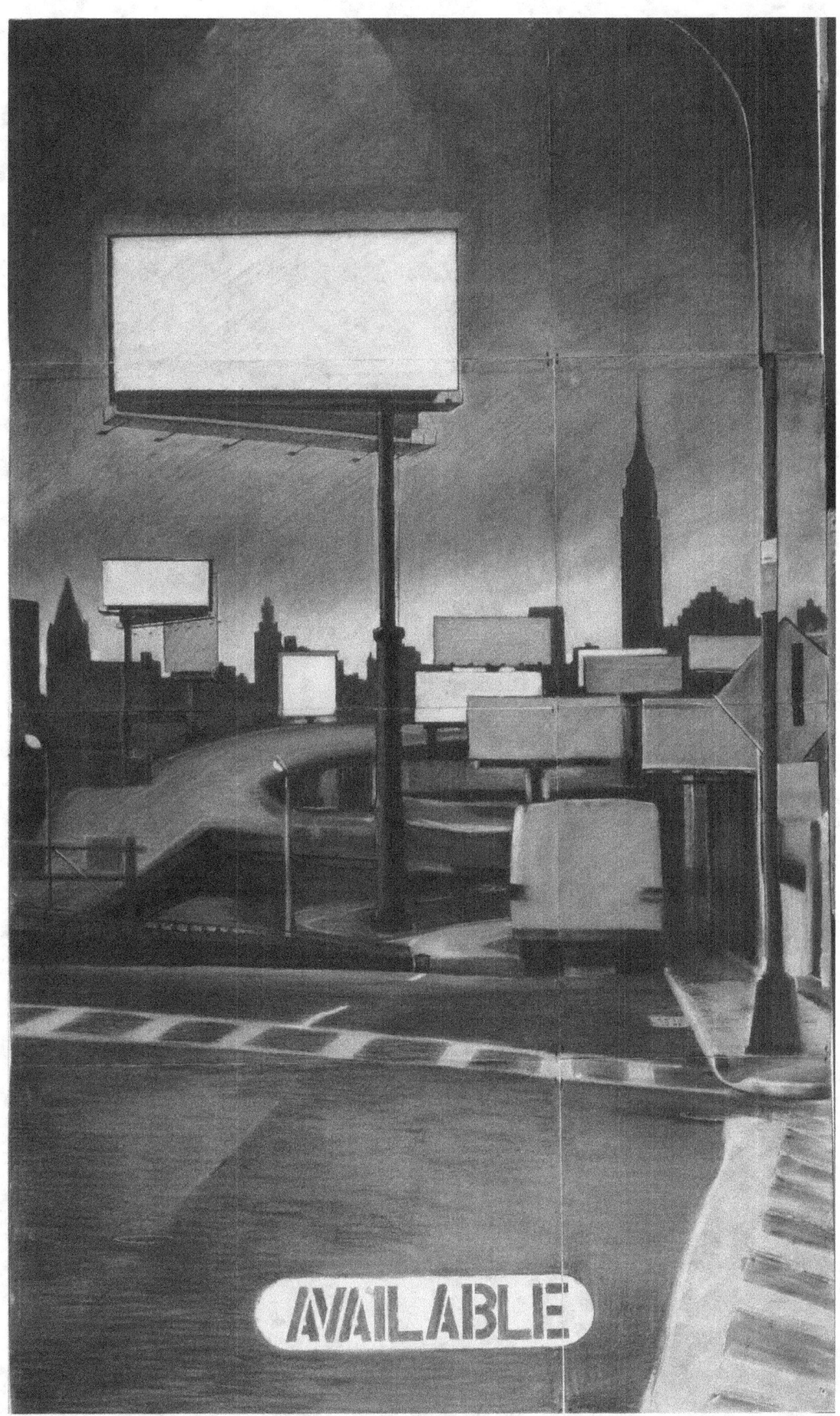

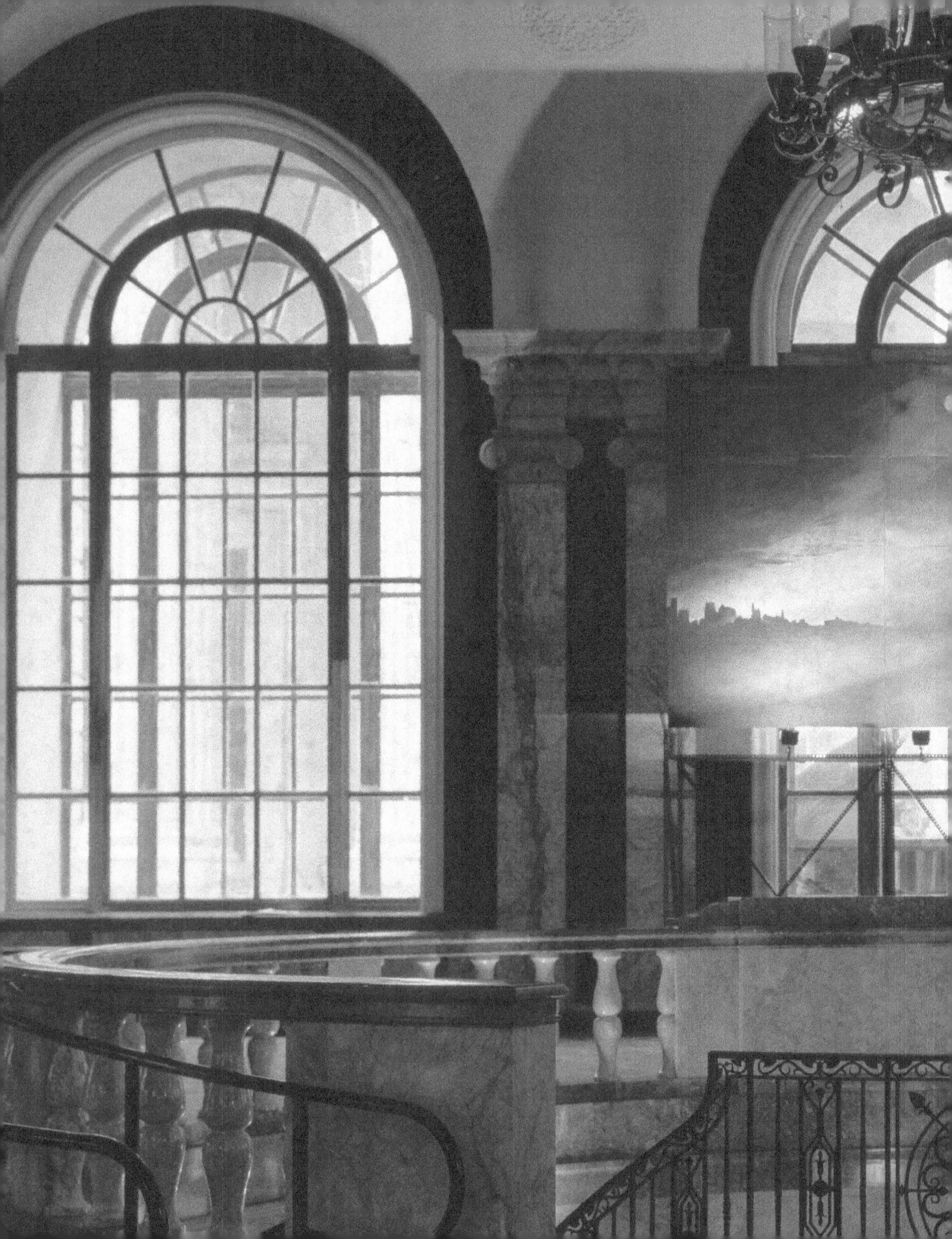

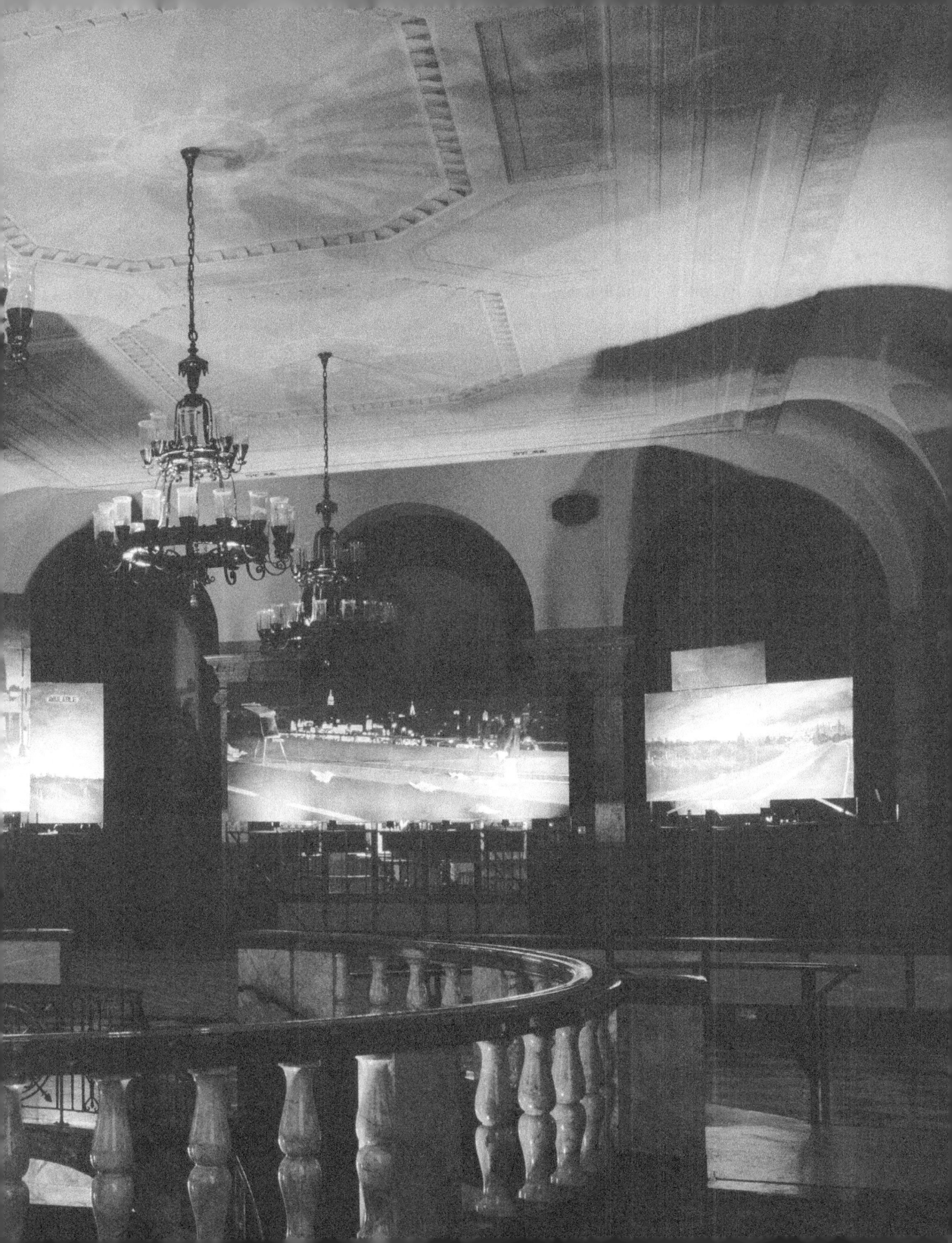

boards, complete with dramatic underlighting. It was an ambitious undertaking, but I once again convinced my "creditor" that it was worth it. The massive lobby in the original Bank of New York building on the corner of two of the city's oldest streets, Wall and Williams, didn't come cheaply for the week, nor did the catalogs, lights, the metal to build the scaffolding, the hundreds of sheets of paper for the drawings, the foam board that backed the drawings and the wood panels that backed the foam board; the electrical wiring, the truck rentals, the assistants hired to mount the show, the money wasted on the publicist with a coke problem I didn't know she had until I found out that she was in Bellevue, all out of money and publicity. But this, the first big show in my hometown, was all gonna be worth it—"I promise"—yes, it had to be. After all, I had managed to convince Clear Channel, who owns half the billboards in America, to provide me, rent free for an entire month, the transformation and mounting of one of The Billboard Series drawings into an actual 50' x 60' billboard smack dab in the middle of Times Square, at the corner Broadway and 48th street. The drawing, titled "New York, New York," was conceptualized as a play on art as life and life in the city as commerce: I sold advertising space within the actual drawing. Corporate sponsorship as tribute to art and commerce. And with proceeds going to Art Start, a NYC nonprofit enriching the lives of inner-city youth through art and culture, the purchase of ad space provided corporations an opportunity to market their philanthropic views. The strategy worked. A number of New York-based companies purchased tiny spaces in the drawing that weren't so tiny when printed for Times Square. The billboard looked great, too. That it also doubled as an advertisement for the show downtown wasn't so shabby either. It was a proud moment in a young artist's life.

The exhibition, however, didn't pan out the way I expected or had Teresa believe it would. After the opening night party with friends, family, and guests of Art Start, nobody else showed up during the remaining days. Sure, I could put a little blame on the cokehead for not promoting the show according to the plan she convincingly sold me, but I and a few friends worked it as best we could with the little time and money left. It was more than that, though. I could count on two hands and maybe one foot how many people came in off the street during lunch or after work during the exhibition's' short run. Each day, from 9AM to 7PM, I stood outside in a futile attempt to solicit viewers—"take a peek at The Billboard Series," I'd say—as if I were P.T. Barnum describing something inside a colored tent. I felt like a sucker instead, offering free catalogs and refreshments to see

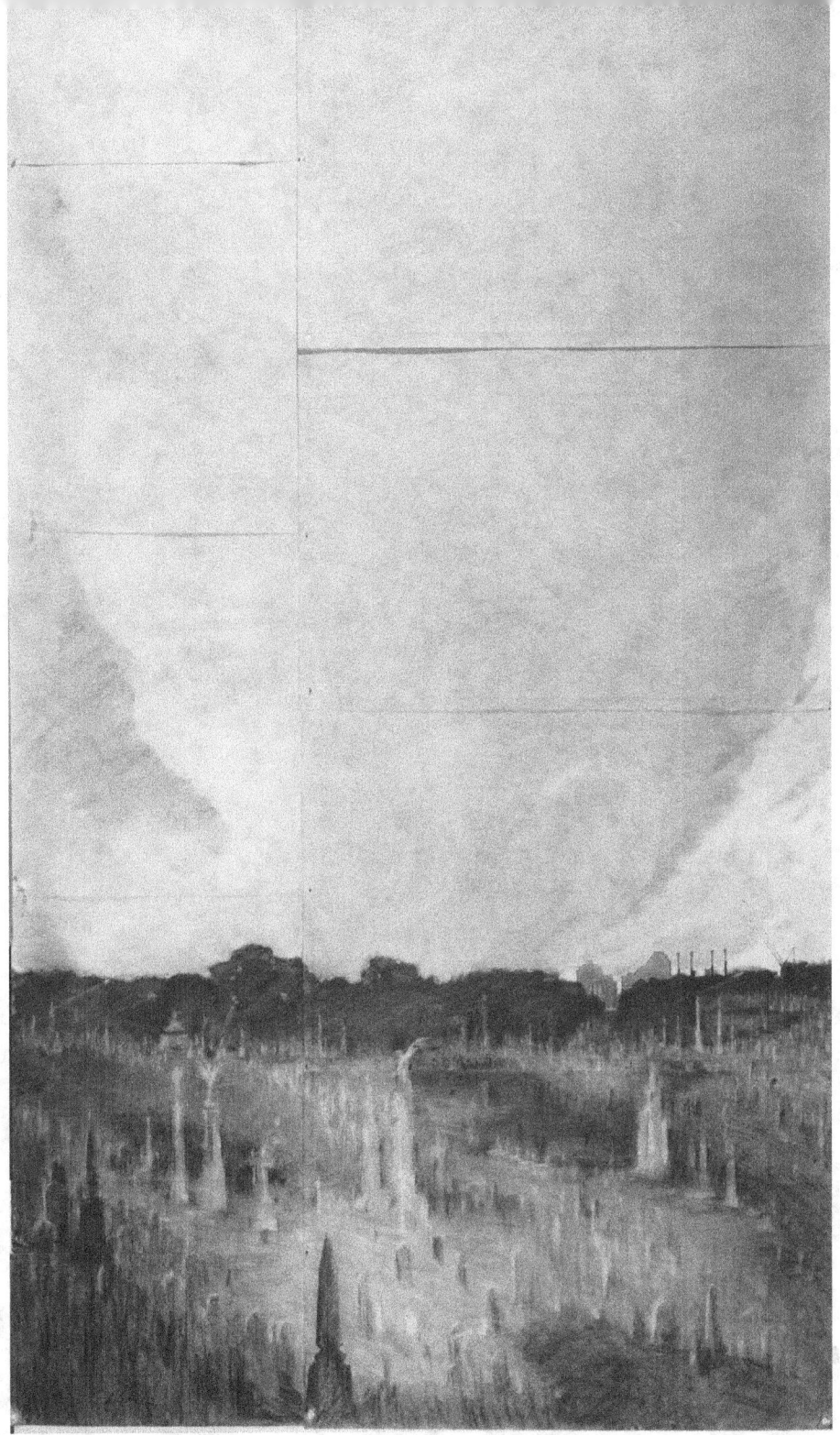

art. But they didn't want to see or hear any of it. And who could blame them? Most were there that

day and most, it seemed, didn't want to stick around downtown any longer than they had to; the

wounds were vivid on their faces as they quickly walked past me, shaking their heads "No, thank

you" or sneering, "You gotta be kidding, 9|11 art?" Which way to egress?

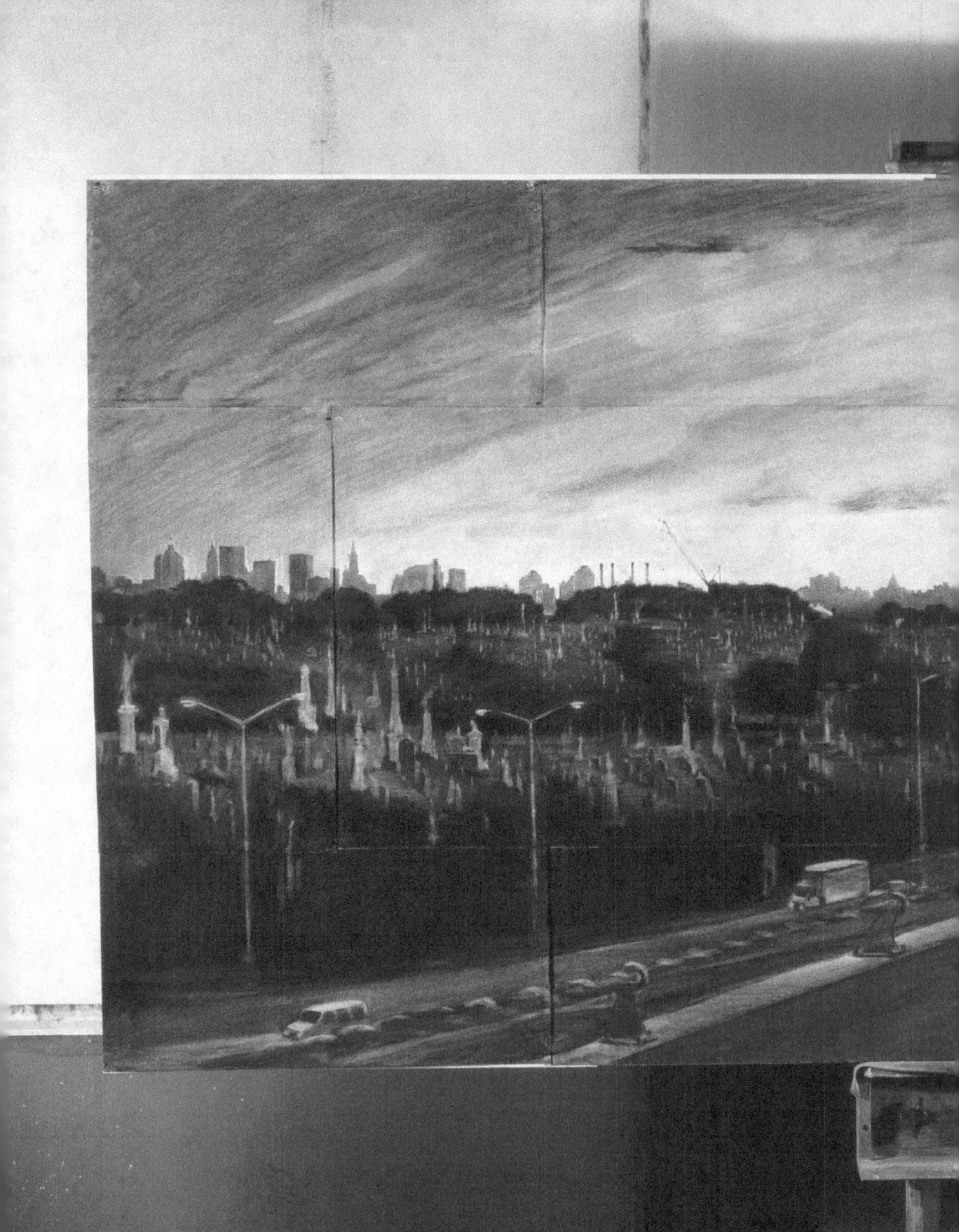

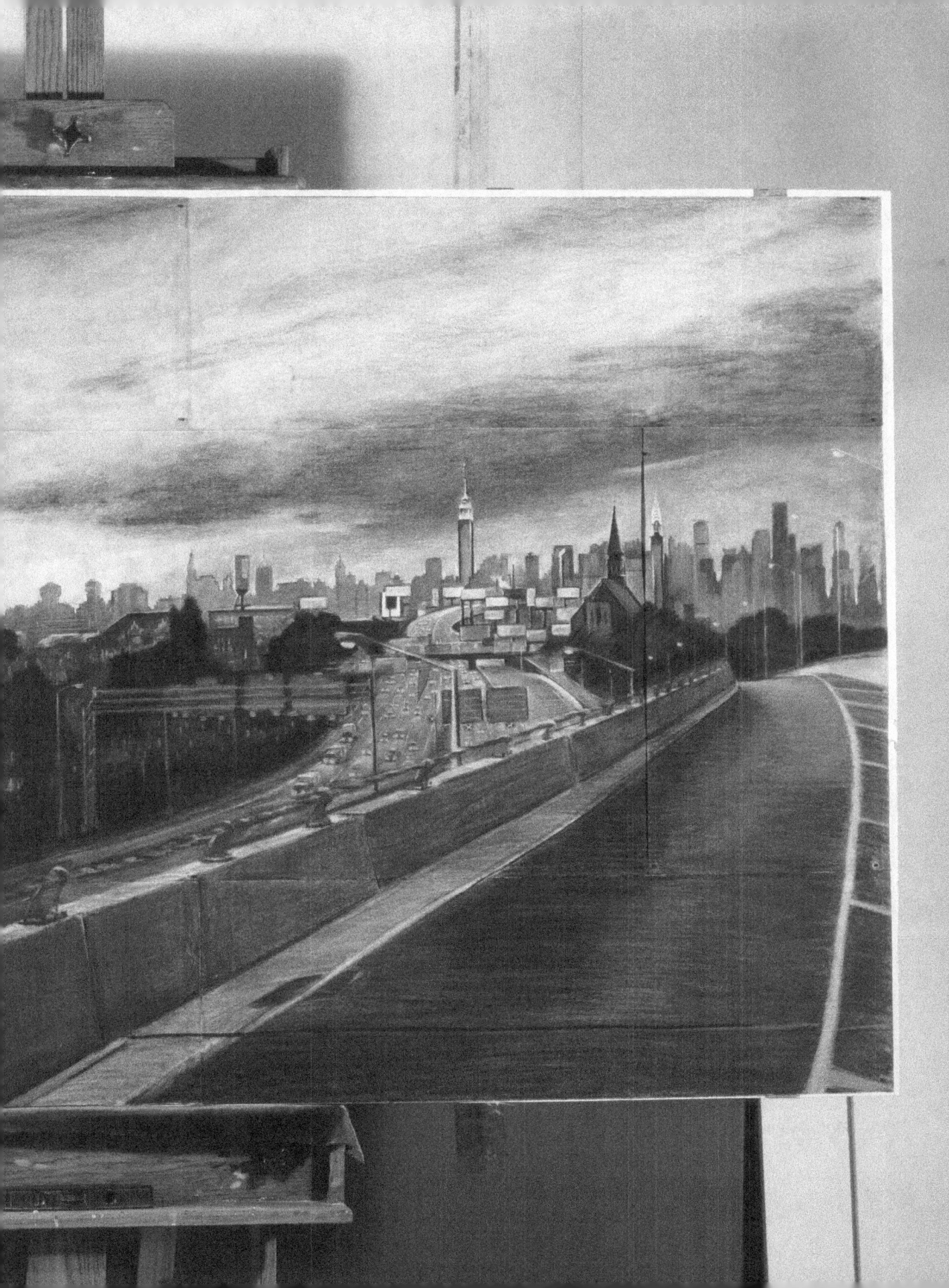

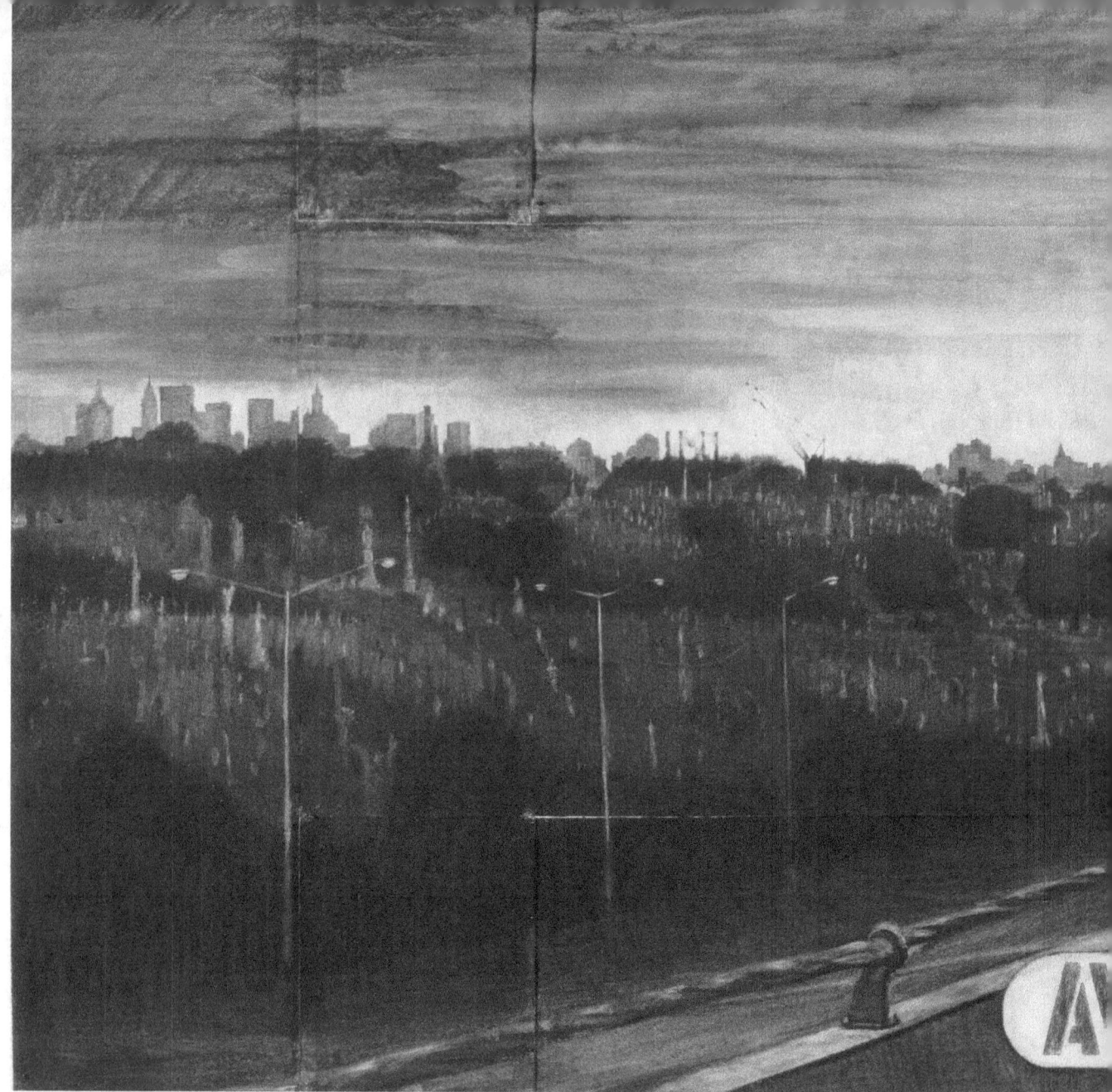

I was too eager to show work too personal. Too dark. My response to 9|11 arrived too soon. I couldn't wait to take the show down and hide. Each day, like a saving grace, Teresa would arrive with Matthew in tow to pick me up. Each day she asked the same questions: "How was your day, Gregory?" and "Did anyone show up today?" At that, I'd cringe.

Once, I answered, "Yes, Becket Logan came in unexpectedly with his camera and shot the installation for me, no charge."

"Well, that was very nice, wasn't it?"

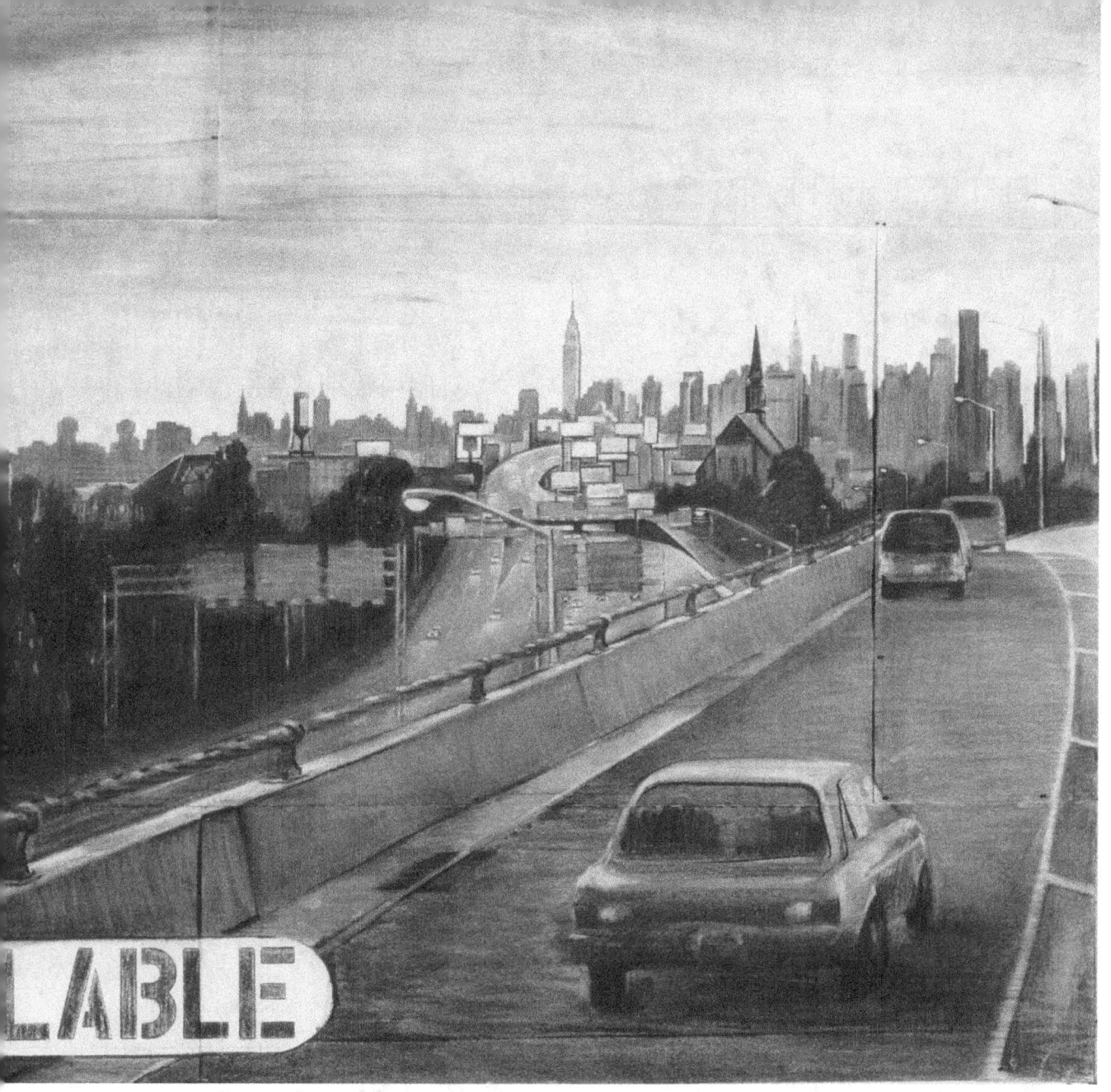

"It sure was, baby." I tried to smile, but the smile went the way of all the people who had passed earlier in the day. It was the lowest point in my life. Even given the success of executing the work, selling the ads, donating money to a good cause, launching the opening, securing the billboard in Times Square, I felt like a failure. The bottom line was that no one showed up after the opening, or wanted to, and nothing ever sold. Months later, The New York Historical Society would acquire "Exodus" for their permanent collection, but somehow it didn't seem to fix anything, didn't adjust my negative vibes into positive ones, or make future prospects appear brighter. It was a cherry on a melted, ice cream sundae.

LIFE LESSONS: PART 2

Be sure of it, give me the ocular proof.

—Shakespeare

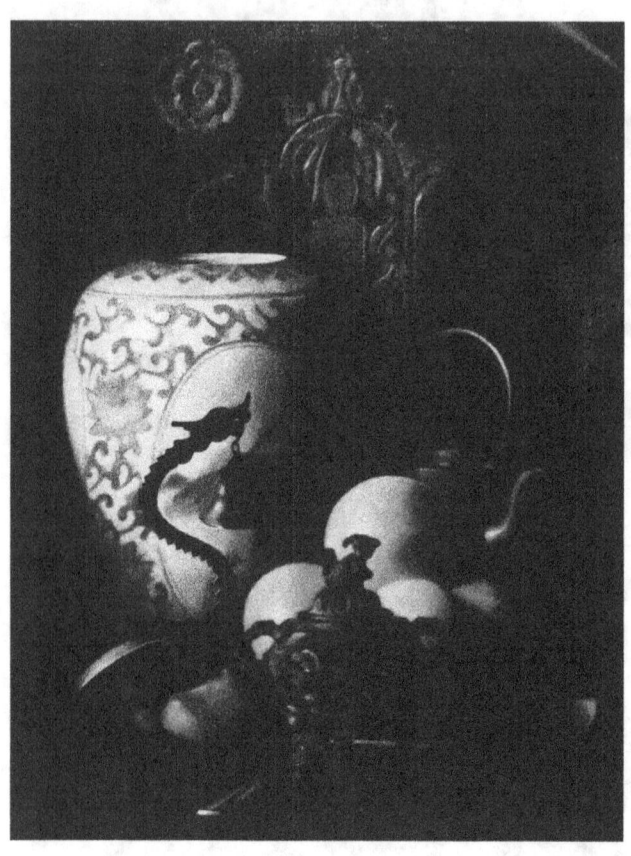

While a student learning to draw and paint life representationally, the whole point was to see and render form, line, and value accurately. To "keep looking" until "truth" comes into focus and is captured honestly, not filtered through imagination or style. There was a week when I was painting fresh oranges. Each morning, entering the studio with eager eyes, thinking I had nailed their form and color accurately the day prior, I discovered how off I was, how poor the painting was, so bad, in fact, that I stood before the easel in disbelief. "Am I blind?" I wondered. Line, color, shape, value—everything was god-awfully off. This time, it was because of my naïveté, and inexperience, that I didn't realize oranges shrink and that their color changes as the days go by. I didn't know that it could be as subtle as clouds moving across the sky, affecting perception of value and hue. I was chasing something transient—a still life on the move, so to speak—and it was an eye opener to say the least. To see simple oranges painted wrong first thing in the morning, I continued to learn from that experience as the years went by. Sometimes we just can't see what's right in front of our eyes: the good, the bad, the indifferent, or the absolutely ridiculous. But when you've been made a fool by fruit in a Delft bowl, you have a little something going for you: humility, combined, somewhat ironically, with an abiding trust in one's own sensibilities.

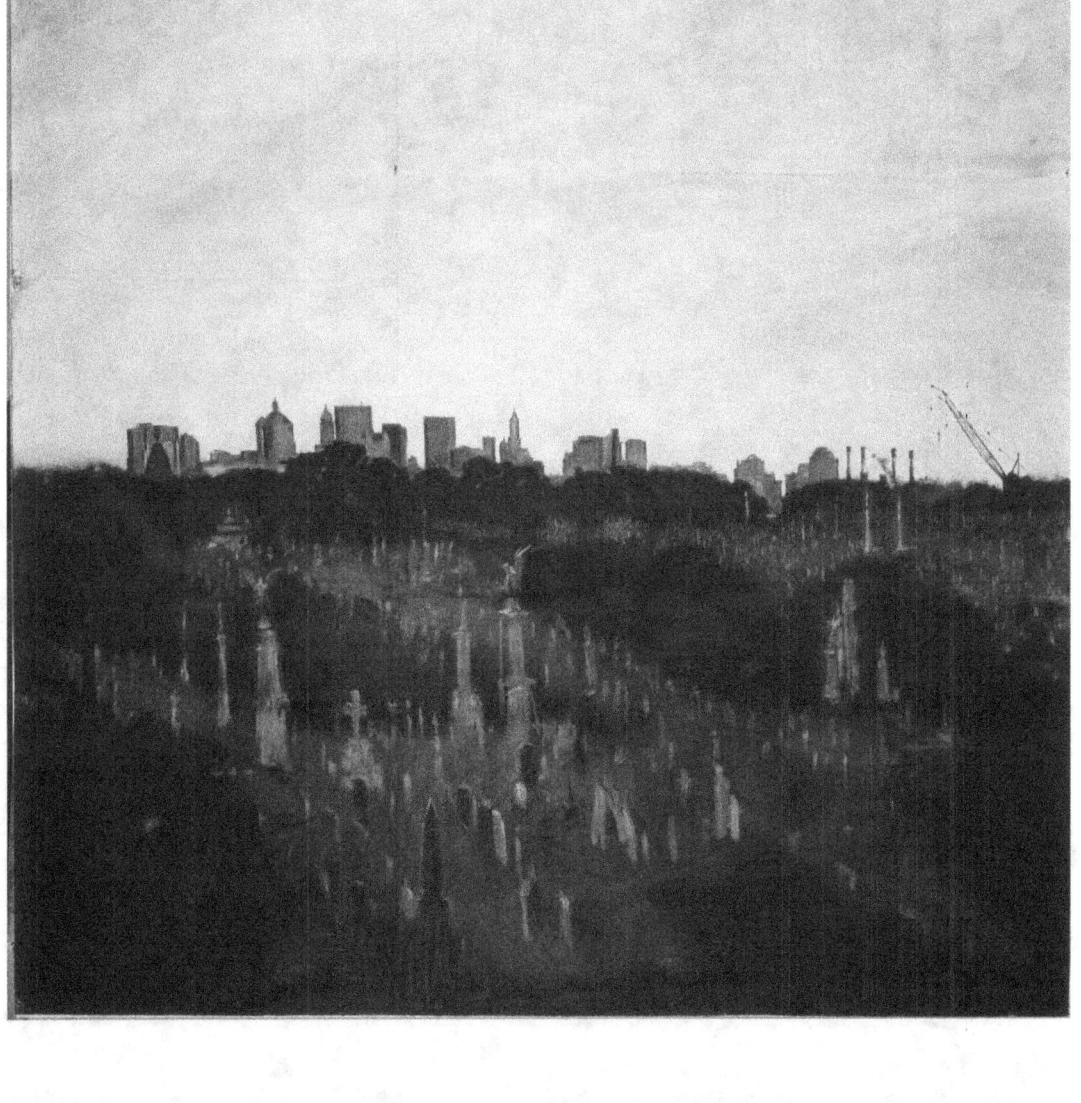

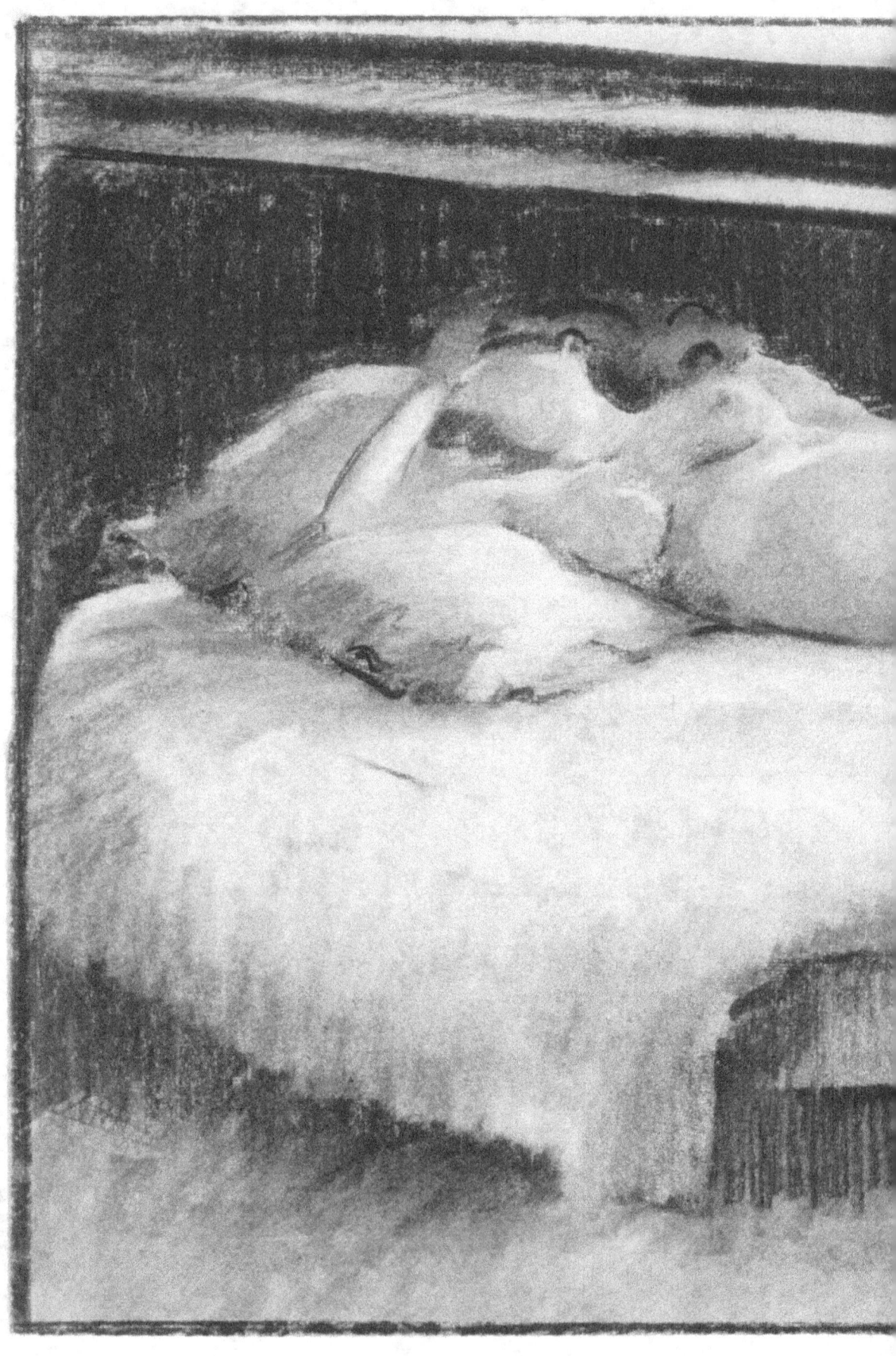

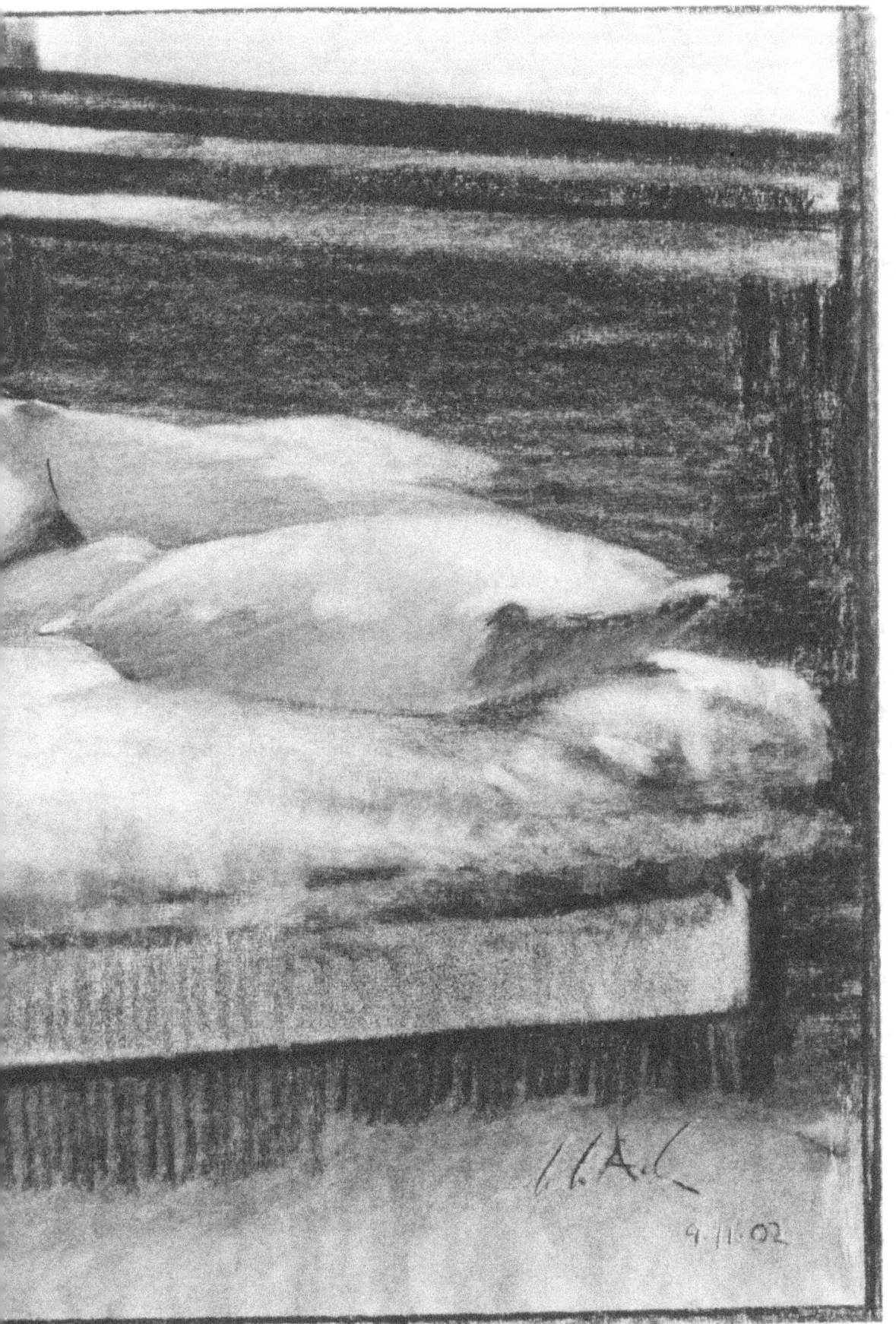

9/11.02

September 11th, 2002

Note: Outside it was clear and sunny.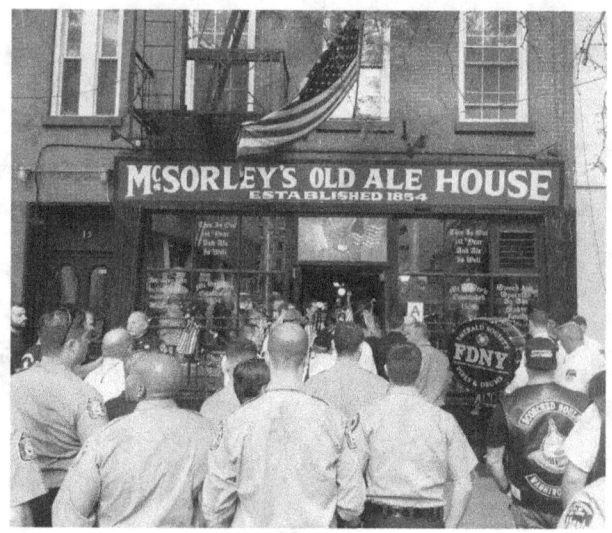
Inside, Teresa laid sound asleep, naked and nine
months pregnant. Knowing that a child was to
enter our lives at any moment made the one-
year anniversary of 9|11 stranger and more sur-
real. The anticipation of fatherhood, combined
with the sight of motherhood, brought joy and
delight to our bedroom scene. I sat there, on the
edge of the bed, and tried looking ahead: would

I go buy two coffees and a cheese Danish for breakfast exactly as I did one year ago? Would my wife
join me at the table and read the paper, or will she feel tired and prefer staying in bed to wandering
dreamily in and out of the maternity ward? By noon, I'd be behind the bar at McSorley's, waiting
for the influx following Ground Zero services. The ancient sound of bagpipes echoed in my head
while images of an uncertain future as "Dad," "provider," and "artist" swirled. Anxiety tightened
its grip on my breath—slowly, stealthily—like the pigeons that sometimes wobbled their way into
the loft through windows left open, only to "swoosh" away. But the anxiety, unlike the pigeons, was
not so easy to detect, and there was no window to slam shut.

Teresa, however, was easy to notice and behold. She was ravishing; voluptuous and wom-
anly lying beside me, still and peaceful. I quietly got up off the bed and moved the French easel
into position, put up the clipboard with a fresh sheet of paper, and started the day the best way
I could, by drawing her—an expecting mother. I worked fast and without noise, save the barely
audible sound of the charcoal stick quickly grinding down against the paper. Halfway through, her
eyes tried opening but their lids fought back, yet not before allowing them a slight glimpse of me at
work, which made her smile and settle comfortably back into her dreams. Normally, I don't sign
my works; a signature can be ruinous to the composition. It's even more rare that I date a piece: it's
a way for me to not remember how many years have passed. But today I didn't care. I etched name
and date across the bottom right.

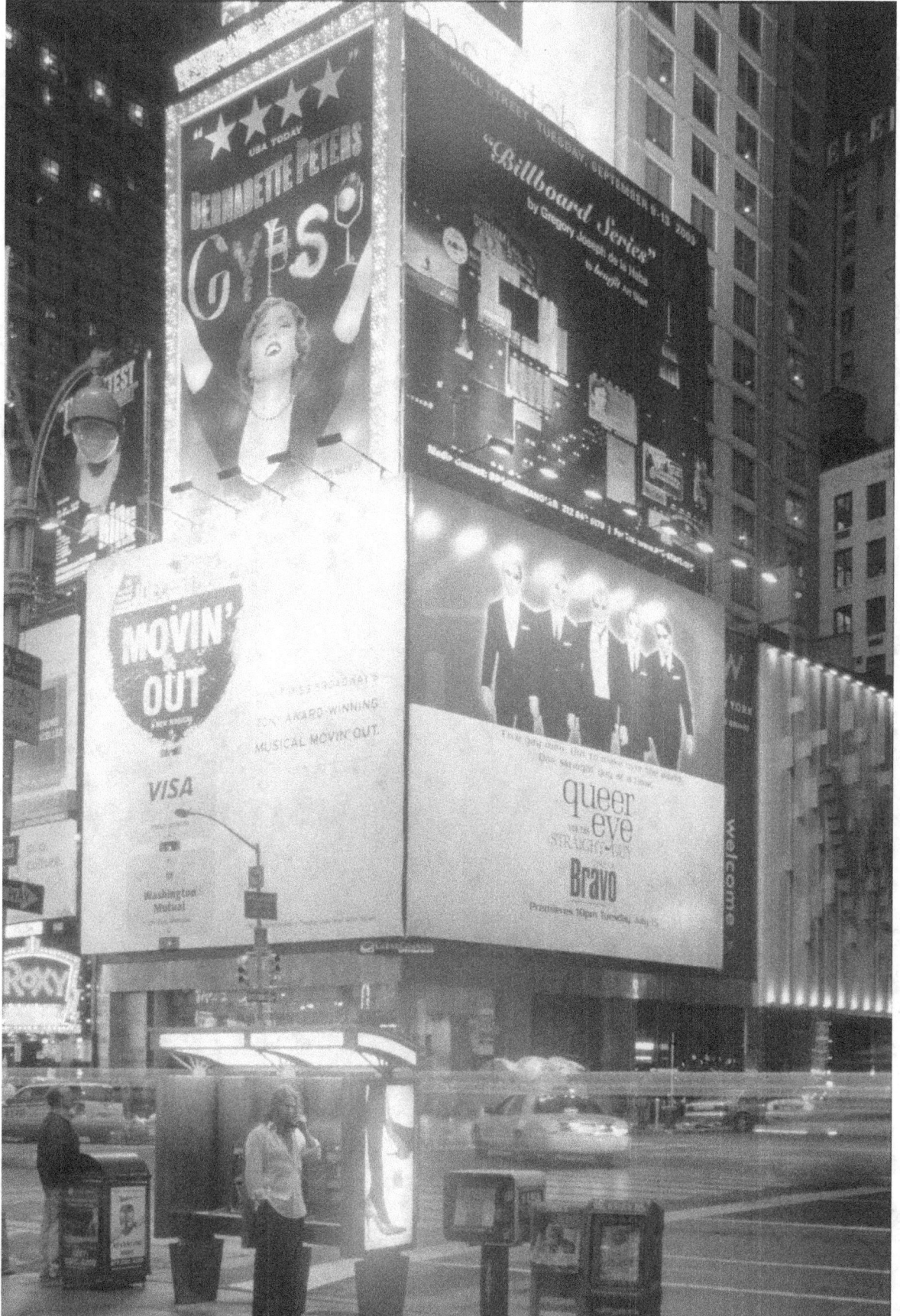

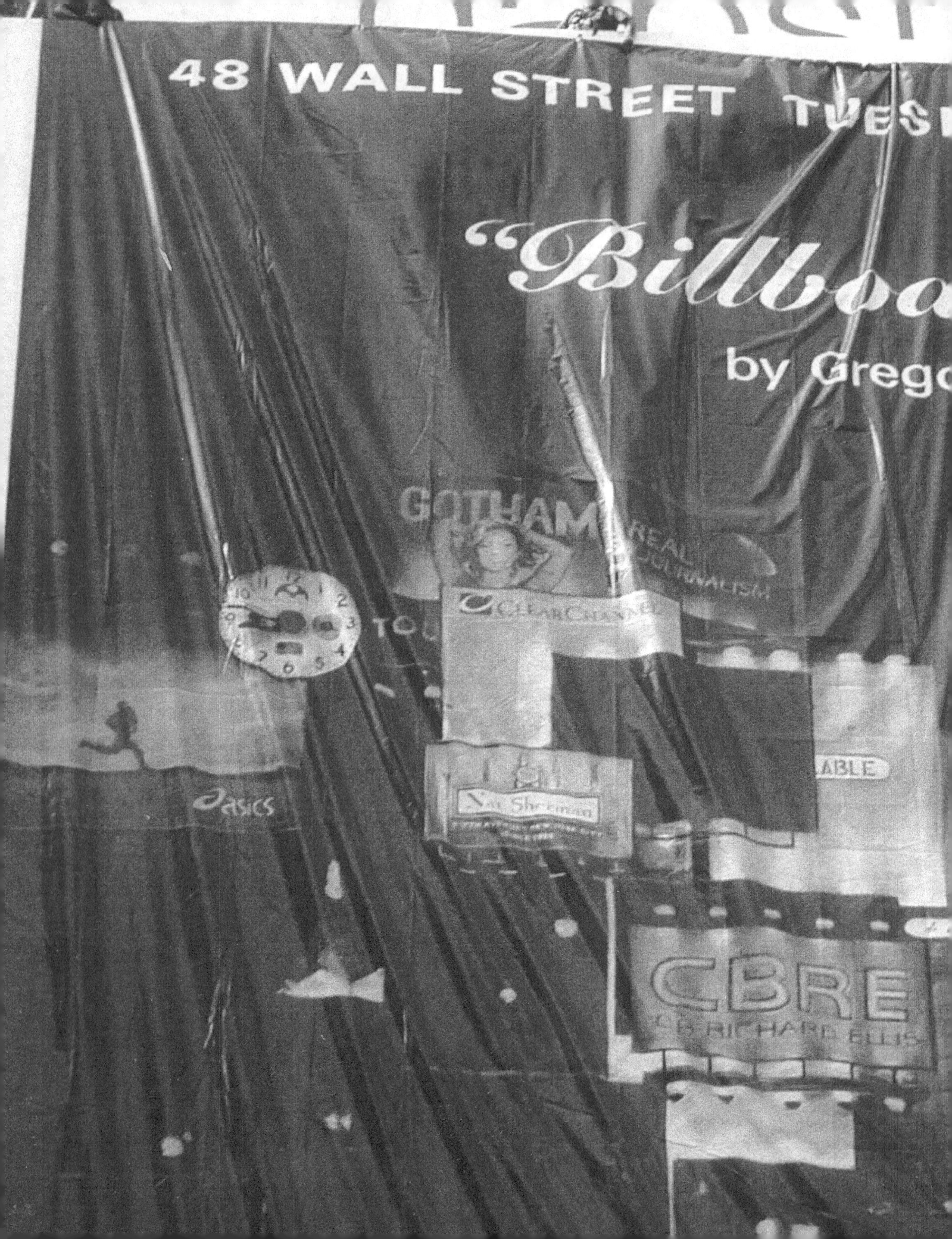
48 WALL STREET TUES
"Billboa
by Grego
GOTHAM
REAL
JOURNALISM
asics
CBRE
CB RICHARD ELLIS

SEPTEMBER 9-13 2003

d Series"

Joseph de la Hab*

to *benefit* Art Start

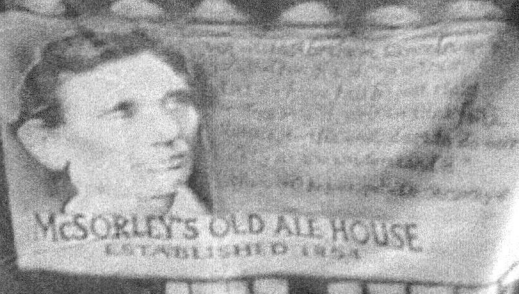

McSORLEY'S OLD ALE HOUSE
ESTABLISHED 1854

CUSHMAN &
WAKEFIELD.

15 East 7th Street, September 11, 2002, 11:00am

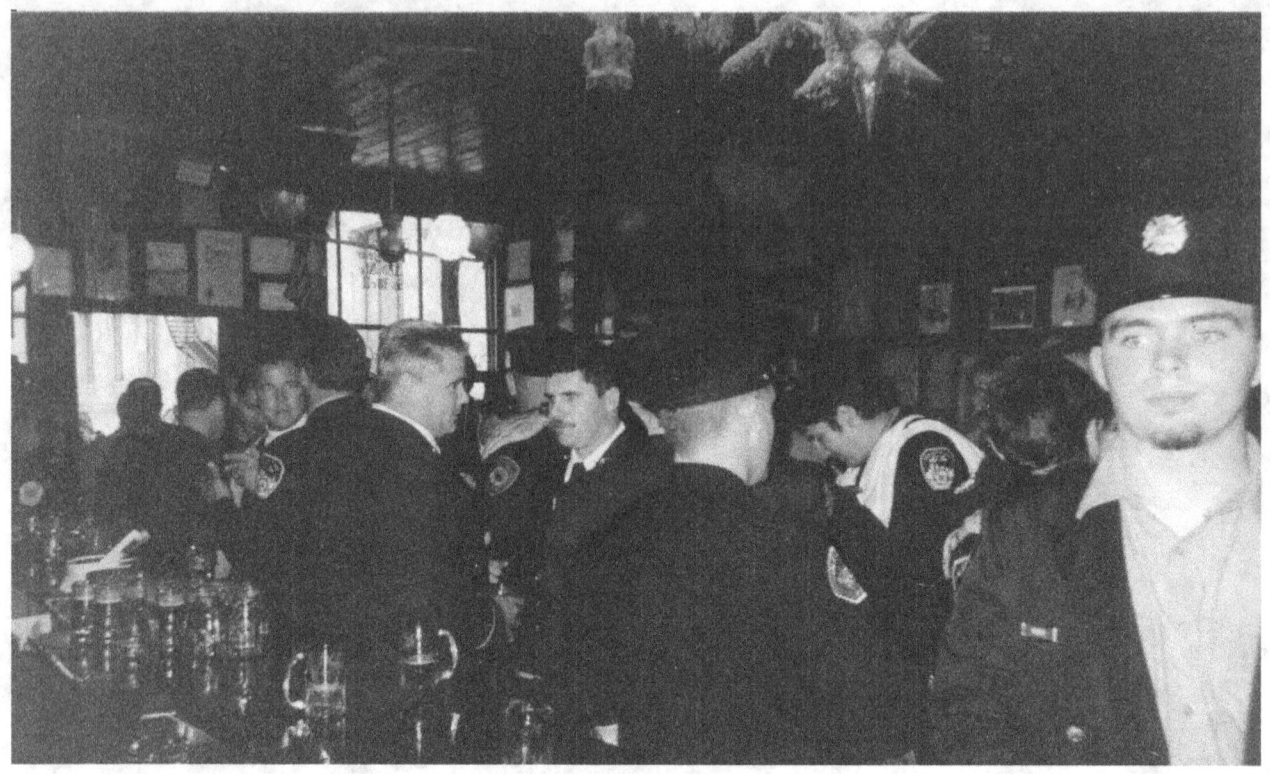

A home away from home for many, McSorley's has been a place of refuge and solace for New York's workingman and for the Finest and Bravest for over 150 years. As expected, the place was packed. Firemen and policemen from the world over filled the bar: from New Zealand, Australia, Great Britain, Germany, Canada, Los Angeles, Chicago, Boston; upstate New York, New Jersey, and Long Island, all decked-out in their finest full-dress uniforms. Out front, it seemed that the crowd of men and women snaked all the way back to West and Vesey streets. Throughout the day, many asked me to mind their caps. I placed them behind the bar, behind the wishbones that hailed from another time of great loss, atop porcelain mugs a hundred years old, in front of pictures of good men who did their best for country during the times they lived, caps piled five, six, ten high across the entire backside of a bar whose history and stories run deep and tight within the fabric that is New York City. Amongst the crowd were friends and familiar faces, like the great guys from Rescue 4 in Queens, a specialized unit that lost six on 9|11 and would lose 3 more in an Astoria, Queens hardware store blaze in a few year's time.

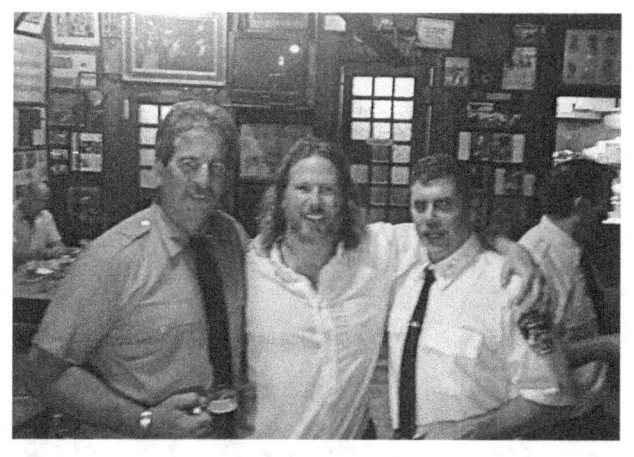

Richie Schmidt, also known as "Big Rich" because of his 6' 5" frame, was one of the Rescue 4 crew. After the attack, he never left the site, searching tirelessly not just for fellow brothers but also for the body of a grief-stricken woman's husband, a man who was also his friend, and fellow firefighter. After 30 days, he found his dear friend's body. So when Big Rich asked permission to stand on the bar to give a speech at precisely 3:43PM, the time signifying the number of men lost, all I could do was offer a heartfelt smile and reply, "Of course, my friend." I pointed to where I thought best for him to stand. But how was he going to fit? His head would surely hit the ceiling, or would it? And then the biggest concern: would the 150-year-old bar support his massive frame? Everything would be OK, I assured myself. McSorley's has a way of watching over itself. The spirits occupying the ale house's soaked walls, floorboards, and bar would also watch over this gentle giant, who suddenly jumped five feet off the ground while standing shoulder to shoulder in a jam-packed room. It was as though the spirits of the fallen, and the spirits of McSorley's, had lifted Big Rich straight up and off the floor; in turn, he mended the spirits of all those in attendance, sharing his fortitude, his generous, brother-ly soul. And there I was, standing behind the bar, watching, serving; minding the old saloon on East 7th street and all its larger-than-life patrons; minding it for my wife's family, minding it for my son, car-ing for a moment that I would one day share with him. The sawdust on the floor soaked up more than spilled ale that day

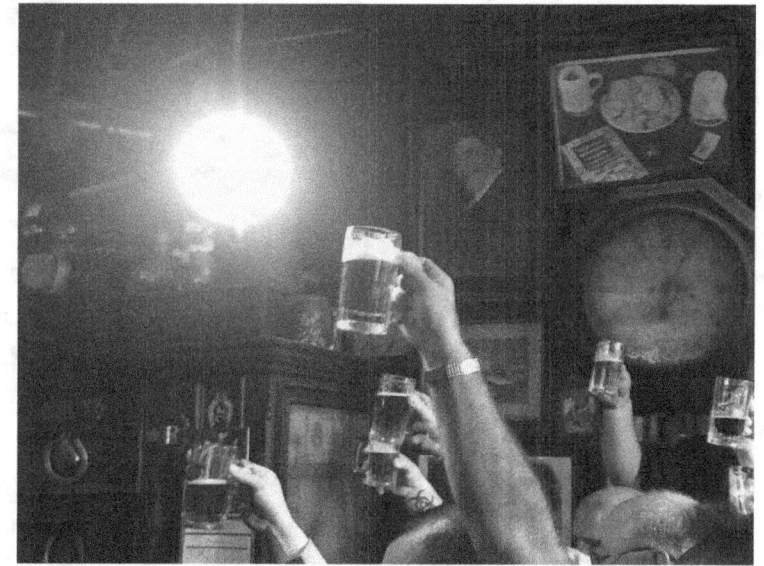

CONTINUING FORMATIONS

"One's art goes as far and as deep as one's love goes."
—Andrew Wyeth

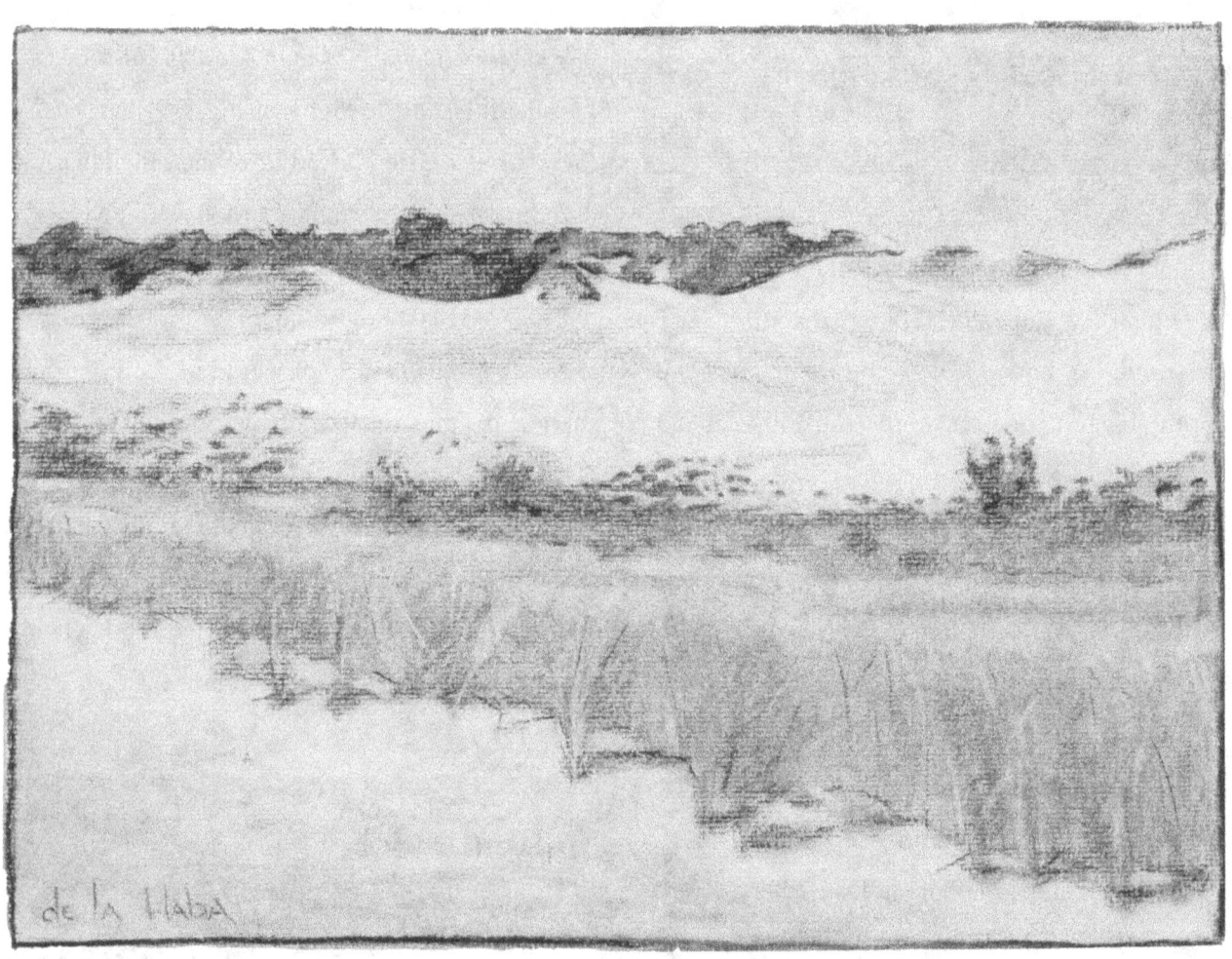

de la Haba

    The perceived ratio of value to cost perpetually readjusts over time. Onward it goes, frenetically, slowed only for intermittent price checks, full-out reality checks and, in some instances, a wish for a total refund on past actions and purchases. But there's no turning back, ever, and there can't be any regrets. How can there be? Regrets are tacks in your pockets. I try to keep as little in mine as possible. The tolls keep adding up but so, too, does the work. What does it all amount to at the end of the day? The paintings on the walls and alongside them, three, four, five deep; the drawings under the bed (the safest place to lay them flat) and those works unseen, in the closet upstairs or in storage, out of sight, like the countless hours tucked forever beneath each surface of every finished work. Retrieving the sweat equity put into them year after year and the constant uphill struggle. Stored paintings by a nobody are not a tradable commodity. If only artists could live off pleasure and joy and pay bills accordingly.

Paternal responsibilities vis-à-vis the circumstances of the emerging artist: If the studio building crumpled to the ground tomorrow, what would insurance cover? Unluckily, down the line, it would turn out that I had the wrong insurance when an "act of God" struck a fire pipe inside a different studio, flooding the place with more water than mops and buckets could handle, ruining drawings, photographs, costly paper, and props left on the floor. All the saved receipts added up to nothing but a pile of dry, wrinkled-up paper, useful to a collage artist but not to me. Who would have thought pipes on the inside of a building are subject to malicious acts by the man himself and that top floors flood as quickly and destructively as bottom ones? There'd be no reimbursements from God or the insurance company for the lost time and value in those items, no payback for damage to self-esteem (artist's suicides come to mind), no restitution for the pain and suffering endured during the crisis (it is a crisis). This, the sad truth about anonymity in the arts and poor insurance choices.

Yet all the works saved, not ruined, at home and still clinging to walls as though on life support for monetary redemption, and those not yet executed but percolating deep in the well awaiting the right time or patron to cover expenses, these are worth more to me than anything I have, save the child in my arms and the beloved mother who carried him—even though she drives me crazy when placing canvases incorrectly against one another, leaning a smaller one against a larger one without putting foam board between them, thereby letting the smaller picture protrude into the larger one, stretching it, and my nerves, in ways neither should be. But this, too, is true: I wouldn't have much of what I have without her, both pictorially and materially. In the years since posing for that first portrait, Teresa never stood in the way of my art and always found a way to help move it along when no one else could or did. She never complained that I worked into the wee hours of the night or on weekends. Or made me feel bad when I lost everything at the track or when what was won disappeared into my art that didn't sell. Nor did she judge a painting unfairly even though, while lying next to each other in bed, she'd question if I had slept with the nude model painted in it. No words offered in response were ever quite as soothing as a simple hug, a gentle caress. And that's the way it should be—unspoken union, a bonding of two meant for eternity, learned only after years of pain and fear and having it out face-to-face, in private and under one roof, with love. And making love no matter what. Teresa melting in my arms, her body fastening weightlessly onto mine, lessened any art-life knockdown, obscured whatever was, at the moment, languishing, or outright rotting, on the studio floor.

Teresa: "So I drive you crazy?"

"Yes."

"But you love me, I see."

"Very much."

"I'm very proud of you, Gregory."

"Thank you. The CV is getting there."

"I'm sorry I ever gave you any grief..."

"Stop, T." I call her that, affectionately, for short. "You're the last person on this planet who needs to apologize. Especially not to me. I should apologize to you for putting art before reality, ideas before bills, paintings before you. For buying the slowest racehorse a credit card could buy. And opening a nightclub without a permit. And for turning our beautiful home into a club in the first place and moving our bed into a closet down the hall so I could make a VIP room with it instead. Is there anything I'm forgetting?"

"Plenty," she says before letting out a chuckle she tries to hold back.

Everytime she laughs she tilts her head to one side and her cheekbones get all red and her eyes swell and fill with water, tears of happiness that come from a well of honest-to-goodness emotion and joy, held captive most days by her serious devotion to work, her honor in caring wholeheartedly for family, and her unflinching commitment to love unconditionally whether stranger, foe, or me.

I look down at Matthew, his birth and the constant changing of diapers the few proud moments of fatherhood thus far. I think: how many measures and dollars will Teresa and I go through, as sane parents must, over the course of his life, to care and protect properly: the helmets, the car seats, the arm floaties, the band-aids. Kids love band-aids. How much would an insurance company offer him if his unknown and auction-record-less artist father never returned from work because of some unforeseeable catastrophe? What is the value of a babbino to a son? An artist to society? I hold the little bugger closer and gaze southwardly from his motionless skull, expecting to see what I've seen on the lower end of Manhattan from my perspective in Queens an entire lifetime.

Yet each day reality rises up ever so large, like an imagined billboard jutting up from the Brooklyn Queens Expressway, violating the altered skyline with a gripping message etched loud and bold: LIFE IS FLEETING, WHAT'S IT WORTH TO YOU? The choking, acrid black smoke that filled the sky that fateful day is gone, dispersed between here and infinity months ago, as the emptiness and undying loss that is Ground Zero lingers powerfully, seared in collective memory. With each glimpse downtown, or each glance at the somber faces of every fireman marching up Fifth on St. Patrick's Day, or at the sight of a black ribbon wrapped around a police officer's badge of honor, I am transported back in time; flashbacks occur at airports, with the unbuckling of a pant belt, and at the scene of a cute black Labrador lying outside the midtown tunnel with his handler. Something mentioned on the radio, some image on a front page, it all brings back the pain. 9|11 is as much behind us as it is next to us.

But in the Towers' wake, in the piercing clarity of their absence, life's true valuation on matters grand and small have revealed themselves most abundantly. What frames would ever suffice in fitting such wonders within their hold? What canvas could ever capture life's humbling greatness within its weave?

The End

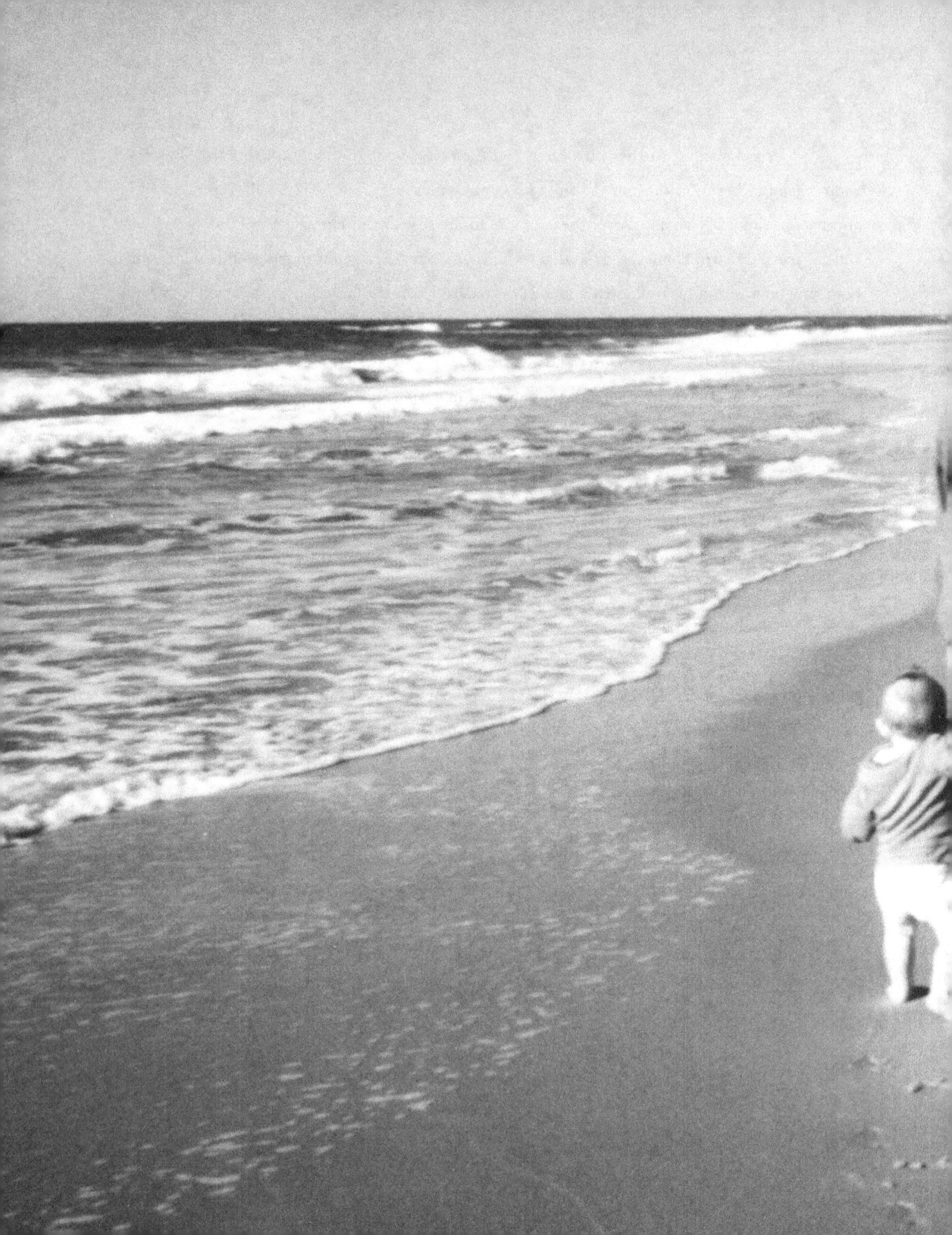

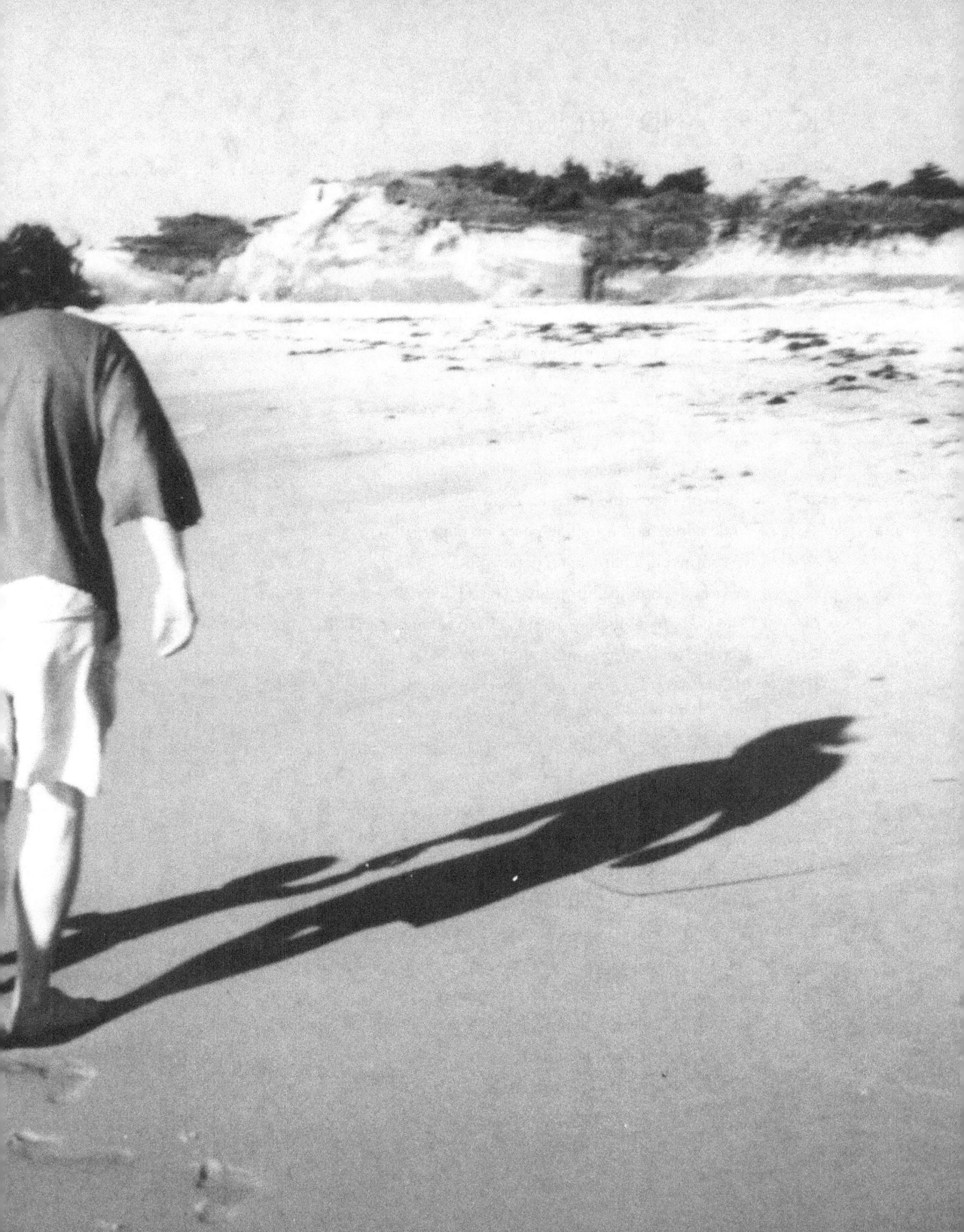

PICTURE AND ART INDEX

All artwork by Gregory de la Haba. All works are in Private Collections unless otherwise noted.

ACKNOWLEGEMENTS

To my late father-in-law, Matty Maher, I'm eternally grateful. Without whose support and belief I'd have so much less to write or care about. To all my artist and poet friends I adore, I eagerly await your next show or book so we can revel and roll in art's magnificent spirit sooner rather than later. To my Publisher, John Gosslee, and Editor, Andrew (Ibis) Sullivan at C&R Press, how cool we've met by chance and believe in art and literature the same way—not by chance. To Mike Pienciak, who enlightened me with his wisdom (on writing and other matters) through endless questioning. To my dear friend, Bryan Thatcher, a part of my creative endeavors for years, always camera and road-trip-ready. To my two older brothers who set the bar for success and kindness. To my father, and late mother, who first brought me to Montauk as a child and encouraged the seeking of wonderment in all things. And lastly, to my wife, Teresa, whose grace has blanketed all my failures and shortcomings described herein and loves completely, still.

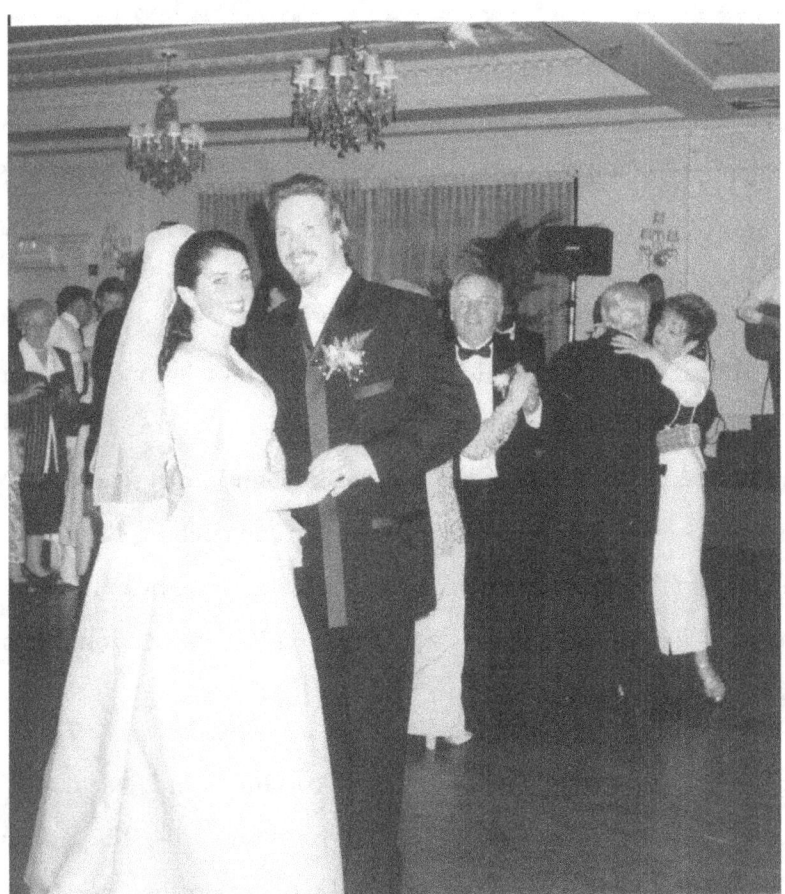

GREGORY DE LA HABA

Gregory de la Haba is an American interdisciplinary artist. A skilled painter with a pedagogical lineage that stretches back to Jacques Louis Davide, he is an exemplary practitioner of fine art whose conceptual practice resists categorization. De la Haba's work explores themes of addiction, contemporary notions of masculinity and Duende, a heightened state of emotion, expression and authenticity derived from pure artistic expression. It is from this place that the artist unlocks his true self—both in art and in life.

Since 2008, de la Haba has produced art-related ventures through his creative platform Bodega de la Haba. Notable projects include hosting literary events with Pulitzer Prize-winning poet Franz Wright, curating a survey of important work by the celebrated artist, Judy Rifka, at Pulpo Gallery in Murnau am Staffelsee, Germany, and producing and narrating Terrence Browne's Irish, art-history musical, *Hazel: Made In Belfast* which premiered at Carnegie Hall.

De la Haba's work has been exhibited internationally, including Salzach Biennial, Salzburg Arts Festival, Queens Museum, Kunsthaus Tacheles, Contemporary Istanbul, Design Week Milan, Mykonos Biennale, SCOPE Art Show, Art Miami, Art Southampton and Sylt Art Fair. In 2009 de la Haba was the Artist-in-Residence at Jack the Pelican Presents in Brooklyn where he firmly cemented his notoriety with a provocative body of work.

A cum laude graduate of Harvard University, de la Haba has written on a number of artists including Billy The Artist, Richie Culver, Marcus Jansen, Cristina BanBan, Oscar Murillo, Al Diaz, California Locos (Dave Tourjé, Chaz Bojórquez, John Van Hamersveld, Norton Wisdom and Gary Wong), Miya Ando, Andy Moses, Timothy Warren Williams, Lance De Los Reyes, Mel Bochner and many others. De la Haba's writings and artworks have been featured in a number of publications including The New York Times, Southampton Review, Rizzoli's Irish America, New York Arts Magazine, and Portray.

De la Haba is represented by Geuer & Geuer Art GmbH in Dusseldorf, Germany. A native New Yorker, the artist lives and works in New York with his wife, Teresa, heir to New York's legendary pub, McSorley's Old Ale House, and their two boys, Matthew and Sebastian